Fashion Supply Chain Management

Fashion Supply Chain Management: Integrating Sustainability through the Fashion Supply Chain provides a comprehensive guide to the entire supply chain management process as it relates to the fashion industry; how fashion supply chains work from raw material to finished product, and how generic supply chain concepts are applied in the fashion context. It focuses on contemporary strategic issues with which the sector is currently confronted, some of its current challenges and the innovative ways the sector has developed to respond to these challenges.

Concepts such as sustainability, fast fashion, raw materials, logistics and reverse logistics, costing, lean and agile manufacturing and other supply chain strategies are expertly covered in this work, with each area underpinned by the new technologies required to support supply chains in the fashion industry. Each chapter is complemented by an in-depth case study from a relevant global organization so that readers can gain real-world insight, alongside pedagogy to aid student comprehension, including quizzes, end-of-chapter activities, and role-play scenarios.

This key work is an essential textbook for students studying fashion supply chain, operations, and logistics as part of fashion management undergraduate and postgraduate degrees. Fully comprehensive on theory yet applied to practice, it will equip students with the tools and understanding for a future career in the fashion industry.

Virginia Grose, *BA Fashion Textiles, MBA, MA-HE, SFHEA, Doctoral Candidate Circularity in Cashmere Supply Chains.* Virginia is currently the Head of Fashion & Assistant to the Head of the School of Arts at the University of Westminster, UK.

Nicola Mansfield, *MA Fashion Futures, SFHEA, FRSA.* Nicola is currently a Senior Lecturer at the University of Westminster, UK.

Mastering Fashion Management

The fashion industry is dynamic, constantly evolving, and worth billions worldwide: it's no wonder that Fashion Business Management has come to occupy a central position within the Business School globally. This series meets the need for rigorous yet practical and accessible textbooks that cover the full spectrum of the fashion industry and its management.

Collectively, *Mastering Fashion Management* is a valuable resource for advanced undergraduate and postgraduate students of Fashion Management, helping them gain an in-depth understanding of contemporary concepts and the realities of practice across the entire fashion chain – from design development and product sourcing, to buying and merchandising, sustainability, and sales and marketing. Individually, each text provides essential reading for a core topic. A range of consistent pedagogical features are used throughout the texts, including international case studies, highlighting the practical importance of theoretical concepts.

Postgraduate students studying for a Masters in Fashion Management in particular will find each text invaluable reading, providing the knowledge and tools to approach a future career in fashion with confidence.

Fashion Marketing and Communication
Theory and Practice Across the Fashion Industry
Olga Mitterfellner

Fashion Buying and Merchandising
The Fashion Buyer in a Digital Society
Rosy Boardman, Rachel Parker-Strak and Claudia E. Henninger

Sustainable Fashion Management
Claudia E. Henninger, Kirsi Niinimäki, Marta Blazquez Cano and Celina Jones

Fashion Supply Chain Management
Integrating Sustainability through the Fashion Supply Chain
Virginia Grose and Nicola Mansfield

Celebrity Fashion Marketing
Developing a Human Fashion Brand
Fykaa Caan and Angela Lee

For more information about the series, please visit https://www.routledge.com/Mastering-Fashion-Management/book-series/FM

Fashion Supply Chain Management

Integrating Sustainability through the Fashion Supply Chain

Virginia Grose and Nicola Mansfield

Routledge
Taylor & Francis Group

LONDON AND NEW YORK

Designed cover image: © Yaroslav Kushta/Getty

First published 2023
by Routledge
4 Park Square, Milton Park, Abingdon, Oxon OX14 4RN

and by Routledge
605 Third Avenue, New York, NY 10158

Routledge is an imprint of the Taylor & Francis Group, an informa business

British Library Cataloguing-in-Publication Data
A catalogue record for this book is available from the British Library

Library of Congress Cataloging-in-Publication Data
Names: Mansfield, Nicola, author. | Grose, Virginia, author.
Title: Fashion supply chain management / Nicola Mansfield and Virginia Grose.
Description: 1 Edition. | New York, NY : Routledge, 2023. | Series: Mastering fashion management | Includes bibliographical references and index. |
Identifiers: LCCN 2022059360 | ISBN 9780367703400 (hardback) |
ISBN 9780367697457 (paperback) | ISBN 9781003145783 (ebook)
Subjects: LCSH: Clothing trade. | Business logistics.
Classification: LCC HD9940.A2 M367 2023 | DDC 746.9/20687--dc23/eng/20221209
LC record available at https://lccn.loc.gov/2022059360

ISBN: 978-0-367-70340-0 (hbk)
ISBN: 978-0-367-69745-7 (pbk)
ISBN: 978-1-003-14578-3 (ebk)

DOI: 10.4324/9781003145783

Typeset in Bembo
by KnowledgeWorks Global Ltd.

Access the Support Material: www.routledge.com/9780367697457

Contents

Chapter 2   Suppliers: From raw materials to finished goods   **29**

Chapter 6   Costing in the fashion supply chain   **127**

Chapter 7   Innovation and the future of fashion supply chains   **153**

List of Figures

About the Authors

Virginia Grose BA Fashion Textiles, MBA, MA-HE SFHEA, Doctoral Candidate Circularity in Cashmere Supply Chains

Virginia has an industry background in design and product development through working in global supply chains from the UK to China, Sri Lanka and EU to create commercially viable products. She has been involved in lecturing since 2007 with several institutions in the UK and EU and is currently the Course Director of the MA Fashion Business Management programme at the University of Westminster, a course which also runs at Informatics Institute of Technology (IIT) Sri Lanka. Virginia is also the Liaison Tutor for the University of Westminster Courses in Fashion Marketing Communication at IED Barcelona and Milan. Her research interests range from product development and sustainability to risk management ethics and circularity in fashion supply chains. She is currently researching her PhD at Robert Gordon University (RGU) Aberdeen, focusing on sustainable product development and recycling in cashmere knitwear supply chains.

Nicola Mansfield MA Fashion Futures, SFHEA, FRSA

After a long career in global supply chains and fashion product development, Nicola is currently sharing her extensive experience and knowledge with UK and international students by fashion business lecturing in London. She is currently a Senior Lecturer at the University of Westminster and her main areas of focus are: garment construction, costings, new materials and textiles and the future of circular supply chains. She is supported by close industry contacts and relationships with both household and niche brands, and always strives to make headway with new business models and methods of production.

Acknowledgements

The authors would like to thank all of their industry contacts that have supported this work with their generous time providing in-depth advice and interviews: Ross Barry of LMB Textiles, Diana Kakkar of MAES London, Ilishio Lovejoy, Henry Hales of Tu Pack and SIRPLUS, Sarah Watkinson of Yull Shoes, Niki Akrivou of Snag Hosiery and Annabel Humphries of Pursuit the Label. Finally, a special thanks goes to Rosanna Mansfield and Hugo Riley at Beige Agency for their support with figures and images.

Foreword by Dain Son Robinson

I was introduced to Nicola and Virginia in 2021 as part of my role in the Sustainability Team within the University of Westminster to identify best practice on sustainability pedagogy within the organization. Although many of our academic colleagues took personal interest in environmental issues, sustainability pedagogy was (and is still) a relatively new concept. There weren't many colleagues who were teaching sustainability to their students in a way that was embedded, relevant, interesting, and applicable, consistently throughout their degree programmes. However, when I met Nicola and Virginia, I learned that they had long been teaching sustainability as part of their Fashion Business Management BA and MA course curriculums. This was incredibly exciting for me considering the importance of sustainability awareness and education within the fashion industry, and since the Fashion Business Management courses attract so many students each year at the University (which isn't surprising when there are two amazing women involved in running the courses).

As sustainability becomes *the* global topic of the 21st century, it is imperative that higher education students must learn about environmental and social issues, how it is relevant to their course curriculum, and how to apply their learnings into practical action once they enter the workforce. But before students can learn about sustainability within universities, the academics themselves have quite a lot of catching up to do to learn about the relevance of sustainability within their own fields, whether they teach fashion, biochemistry, criminology, literature, marketing, or even film. However, in Nicola and Virginia's case, this isn't true. They had already understood the importance of sustainability pedagogy and had taken it upon themselves to teach their Fashion Business Management students about this topic, despite the lack of external pressures (although, thankfully now growing across the sector) to embed sustainability into the curriculum. Their pioneering journey has led to this textbook on sustainable fashion supply chain management that I am so personally excited about, knowing how much passion has gone into the publication of this book.

I hope this book will inspire readers to take action like Nicola and Virginia have, whether it is through sharing your knowledge to others, making personal changes to your daily actions, or pursuing a career in sustainable supply chain management to create positive changes from within. It's these catalytic actions that make a difference and brings me hope in these uncertain times to keep going and continue pushing within my own sustainability journey. For this, I thank Nicola and Virginia for being their incredible and inspiring selves, and for writing this textbook that provides clarity in understanding the overly complex world of sustainable fashion supply chain management.

Oct 2022

Preface

This book was conceived after a decade of teaching fashion business students at undergraduate and post-graduate levels in the fields of fashion supply chain management, sourcing, and sustainability. It is the subject area of the authors who wanted to bring together some of their key teaching areas and industry practice in the areas of risk relationships, costings, auditing and sourcing logistics in addition to looking to the future integration of digital innovation in the fashion supply chains. The shift towards a more transparent sustainable industry has gathered pace and resulted in newer brands doing things differently in the mainstream fashion industry and supply chains. There has been a significant shift to online retailing that has impacted the way brands source and manufacture fashion, and the over-arching impact of the COVID-19 global pandemic and Brexit has impacted the way fashion brands do business and set up their supply chains.

The textbook provides an overview of the contemporary 21st century fashion supply chain and provides insight through case study interviews into important areas such as: recycling textiles, CMT and UK manufacturing, zero waste and closed-loop manufacturing as well as in-depth explanations of costing fashion, risk management and the different type of relationships, with supply chain models applied in a fashion context.

As we write this book, we are witnessing a change in our planet and our world of fashion and the supply chains that cross the globe. The disruption created by the pandemic has accelerated a need for change, and the fashion industry is under the spotlight in terms of waste and environmental and social impacts. This disruption means the need to move from a linear to a circular model in fashion supply chain management is not optional. A circular economy promotes the extended life of textiles and finished used goods, recycling and reuse to minimise waste and keep raw materials in circulation, if possible.

We have underpinned this textbook with sustainability and our view is that all supply chains should be sustainable and ideally move to circular models to support the planet and people involved in this global industry. We also refer to the UN Sustainable Development Goals in the book and each chapter links to those most relevant. This framework supports the move to a circular supply chain model.

CHAPTER 1

Fashion supply chains

Overview and context

This chapter will discuss how fashion supply chains have evolved and highlights key milestones in the fashion industry such as globalisation and international sourcing. Fashion supply chains progressed as a business model due in part to accelerated globalisation over the last 30 years. Fashion supply chain became a key and critical determinant of success in the fashion business. We need to consider the history and context of the supply chain holistically and the origins of key concepts in supply chain management (SCM) as we investigate the topics in this book.

Summary

This chapter discusses how fashion supply chains have evolved, linked to key milestones such as globalisation and sourcing "super sourcers" such as Li & Fung and influential global retailers such as Zara, H&M and Primark. Luxury brand conglomerates who have a wide impact on global fashion supply chains and their different business models will also be discussed. This chapter will also include an appraisal of vertical, semi- and non-vertical supply chains and the influence of key retailers' sourcing policies will be critically examined and evaluated alongside relevant theoretical concepts in the field.

However, the past few decades have seen the evolution and importance of sustainability in supply chain management as a direct result of global sourcing and the "fast fashion" model integration by most fashion brands, which has created excessive consumption driven by agile, fast and flexible supply chain management processes.

Learning outcomes

At the end of this chapter, you will be able to:

- Define and understand the chronology of the supply chain and the key business models that exist over time

- Identify the key milestones, drivers and influences of supply chain management (SCM) and sourcing policy in the fashion industry

- Apply and understand the merchandising or procurement mix in the context of the fashion supply chain

- Understand and apply the R's of supply chain to any fashion supply chain to determine success

9 Industry, Innovation and Infrastructure

16 Peace, Justice and Strong Institutions

17 Partnerships for the Goals

SDG GOAL(S) – THIS CHAPTER LINKS TO:

8 Decent Work and Economic Growth

What is a supply chain?

There are many formal definitions of supply chains and it is important to reflect on a couple of these to understand what a supply chain is. For example, one definition of a supply chain is a "network of facilities and activities that performs the functions of product development, procurement of material from suppliers, the movement of materials between facilities, the manufacturing of products, the distribution of finished goods to customers and after-market support for sustainment" (Mabert and Venkataraman 1998).

A further explanation of a supply chain is a "set of organizations directly linked by one or more of the upstream and downstream flows of products, services, finances and information from a source to an end customer" (Christopher 2014).

We can see that SCM is the management of a network of interconnected businesses involved in the ultimate provision of product and service packages required by end customers. It is a management process that is outside the brand or retailer – and can involve many organisations working together and coordinating activities to deliver fashion clothing to an end customer (Lambert and Garcia-Dastugue 2011). One of the earliest recorded supply chains was the Silk Route made famous by Marco Polo's journey across the alps from Venice in Italy to China where he found silk, cashmere and other luxurious textiles and brought the fibres back to Italy. This was the start of one of the first global sourcing hubs and in Northern Italy today, the cities of Como and Prato are still famous for cloth made from silk, wool and cashmere fibres and are part of the world-recognised fashion industry in Italy (Cooper, Lambert, and Pagh 1997; Jacoby 1997).

The concept of SCM has origins within military logistics where, historically, the army is able to set up camps and small villages with all the necessary infrastructure quickly and efficiently (Fernie 2002). An effective fashion supply chain strategy is market driven and customer focused and the supply chain links with fashion retailers' buying and product development processes. This means that every strategic supply chain decision should consider the customer needs in addition to the market segment for the brand. One supply chain size and type does not fit all brands in all market segments such as luxury, fast fashion and value ranges – the decisions about where to invest in raw materials or where to focus on one specialist supplier of materials can be crucial to success and sales.

These decisions should be tailored to an individual retailer and careful consideration paid to location of raw materials and the manufacturing of the end product.

The day-to-day management of the critical path for each product is equally crucial to SCM success and linked to this are effective supply chain relationships (see Chapter 3).

However, it is important to note that fashion supply chains were initially designed along a linear process and should move to embed sustainability in the 21st century, ideally becoming completely circular to include reuse of both pre- and post-consumer waste (www.commonobjective 2019).

An effective fashion SCM starts by understanding the market and customers. In planning a supply chain, we should begin by understanding the fashion customer and ensure that the fashion supply chain is created with the customer in mind (Kathiala 2020). The main elements to be considered in creating a supply chain include the following points and can be used as a starting point for any fashion brand:

- ■ The context of fashion retail
- ■ Macro- and micro-environment disruptors
- ■ Consumer demographics
- ■ Lifestyle
- ■ Reverse logistics and waste

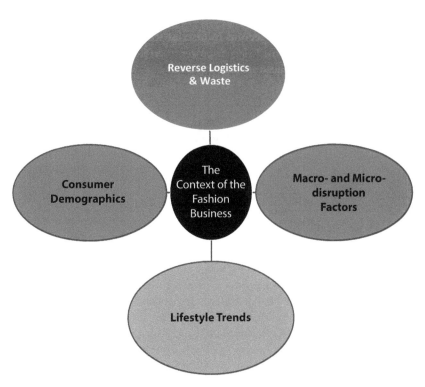

Figure 1.1

The Supply Chain Mix

Context of fashion supply chains

The size of the fashion industry is not easy to estimate, but according to McKinsey (2020), was worth over $2.5 trillion before the COVID-19 pandemic. However, it is hard to be completely accurate in some sectors of the industry, especially because there are approximately 60 million workers in the garment manufacturing industry worldwide. More than half of these workers are women and includes many subcontractors and "cottage" industries that remain a large part of some countries' supply chains.

First to fourth Industrial Revolutions

The cotton industry was one of the first industries to "globalize," forming the "first" industrial revolution centred in Lancashire in the UK. Manchester was known as "Cottonopolis," and is recognised as the first global industrial city; the industrial revolution subsequently spread to Europe and the United States (Dicken 2007).

- **The first Industrial Revolution**
  It used water and steam power to mechanize production. It was in the 18th and 19th centuries when the first industrial revolutions used water power to make clothing. "Cottonopolis" in the north of England, one of the first global cities of Manchester, was born out of the cotton industry (Ronayne 2015).

- **The second Industrial Revolution**
  It used electric power to create mass production and clothing began to be produced at scale.

- **The third Industrial Revolution**
  The 1980s and 1990s saw the invention of technology and the introduction of the Internet. These radically changed the business of fashion once again, supporting innovation and inspiration behind today's successful fashion SCM. This was driven by successful fashion and online players such as Inditex and Amazon, both of whom can attribute success to both agile and "just-in-time" production and supply chain logistics.

- **The fourth Industrial Revolution**
  Brands such as Apple have become influential in digitisation, creating the fourth Industrial Revolution and furthering innovations garment manufacturing (Gökalp, Gökalp and Eren 2018). Such initiatives include radio frequency identification (RFID) tags and blockchain technology used to re-create the transparency missing from so many of today's supply chains, which have become fragmented by the global sourcing policies of fashion retailers. Additionally, brands such as Adidas have introduced robotics in manufacturing through a so-called "speed factory" in Ansbach, Germany. Other initiatives include three-dimensional (3-D) printing of garments, pioneered by several brands. In China, many brands are investing in this technology and using it for fashion items (Chan et al. 2018).

However, the fourth Industrial Revolution does not just include technology in the innovation process. A clear demonstration of this are new sustainable and biodegradable fibres, such as Pinatex, made from pineapples and the repurposing of natural fibres to create beautiful, sustainable raw materials (see Chapter 2 for more on textiles).

Globalisation and the move to an outsourced model in fashion supply chains

The trend of globalisation and the move from localised, integrated, global sourcing in fashion supply chains was largely driven by retailers in the late 1980s as pressure from overseas manufacturers created competition in the markets. American and British retailers and manufacturers lost out on business to cheaper imports from Southeast Asia (Abecassis-Moedas 2007; Gereffi 1994).

Meanwhile, fashion customers continued to demand lower prices and faster product turnaround, which further accelerated the globalisation of fashion supply chains. Initially, China was the first main overseas sourcing location for many Western retailers, but over time, low-cost fashion clothing production typically became much wider, centred around even-lower-cost locations such as India, Turkey, Cambodia, Vietnam and Bangladesh. More recently, Chinese companies have invested in Myanmar and parts of Africa, such Lesotho, as part of lower cost-sourcing strategies.

The 1980s and 1990s also witnessed the rise of the retailer's own label or private label brands. The internationalisation process became influential on the design and strategic direction for fashion supply chains. New entrants such as Zara and the Arcadia group besides big US retailers such as Nike and Gap added to the fashion supply chain revolution at the time. However, this flexibility and response to changing consumer demand resulted in shorter runs, perhaps only 500 units, and product "drops" became more frequent. According to Barnes & Lea-Greenwood (2006), "This caused some shift in the supply chain as sourcing moves away from China who favour long production runs, towards more flexible and small production units, such as those in Europe and the Middle East. However, respondents suggest that the Far East is responding to this new demand."

In the 1990s and 2000s, the vertical model of supply became one of disintegration as this evolved into mass-market outsourced fashion supply chains, creating a throwaway culture and disposability in fashion clothing. This was a direct result of the fragmented global supply chain business model and the increased volume of low-cost fashion (Perry and Wood 2019). Clothing firms and retailers faced the growing pressures of rising costs, a downward spiral of retail prices and a turbulent economic climate. The garment and textiles industry in the UK depended on low capital- and labour-intensive operations and as production costs increased with little opportunity to pass these costs on, many branded fashion manufacturers were forced to reconsider their business models.

Firms looked to source more of their products overseas and to subcontract production in more economically viable locations; manufacturing in low-cost labour regimes became the norm for clothing firms based in developed economies

(Christopher 2004a; Dicken 2007). It was during this time that the once–dominant UK clothing sector suffered its greatest decline, a move underlined by the symbolic decision by Marks and Spencer, one of the country's stalwart procurers of British-made fashion, to licence production overseas (Allwood et al. 2006). From the mid-1990s onwards, UK clothing firms adopted the strategy of outsourcing production to low-wage countries (Lane and Probert 2006).

The aim of most supply chains was initially designed to mitigate any inventory risk and to increase cash flow; this means that value should be created across all tiers of the supply chain, from the first to the last mile, by keeping the product moving at all stages of the supply chain. Inventory standing still attracts cost and makes the inventory open to theft and damage. The last mile to the customer can often be most problematic – customers are now very much part of the supply chain due to online door-to-door deliveries and returns (Crisell 2020).

Key contextual changes in the environment

One of the biggest factors in the last 30 years was the elimination of the Multi Fibre Arrangement (MFA) in 2005, which imposed quotas on developing countries (Appelbaum 2004). The World Trade Organization (WTO) had established the 1995 Agreement on Textiles and Clothing (ATC) and this mandated a 10-year phase out of the quotas.

Within fashion SCM, especially in the luxury segment and some middle market retailers, vertically integrated manufacturing was commonplace before globalisation occurred until the impact of global sourcing pressurised fashion retail margins. Globalisation, together with intense market competition, the introduction of technology and changes in consumer behaviour resulted in a highly complex turbulent market – hence, "flexible modular organisations in supply chains were viewed as more effective than vertical integration" (Djelic and Amiano 1999).

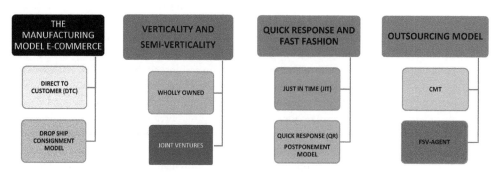

Figure 1.2

Supply Chain Models

Global environment and key macro-factors

The global environment for sourcing products is extremely volatile. Understanding the markets and balancing the risk, distance, cost and quality is a delicate juggling act for retailers and fashion brands. One of the most important concepts in fashion supply chains is that of "trade offs" (Christopher 2001). Trade off tactics are usually found between cost versus quality and time versus cost. Having a global perspective and considering strengths and weaknesses of suppliers of finished goods and materials in developed and developing countries are important elements of fashion SCM. These need to be balanced against location and skills in addition to the availability of raw materials to make business decisions on the most appropriate balance of supply chain locations and costs involved for a fashion brand and customers.

Ending the MFA to Brexit

Equally, gaining an understanding of trade agreements, duty and other import taxes from the source to the market is crucial to the success of fashion supply chains. Trade agreements need careful consideration and the impact of duty and taxes between the country of origin and the importing nation may differ considerably (Fixing Fashion Report 2019). They can also fluctuate for political and economic factors, such as the recent changes in the European Union (EU) as a direct result of the Brexit trade deal with the UK withdrawal from the trading bloc. This created overnight changes for retailers manufacturing goods in the EU with new and different rules and regulations imposed as part of the revised trade deal implementation. As a direct result, there were many immediate positive benefits of globalisation affecting fashion supply chains, such as cheap imports and greater supply chain efficiency, resulting in the creation of the fast fashion business model and decades of continued increased demand for goods.

These benefits created jobs in developing countries and an increase in different types of employment, such as the creation of service industries in developed and mature markets. In fact, the sourcing policies of major global retailers such as Gap and H&M helped move the Western world into a post-industrialised phase (Fernie and Sparks 2019; Perry and Wood 2019). The demand for volume and speed to market for fashion clothing also increased flexibility in apparel manufacturing and created a highly skilled workforce in parts of Asia, for example in Sri Lanka.

An alternative perspective is based upon the negative effects of globalisation and a loss of jobs and industry in clothing manufacture in the UK and North America (Dicken 2007). In fashion supply chains, we have to consider which model of sourcing is most appropriate for our brand and customers and. If global sourcing is part of that, fashion brands need to act responsibly and consider how this strategy will contribute to the economic development of a region in which it operates and also consider how the overall environmental impact of the brand may be reduced.

Certain business model concepts in fashion production and manufacturing emerged in the globalised world. Some fashion retailers helped to shape these concepts through business model innovation and significant work on the development of fast moving and proactive supply chain models. The origin of quick response (QR) manufacturing evolved into what we now call the fast fashion business model developed from the concept of "postponement" and has further moved to "just-in-time' (JIT) manufacturing. All of these concepts stem from the Japanese manufacturing industries that evolved after World War II (Christopher 2004b; Hines, Lea-Greenwood, and Barnes 2006).

Fast fashion and super sourcers

Fast fashion grew from postponement, a technique used by Benetton in the 1980s. This predominantly knitwear brand perfected this sourcing model by designing knitwear in a "greige" form for the purpose of garment dyeing different silhouettes.

This gave them the ability to react to sales and forecast fast-selling styles. This technique was replicated and perfected as a business model by Inditex and the global Zara brand emerged as a market leader with headquarters in La Coruna in northern Spain.

Zara practiced a similar technique several decades later using greige and stock materials while also testing out new silhouettes in stores. The success of this was partly due to their ability to send electronic point-of-sale data back to its headquarters for instant manufacturing and decision making. The democratisation of fashion is generally attributed to Zara and Inditex. The fast fashion model is responsible for a shift in consumer behaviour and fast fashion is in itself a supply chain model (Aftab, Yuanjian, and Kabir 2017). There are also other business models with multi-faceted global sourcing known as the so-called "super sourcers" Li & Fung and influential global retailers such as H&M and Primark (Christopher 2016).

See now buy now and drop culture

More recently, other supply chain models such as selling directly from catwalk to customer emerged that had a direct impact on the supply chain and sourcing in fashion, effectively creating new models of supply (Perry and Wood 2019). Burberry began this tactic in 2016, and since then, the "see now buy now" (SNBN) business model of selling has been integrated into the manufacturing of collections and ranges by many fashion brands.

Online retailing or e-tail is another business model that has affected the way brands design and develop products and where they locate their overall manufacturing and supply chains. The growth of the e-commerce business model has led to a tactic employed by many online retailers, especially large platforms – known as the "drop ship" model (Wen Choi, and Chung 2018).

This model is used by large retail platforms and their brands. Essentially, orders are made via the platform, but the brand takes care of order fulfilment and delivery to the end customer. The platform is merely an advertising space where the order can be made – stock is held by the brand. This business model has become popular as part of an overall e-commerce strategy and was pioneered by large global online retailers such as Net-a-Porter and Farfetch, but is now a widely adopted business model by many on line retailers.

Ultra-fast fashion model

The production of new products sold at low cost encourages overconsumption. Pereira and Scarpin (2020) suggest that such brands have sped up the production processes to an extent that has not been seen previously using onshore and offshore sourcing. The primary focus is to create consumer demand for fashion based on data gathered mainly from social media. These brands usually follow a direct-to-consumer (DTC) approach, maximising a blend of trend information and using style scouts to identify what influencers and celebrities are wearing to create instant fashion with minimal stock holding.

Supply chain theory – for different business models

The theory in SCM tends to be generalised across industries and is extensive. In fashion supply chains, there are two essential theoretical models that should be considered:

One of the most well-known frameworks concerning SCM comes from Martin Christopher and is known as the R's of SCM.

R's of supply chain management

It was developed by Emeritus Professor at Cranfield University Martin Christopher, M., 2016. Logistics & supply chain management. Pearson UK. In the era of intensive supply chain competition, several principles emerged to guide the supply chain manager that remain useful tools. These can be conveniently summarised as the R's of SCM:

- Responsiveness
- Reliability
- Resilience
- Relationships

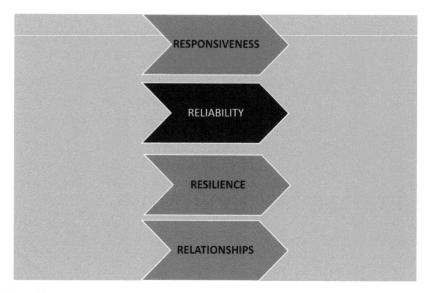

Figure 1.3

R's of Supply Chain – Martin Christopher 1998

These ideas should be applied to the entire supply chain of a fashion business to determine how effective these measures are. As noted by Christopher (2015), an excellent current example of this is Zara with highly integrated sales and supply chain processes in place that can "flex" the entire supply chain.

Procurement and merchandising mix

Another framework that is often applied is known as procurement or merchandising mix and can also act as a framework to design or redesign a supply chain in the fashion industry: "The process of planning, implementing, and controlling the efficient and effective forward and reverse flow and storage of goods, services, and related information from point of origin to point of consumption for the purpose of meeting customer requirements" (Council of Logistics Management 1991; Stone 2012).

This is a useful model for retailers who can apply it to monitor the effectiveness of the supply chain and entire procurement process.

- **Right goods**
- **Right place**
- **Right time**
- **Right quality**
- **Right quantity**

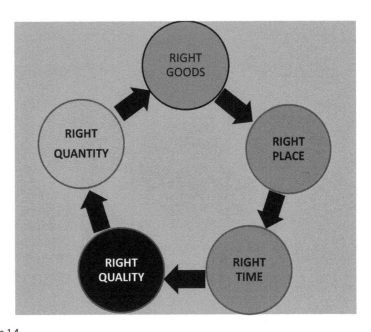

Figure 1.4

Merchandising & Procurement Mix 1991 – Council of Logistics Management

Vertical fashion supply chains

This section is an appraisal of different types of supply chain models: vertical, semi- and non-vertical and outsourced. Initially, most fashion supply chains were vertical – owning the entire process of manufacturing garments, including the spinning, dyeing, weaving and knitting of the raw materials (Caniato et al. 2011). Such vertical models of supply date back to the Industrial Revolution and businesses such as Coats, Patons, Courtaulds, Carringtons and many other large-scale textile manufacturers emerged in the UK. In the United States, the cotton industry had a similar impact on companies such as Levi Strauss and Fruit of the Loom.

Vertical manufacturing is simply a manufacturer that has most parts of the value chain under its roof and is wholly owned, rather than just one process of the garment manufacturing process. These include manufacturers that makes the fabric and often buy or own all the raw materials directly to turn into yarn, textiles and finished goods. They may even own the source of raw materials or at the very least have extremely close relationships with the key source. This type of manufacturer is much less common in the 21st century than previously, with the majority of vertical supply chains in the fashion business now found largely in the field of luxury brands. This is because direct control, quality and visibility are crucial to maintaining high standards of craftsmanship and heritage in such items as leather goods, silk and accessories and where very specific and often iconic yarns, intricate finishes, fabric and trims are required (Caniato et al. 2011).

Brands such as Chanel, Louis Vuitton and Gucci (part of the Kering Group) still have high levels of verticality and control in their supply chains. Chanel invested in their supply chain through long-term relationships with textile mills, such as Linton Tweeds, and strategic acquisitions such as Montex and Maison Lesage embroidery companies created semi-vertical relationships (Crisell, 2020; see more on supply chain relationships in Chapter 3).

Fashion business model – semi-verticality and outsourcing

The breakdown of vertical supply chains due to market pressure and globalisation led to semi-verticality in fashion supply chains, which in turn created completely outsourced and highly fragmented fashion supply chain models (Perry and Woods 2019).

In the era of global sourcing, most retailers set up their own supply chains with extensive networks of suppliers and logistics partners as well as many raw material suppliers. The alternative to this outsourced model is to own manufacturing, as discussed, creating verticality, which is expensive and now largely only used by luxury brands. There is, however, a further model, the full-service vendor (FSV) model, which uses a sophisticated manufacturer as an intermediary to arrange everything for you (Shen et al. 2016). Some large manufacturers offer this full service and source raw materials (depending on the product). Further alternatives are those that operate as "cut, make and trim" (CMT) manufacturers who do not have time or resources to research fabrics, trims, or any other components to make up a product (www.makeit british.co.uk; Perry and Towers 2013). The full-service manufacturer will do everything for the brand or retailer and key tasks include:

- Source the fabric and trims
- Manufacture the product
- Package the product for distribution

The full-service model

Sometimes referred to as a fully factored or full package production manufacturer, the FSV will look after an entire order from design through to delivery to the freight on board (FOB) point.

They can do everything from design assistance, pattern making, grading, sourcing materials and components, sampling, bulk production, packing and freight forwarding. They can provide economies of scale with a "one-stop shop" approach, usually with fewer delays and choices of materials and finishes. However, they also can create a lack of control, less flexibility and sometimes less transparency.

An FSV will also handle the distribution – full-service manufacturers are set up to produce high-volume quantities and work with established and often global businesses, leaving small brands often with no choice but to find CMT manufacturers to produce their products. One of the most well-known global sourcing companies for many large retailers and brands across the globe is Li & Fung of Hong Kong, which is often referred to as a "super sourcer" (Magretta 1998). In 2017, Li & Fung created the "supply chain of the future" model. This was designed to completely digitize supply chains linking the 3-D digital product development arm of the company directly with customers and manufacturing. Li & Fung underwent a major reorganisation to become leaner and more focused on these separate divisions within the company:

- **Logistics:** Covering China and Asian local customers and includes three new centres of excellence, this focuses on new sourcing locations, transportation and e-logistics
- **Raw materials:** Based on its extensive experience in manufacturing and sourcing raw materials
- **Costings:** Due to scale, the ability to provide efficient costings

Li & Fung has a vendor platform for the 10,000 suppliers it refers to as partners. Dynamic costing tools use the history of costing and forecasting to match the most appropriate manufacturing location for client orders. Working with such a large agent for full outsourcing creates the opportunity for retailers to pass on the administrative side of procurement, which include credit services, letters of credit, compliance and management systems in factories. It is important to note that these third-party large agent suppliers provide a real alternative to retailers finding their own manufacturers, but this model can also remove transparency and visibility in the supply chain and create risk for a brand (Barnes and Lea-Greenwood 2006; see Chapter 5 for more on risk management).

The cut, make, and trim model

Once regarded as a "secondary" and inferior model of outsourcing compared with the FSV model, CMT has seen a rise in popularity once again in the production industry. A CMT manufacturer will usually only handle the manufacturing element, leaving full responsibility for ordering the fabric, trims and all of the other associated components with the brand or retailer. They do not have the manpower to spend time sourcing materials, although they may be able to provide advice on this based on their experience. It is also the responsibility of the brand that all of the components arrive for the allotted production schedule, otherwise production slots may be missed. In the UK, there are many CMT suppliers who work with large mass-market brands and produce in volume for fast fashion retailers and smaller bespoke brands in the premium sector. The case study in this chapter looks at a unique CMT atelier-style sustainable manufacturer in the fashion industry – MAES London.

The move from supply chain management to sustainable supply chain management

All the SCM models discussed, their techniques of agility and flexibility together with profit and high levels of competitive advantages influenced the push for fashion brands and their supply chains to become more sustainable. The fashion supply chain and the entire fashion industry as we see it today grew as result of techniques such as QR and JIT (Pookalungura 2013). Initially, green supply chain management (GSCM) was discussed prior to sustainable supply chain management (SSCM) as a way to evaluate the environmental impacts on efficient supply chain operations. Srivastava (2007) defines this as:

> "...integrating environmental thinking into supply-chain management, including product design, material sourcing and selection, manufacturing processes, delivery of the final product to the consumers as well as end-of-life management of the product after its useful life."

This led to the evolution into and establishment of SSCMfrom 2010 onward and includes social as well as economic and environmental sustainable factors. SSCM is defined as:

> "The creation of coordinated supply chains through the voluntary integration of economic, environmental, and social considerations with key inter-organizational business systems designed to efficiently and effectively manage the material, information, and capital flows associated with the procurement, production, and distribution of products or services in order to meet stakeholder requirements and improve the profitability, competitiveness, and resilience of the organization over the short- and long-term"
>
> (Ahi and Searcy 2013)

This push in SCM led to sustainability becoming prioritized by businesses and implementation in their supply chain processes as noted by Henniger et al (2016). Sustainable fashion and the supply chain takes into consideration the social, natural and economic price associated with fashion production.

SSCM has strong similarities to a traditional SCM, but SSCM incorporates not just the issues surrounding economic benefits of a business and supply chain, but also social and environmental concerns. Thus, SSCM can best be described as "the management of material, information and capital flows while taking goals from the three dimensions of sustainable development, i.e. economic, environmental, and social, into account" (Seuring and Müller 2008). The focus of SSCM research has been focused on environmental performance (De Burgos Jiménez and Céspedes Lorente 2001) or green product development (although both environmental and social aspects are associated with SSCM, both concepts emphasise the social dimension within SSCM). The slow fashion industry provides an opposing perspective to fast fashion. Slow fashion, whilst it can remain fashionable, is a lifestyle philosophy, not a supply chain model. Slow fashion runs opposite to fast fashion and was derived from the slow food movement (Fletcher 2008). It has, however, influenced the implementation of life-cycle models and the move to closed-loop or circular models in the fashion SCM.

The transition from fast fashion to sustainable fashion supply chain management (SSCM)

The fashion industry grew significantly because the transition to a pull system (where production of goods is initiated by the consumer) from a push system (producing goods based on a prediction of market expectations) was made possible.

Despite challenges connected to the transition from fast to sustainable fashion, since the late 1990s, a marked increase in sustainability and concerned parties linked to global sourcing occurred as well as early discussions on sustainability focused on solving environmental problems. From the early 2000s, sustainable operations management developed as an area that integrates environmental and social issues with economic aspects of supply chains into a common framework (Seuring and Müller 2008).

The main drivers for this transition were the rapid pace of production and consumption aided by advanced technologies, and the increased exploitation and pollution of natural resources for economic development (with hindsight provided by the various industrial disasters). Over recent years, more stringent laws to protect the environment have been implemented, including laws that mandate binding environmental legislation.

Sustainable or green management initiatives were initially adopted to reduce costs and to increase efficiency, resulting in more effective risk management (see Chapter 5 for more detail on risk).

Importance of the inclusion of the 7R model in the fashion supply chain

The 7R framework is a model that is directly linked to SSCM and can measure pollution prevention in a business by focusing on the seven R's: reduce, reuse, recycle, restyle, rewear, redesign and reimagine. In this way, a business can investigate their supply chain and highlight the aspects that are particularly well managed or may have a lower impact on the environment, and equally highlight areas in the supply chain that require improvment (Henniger et al. 2015; see Chapter 4 for more detail on this framework).

SSCM theory emerged in the 1990s driven by the work of key authors such as Braungart and McDonough's *Cradle to Cradle: Remaking the Way we Make Things* (2002). In the book, they proposed that the integration of design and science can provide enduring benefits for society from materials, water and energy through creation of a circular economy and by eliminating the concept of waste or treating it as a resource. SCM as a concept has been influenced by the move to closed-loop cradle-to-cradle manufacturing and other concepts, such as corporate social responsibility (CSR) (this will be discussed in Chapter X).

The most recent push for cradle-to-cradle SCM can be viewed through the lens of the circular economy; it is increasingly evident that the current linear economy model (take-make-dispose) has substantial limitations and will not be able to attain the sustainable development goals that now dominate the agenda of policy-makers at a global level (Jacometti 2019). In fact, the circular economy model is shaped by the 7R model's principles that should be applied throughout the whole cycle of production, consumption and return of resources (Koszewska 2018; Jacometti 2019; see Chapter 4).

Priorities in the fashion supply chain therefore should be:

- Waste management
- Enhancement of by-products and the connection of waste with the production and use of new raw materials (end-of-waste)
- Transition to a sustainable economy model with raw materials from renewable sources replacing raw materials from non-renewable resources, such as fossil fuels, to abandon the model of a linear supply chain economy

Conclusion

This chapter has provided the context of the fashion supply chain and the recent most dynamic history over the last 30–40 years, where speed and volume together were used as critical success factors to create a competitive advantage. The frameworks provided should be used throughout the book as starting points and basic frameworks for fashion SCM planning. For example, a customer-focused, market-driven supply chain with the right products in the right place at the right time is often referred to as the "holy grail" of retailing and both of these models can support supply chain design in the complex globalised fashion business.

However, this chapter sets the scene as a backdrop to further discuss the importance of the integration of sustainable processes and considerations in any contemporary fashion supply chain. These sustainability factors should not be optional and the fashion overall SCM process needs to be a holistic sustainable version for the future.

The SCM models of the past discussed in this chapter are relevant to define the evolution and the drivers of SCM, but these linear economy SCM models in the fashion industry are limited by the current need to move to circular economy models of supply. The circular economy is viewed as one of the strategic areas of innovation for the future development of the textile and fashion business. This means integration throughout every fashion supply chain process is applied when considering a new supply chain and suppliers, raw materials and transportation of goods across the globe.

CASE STUDY

MAES London interview with founder Diana Kakkar (a CMT manufacturer's quick response for luxury fashion)

Figure 1.5
MAES Logo

Figure 1.6
Diana Kakkar

1. Tell us why you set up MAES London and the Unique Selling Point (USP).

■ I set up MAES London (MAES is "SEAM" spelt backward) to make luxury manufacturing more accessible to fashion designers. I wanted to create a highly skilled atelier that works closely with and speaks in the same language of fashion as the designers we are catering for. In doing so, we could effectively act as a seamless extension of the designer's inhouse atelier and the end product we create would more closely match their vision.

■ We launched in January 2018 in a small 500-square-foot studio in Hackney Wick. In three years, we have expanded dramatically, most recently moving our studio to Tottenham Hale in a 4,000-square-foot space, significantly increasing our capacity so that we can expand our offering to luxury designers across the UK and Europe.

2. What is the MAES USP?

■ Having been a fashion designer myself, I can guide designers through the process. I also studied economics so my approach to fashion is beyond just *creativity*, it also has to make good *business* sense.

■ One of the core services I offer to start-ups and designers is consultancy, helping them set up systems and processes that they find easy to follow through the manufacturing process. It starts with what they are designed to, how much it will cost them, what their margins would be and what they should be selling at according to the make price and respecting the competition.

■ We have a strong value system and people, including internal and external stakeholders, are at the centre of this value chain. This appreciating of the human element is what makes fashion. It is the essence of all our conversations.

■ At the end of the day, fashion is a creative process. It is also subjective. So, one really must have the skill and take the time to understand the client's needs in order to deliver the project. This special empathy toward our designers and clients makes us unique in our approach and method of working.

3. What is your view on fashion supply chains in the UK in general?

A fashion or clothing supply chain is complicated. Some even compare it to the automotive supply chain. To make a garment, you have multiple components that traverse businesses and borders. The supply chain traces all parts of the process, from concept to customer, which go into creating a consumer product. This includes what materials are sourced and where, how they are developed into something larger and the journey the finished item takes in order to arrive in-store or on someone's doorstep. It is truly a team effort to make one garment possible, and definitely not an easy task.

Our core clientele is luxury designers. They would have developed their first samples or prototypes in-house. To manufacture multiples of their designs, they would need a trusted manufacturer who would reproduce multiples of these in order for it to be sellable. We are those trusted manufacturers. We are classified as CMT manufacturers, but we are not the average CMT manufacturer. We have carved out a niche in the crowded industry with our talented team of makers, and their years of experience lends us to help these designers.

A CMT manufacturer will be responsible for cutting, making, and then adding the trims on to the garment. The fabric, patterns and any other relevant trims are supplied by the designers. This allows us to work in a close partnership with our designers to produce orders closer to their selling season.

We are nimble enough to work with them to top up their orders or work on bespoke collections. We have carved out a niche in the CMT manufacturing sector for us in the industry. Apart from the CMT production, we also help develop collections for designers who may be in the early stages of their business and still setting up their team. We act as an extension of their own atelier where we launch brands and set systems for them in terms of pattern or range development. We take pride in their growth and quite enjoy growing with them and are comfortable handing them over to larger CMT factories for products we may not be producing.

4. As a business model, what are the benefits of CMT and the drawbacks?

Advantages of CMT

■ Smaller orders: Fully factored or larger factories demand higher quantities because of high fabric minimums dictated by mills. When designers work with a CMT manufacturer like us, they are not restricted by minimums because they source the fabric, which means they have more options and greater flexibility over quantities.

■ Supply chain transparency: It's ideal for designers and brands looking to work closely with their manufacturers and have more control and visibility over their entire supply chain. This can be communicated in their marketing stories with their customers.

■ Less waste: CMT can be seen as a more responsible option as there is more control over wastage and the use of sustainable resources.

■ Closer to market: CMT manufacturers have a shorter lead time. This reduces the risk for the designers of removing the chance of incorrectly anticipating what the market will want by the time the product hits the shop floor.

■ More control: Designers retain more control with CMT manufacturers as we are using their fabric and components to give them exactly what they are looking for, and there is less need to compromise. With fully factored manufacturers, their network of mills and suppliers is often more limited and made up of pre-existing relationships. This can mean they may not be able to find exactly what you are looking for or that the quality of fabric or components might not always meet expectations.

- Specialisation: CMT manufacturers like us would usually have a specialisation. This is a defining factor for luxury designers choosing to work with us.

Disadvantages of CMT

- Limited scale: CMT factories are usually smaller setups, which means they can't necessarily keep up with the demands of your business as it grows. They may not be able to manufacture the entirety of your collection, for example, as they may specialise in certain categories.

- Cost: Choosing to produce with a CMT manufacturer means designers need to purchase all the fabrics, raw materials and trims while also developing patterns and investing in grading. Designers need to watch the cost of the product in order to maintain their margins.

- Delays: CMT manufacturers are usually the last part of the supply chain. This means any delays higher up in the supply chain have a compound effect on us. You can't always anticipate delays in garment production. Materials stuck in customs, labels made incorrectly or zips delivered to the wrong address are common problems. Fully factored manufacturers will be able to source materials and components faster and have the ability to fix problems quicker.

- Knowledge of fashion: Fully factored factories may be able to cater to start-ups as they will source everything needed to make a garment. If you choose to work with a CMT manufacturer, you need to provide tech packs and spec sheets in order to get your desired product, so having someone with garment technical knowledge in your team is ideal.

5. What kind of clients?

We cater to luxury womenswear designers. Nearly 75% of our current clients are designers who showcase at London Fashion Week, Paris Fashion Week and Copenhagen Fashion week. These designers are sampling their runway collection with us and, eventually, we produce these pieces to be sold at major retailers across the world like Net-a-Porter, Matches or American department stores like Neiman Marcus. The remaining 25% of our clients are designers with successful e-commerce labels who may not necessarily be showcasing at any major runway yet but are still selling globally at major retailers.

Apart from that, we have a few costume designers who work for big production houses, so we make costumes for films.

6. How does work arrive?

CMT manufacturers are often at the end of the supply chain. Finished goods will typically leave our factory and go directly to a fulfilment centre. Lead times are often very short, so management and organisation of operations are key to a successful CMT manufacturer.

Generic workflow for the garment-making process at MAES LONDON

1. The client sends a tech pack along with a spec sheet and pictures of the garment.
2. Fabric and patterns follow once the project is discussed.
3. A sample, Salesman sample (SMS), or a prototype, is launched in the desired fabric.
4. The sample is costed for CMT production based on the minimum order quantity (MOQ).
5. An order is sent by the client for production.
6. A bill of materials for the order will follow from the client with a list of raw materials.
7. Raw materials arrive at the factory.
8. A pre-production sample (PPS) is launched for approval with final fabric and trims.
9. Once the PPS is approved, CMT production begins.
10. CUT: All fabric is cut.
11. MAKE: The garments are assembled on the sewing line.
12. TRIM: All trims are added.
13. A quality check is performed internally.

14. An external quality check happens at the factory or offsite at a location arranged by the client.
15. All finished garments are packed.
16. The order is collected and sent to the distribution centre.
17. All raw materials and patterns are returned to the client.

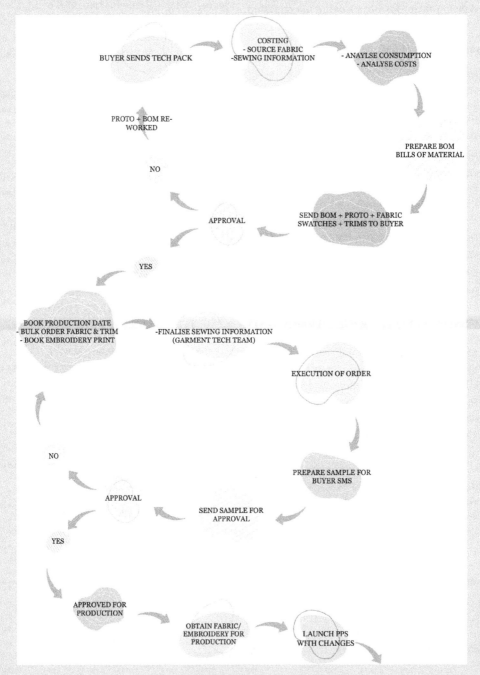

Figure 1.7
Flow Chart MAES 1

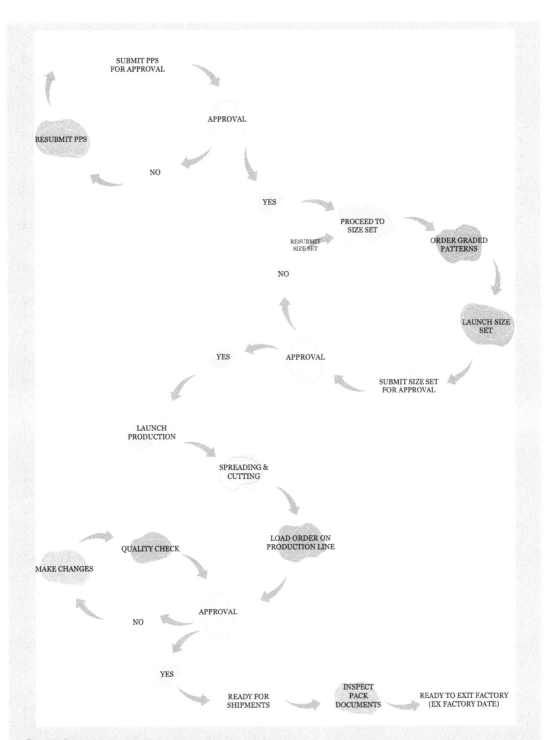

Figure 1.8
Flow Chart MAES 2

7. What is the average lead time from design/order to delivery?

A sample can be finished in as little as two days during peak times such as London Fashion Week but the average time is just under two weeks.

The lead time for production is calculated from the approval of PPS or final raw materials arriving at the factory. Our lead time for production was four weeks, but since Brexit, we have had to extend our lead time to four-to-six weeks. This is to accommodate for fabric delays as most of our fabric comes from the EU.

Brexit has also caused extra paperwork and more logistics help is needed for small businesses like ours. Currently, we do not have a logistics department and this new additional process is taking a lot of our time.

8. Where are most brands located?

Our clients are global businesses selling across the world. Geographical location plays a small role to where you are running your business from. We have clients who contact us from Australia, the United States and Nordic countries, as there may not be an atelier like ours to help them with their product. Having said that, most of our clients are local to the UK and believe in the quality of British-made goods.

9. What is your MOQ?

We are flexible with our MOQ, however, we have found that we are most efficient when producing 40 units per style. This efficiency translates into savings and better pricing of the garments, which is passed onto our clients. Producing lower than 40 units comes at a premium as it may be treated as sampling.

Our clients have chosen us for our standard of quality. We believe in their product and work closely with them throughout the production to ensure the best possible results.

10. Can you tell us how you see the future of CMT?

Digitisation, customisation and social media will prompt designers to rethink their impact of the environment when producing their garments. The need to reduce their carbon footprint will lead to micro-factories closer to the market supply chain.

Short product development calendars, sourcing of small batch sizes and nearshoring are key to the financial viability of fashion businesses opting for CMT manufacturing.

With Brexit and import duty levied on finished goods, designers will be forced to look inward to find solutions to save those extra costs that affect the bottom line.

Luxury designers thrive on having creative control over their products and that comes with ongoing partnerships with their manufacturers. These partnerships, whether it is CMT manufacturers or mills or print developers, will be the key to their success. In return, the concept of micro-factories with specialisations will emerge in local supply chains, which will make this partnership flourish even more.

11. Can you tell us your opinion on the impact/changes on fashion supply chain (FSC) post pandemic?

Prior to the pandemic and Brexit, production managers and quality control managers would frequently visit their factories to ensure production is running smoothly. Fabric faults, trim shortage and pattern problems are common and can halt production. These can be resolved through active communication and interaction with the clients.

What we are seeing post-pandemic is that our clients are heavily relying on us to proactively resolve these issues for them. This comes after years of trust working together.

Travel to factories, both locally and internationally, will remain limited whilst travel restrictions and social distancing rules are in place, so reliance on video conferencing tools will be paramount. Spec sheets and tech packs will need to be thorough.

Transparency in timelines, payments and deliveries will be ever more important to build trust for ongoing partnerships.

We had to pivot very quickly during the pandemic to keep the team safe and keep our clients work uninterrupted. This led to us taking an additional space to adhere to the government's social distancing guidelines. The additional rent was the last thing we needed during the pandemic, but it was the right move for our company and the team. Ultimately it led us to move to our new, larger studio in North London.

12. Anything else to add?

During the pandemic, I had started to observe the fashion industry inside and out. I knew things would be changing on a grand scale. Lots of creatives and freelancers were suddenly without a job.

We were being approached by textile designers looking to start their own fashion line, but they didn't know where to start as their expertise was in surface design and not patterns and fits. This is when I decided to launch Greige Prints, our own inhouse brand catering exclusively to textile designers, making fashion manufacturing more accessible.

If MAES London makes manufacturing more accessible to fashion designers, then Greige Prints keeps the art of fashion alive.

With pre-developed styles, we work with textile designers to print the fabric, and then produce mini exclusive prints collections for them to sell via their website or our website greigeprints.com.

Figure 1.9
Greige

Activities & exercises

1. Develop a flow chart-critical path for fashion knitwear manufactured in Italy and delivered to the UK. Map out each stage and research from raw material to delivery.

2. Investigate a brand with a vertical supply chain and one that is completely outsourced, noting these need to be types of product, and compare. What are the key differences?

3. If you were setting up a fashion brand, what type of supply chain model would you want to incorporate and why?

4. Can a linear fast fashion supply chain model be sustainable? Compare a linear supply chain with a circular/closed-loop supply chain. What are they key differences?

References

Abecassis-Moedas, C. (2007). "Globalisation and regionalisation in the clothing industry: survival strategies for UK firms," *International Journal of Entrepreneurship and Small Business*, 4(3), 291–304.

Aftab, M., Yuanjian, Q., and Kabir, N. (2017). "Postponement application in the fast fashion supply chain: a review," *International Journal of Business and Management*, 12(7), 115. doi: 10.5539/ijbm.v12n7p115

Ahi, P. and Searcy, C. (2013). "A comparative literature analysis of definitions for green and sustainable supply chain management," *Journal of Cleaner Production*, 52, 329–341.

Allwood, J.M., Laursen, S.E., Malvido de Rodriguez, C., and Bocken, N. (2006). *Well dressed? The present and future sustainability of clothing and textiles in the United Kingdom*. Cambridge, UK: University of Cambridge, Institute for Manufacturing.

Appelbaum, R.P. (2004). Assessing the Impact of the Phasing-out of the Agreement on Textiles and Clothing on Apparel Exports on the Least Developed and Developing Countries. https://escholarship.org/uc/item/6z33940z

Barnes, L. and Lea-Greenwood, G. (2006). "Fast fashioning the supply chain: shaping the research agenda," *Journal of Fashion Marketing and Management*, 10(3), 259–271. doi: 10.1108/13612020610679259

Braungart and Mac Donaugh. (2002). Cradle to Cradle: Remarking the Way We Make Things. New York: North Point Press.

Cagri, H. and Damla, U. (2011). Silk road supply chains: A historical perspective. 10.1201/b11368-3

Camargo, L.R., Pereira, S.C.F., and Scarpin, M.R.S. (2020). "Fast and ultra-fast fashion supply chain management: an exploratory research," *International Journal of Retail & Distribution Management*, 48(6), 537–553. https://doi.org/10.1108/IJRDM-04-2019-0133

Caniato, F., Caridi, M., Castelli, C., and Golini, R. (2011). "Supply chain management in the luxury industry: a first classification of companies and their strategies," *International Journal of Production Economics*, 133, 622–633. doi: 10.1016/j.ijpe.2011.04.030

Chan, H.K., Griffin, J., Lim, J.J., Zeng, F., and Chiu, A.S.F. (2018). "The impact of 3D printing technology on the supply chain: manufacturing and legal perspectives," *International Journal of Production Economics*, 205, 156–162. https://doi.org/10.1016/j.ijpe.2018.09.009

Christopher, M. (2022). *Logistics and Supply Chain Management* (6th ed.). Harlow, United Kingdom: Pearson Education. https://www.pearson.com/en-gb/subject-catalog/p/logistics-and-supply-chain-management/P200000007134/9781292416205

Christopher, M. (2000). "The agile supply chain - competing in volatile markets," *Industrial Marketing Management*, 29(1), 37–44.

Christopher, M. and Holweg, M. (2011). ""Supply Chain 2.0": Managing Supply Chains in the Era of Turbulence," *International Journal of Physical Distribution & Logistics Management*, 41, 63–82. http://dx.doi.org/10.1108/09600031111101439

Christopher, M., Lowson, R., and Peck, H. (2004a). "Creating agile supply chains in the fashion industry," *International Journal of Retail & Distribution Management*, 32(8), 367–376. https://doi.org/10.1108/09590550410546188

Christopher, M. and Lee, H. (2004b). "Mitigating supply chain risk through improved confidence," *International Journal of Physical Distribution & Logistics Management*, 34(5), 388–396. https://doi.org/10.1108/09600030410545436

Cooper, M.C., Lambert, D.M., and Pagh, J.D. (1997). "Supply chain management: More than a new name for logistics," *International Journal of Logistics Management*, 8(1), 1–14.

Crisell, H. (2020). https://www.thetimes.co.uk/article/maison-lesage-behind-the-scenes-at-chanels-embroidery-atelier-p8vzhlc0p

De Burgos Jiménez, J. and Céspedes Lorente, J.J. (2001). "Environmental performance as anoperations objective," *International Journal of Operations & Product Management*, 21(12), 1553–1572.

Dicken, P. (2007). *Global shift: Mapping the Changing Contours of the World Economy*. New York: Guilford Press.

Fernie, J. (2017). "Retail Logistics," in Brewer, A.M., Button, K.J., and Hensher, D.A. (eds.), *Handbook of Logistics and Supply-Chain Management* (Vol. 2, pp. 379–391), Bingley: Emerald Group Publishing Limited. https://doi.org/10.1108/9780080435930-024

Fernie, J. and Sparks, L. (2019). *Logistics and Retail Management*, 5th Edition. London: Kogan Page.

Fixing Fashion Report. (2019). https://publications.parliament.uk/pa/cm201719/cmselect/cmenvaud/1952/report-summary.html

Fletcher, K. (2010). "Slow fashion: An invitation for systems change," *Fashion Practice*, 2(2), 259–265. 10.2752/175693810X12774625387594

Gereffi, G. (1994). "The organization of buyer driven global commodity chains: How US retailers shape overseas production networks," in Gereffi, G. and Korzeniewicz, M. (eds.), *Commodity Chains and Global Capitalism*, Westport, CT: Praeger.

Gökalp, E., Gökalp, M., and Eren, P. (2018). "Industry 4.0 Revolution in clothing and apparel factories: Apparel 4.0," in *Industry 4.0 from the Management Information Systems Perspectives*, pp. 169–183. doi: 10.3726/b15120/21

Henninger, C., Alevizou, P.J., Goworek, H., and Ryding, D. (eds.). (2017). *Sustainability in Fashion - A Cradle to Upcycle Approach*. Palgrave Macmillan Ltd. https://link.springer.com/book/10.1007/978-3-319-51252-5. Accessed 27 Feb. 2023.

Hines, T. (2004). *Supply Chain Strategies: Demand Driven and Customer Focused* (2nd ed.). London: Routledge. https://doi.org/10.4324/9780203631669

Huq, F.A., Chowdhury, I.N., and Klassen, R.D. (2016). "Social management capabilities of multinational buying firms and their emerging market suppliers: An exploratory study of the clothing industry," *Journal of Operations Management*, 46, 19–37. https://doi.org/10.1016/j.jom.2016.07.005

International Journal of Physical Distribution & Logistics Management, 43(5–6), 478–501. https://doi.org/10.1108/IJPDLM-03-2012-0107

Jacoby, D. (1997). *The Migration of Merchants and Craftsmen: A Mediterranean Perspective (12th–15th Century).* Routledge Publication. SBN 10: 086078620X; ISBN 13: 9780860786207.

Jacometti, V. (2019). "Circular Economy and Waste in the Fashion Industry," *Laws*, 8, 27. https://doi.org/10.3390/laws8040027

Kathiala, R. (2020). Supply Diversification — A Luxury for Luxury? WWD. April 23. Available at https://wwd.com/business-news/business-features/supply-diversification-luxury-1203565590/

Koszewska, M. (2018). "Circular economy—Challenges for the textile and clothing industry," *AUTEX Research Journal* 18(4), 337–347.

Lane, C. and Probert, J. (2006). "Domestic capabilities and global production networks in the clothing industry: A comparison of German and UK firms' strategies," *Socio-Economic Review*, 4(1), 35–67. https://doi.org/10.1093/SER/mwj030

Mabert, V. and Venkataramanan, M. (2007). "Special research focus on supply chain linkages: Challenges for design and management in the 21st century," *Decision Sciences*, 29, 537–552. https://doi.org/10.1111/j.1540-5915.1998.tb01353.x

Magretta, M. (1998). https://hbr.org/1998/09/fast-global-and-entrepreneurial-supply-chain-management-hong-kong-style

McKinsey. (2020). The State of Fashion 2023. https://www.mckinsey.com/industries/retail/our-insights/state-of-fashion

Perry, P. and Towers, N. (2013). "Conceptual framework development: CSR implementation in fashion supply chains," Pookulangara, S. and Shephard, A. (2013). "Slow fashion movement: Understanding consumer perceptions—An exploratory study," *Journal of Retailing and Consumer Services*, 20(2), 200–206. https://doi.org/10.1016/J.JRETCONSER.2012.12.002

Perry, P. and Wood, S. (2019). "Exploring the international fashion supply chain and corporate social responsibility: Cost, responsiveness and ethical implications," in Fernie, J. and Sparks, L. (eds.), *Logistics and Retail Management* (5 edn, pp. 97–128). London: Kogan Page.

Seuring, S. and Müller, M. (2008). "From a literature review to a conceptual framework for sustainable supply chain management," *Journal of Cleaner Production*, 16, 1699–1710.

Shen, B., Li, Q., Dong, C., and Quan, V. (2016). "Design outsourcing in the fashion supply Chain: OEM *versus* ODM," *The Journal of the Operational Research Society* 67(2), 259–268. http://www.jstor.org/stable/43830670

Srivastava, S.K. (2007). "Green supply-chain management: A state-of-the-art literature review," *International Journal of Management Reviews*, 9, 53–80. https://doi.org/10.1111/j.1468-2370.2007.00202.x

Stone, E. (2008). *The Dynamics of Fashion.* 3rd Edition. New York: Fairchild.

Stone, E. (2012). *In Fashion.* 2nd Edition. New York: Fairchild.

The Chartered Institute of Logistics & Transport UK. (2019). Glossary of terms and dictionaries. [online] available from https://ciltuk.org.uk/Knowledge/Knowledge-Bank/Resources/Other-Resources/Useful-glossaries [6 August 2022].

Venkatraman, N. (1989). "Strategic orientation of business enterprises: The construct, dimensionality and measurement," *Management Science* 35(8), 942–962.

Wen, X., Choi, T.M., and Ho Chung, S. (2018). "Fashion retail supply chain management: A review of operational models," *International Journal of Production Economics*, 207, 34–55. https://doi.org/10.1016/j.ijpe.2018.10.012

Websites

http://www.ecouterre.com/a-robot-just–made-an-entire-t-shirt
http://www.makeit british.co.uk
http://www.wto.org
https://publications.parliament.uk/pa/cm201719/cmselect/cmenvaud/1952/report-summary.html
https://www.commonobjective.co/article/what-is-circular-fashion
https://www.just-style.com/comment/the-future-of-fashion-supply-chains-part-i_id139237.asp
https://www.lifung.com

CHAPTER 2

Suppliers: From raw materials to finished goods

Summary

This chapter will focus on the different types of business engagement within the supply of fashion clothing and accessories. This chapter will cover steps required in the procurement and acquisition of raw materials, yarn, fabric manufacturing and the components used in the manufacture of clothing and accessories. There are complex connections with tiers and layers of participants and the chapter will explain how these connections work successfully and how to best manage centres of excellence and localised systems. It is important to communicate what your process to customers for each product or material, identifying the environmental cost and the benefits for every item. Doing this will result in a customer who can make an informed decision based on their principles and values. It could be argued there is a danger in overloading consumers which may have little effect on their actions and more could be done at the business strategy level with clear Environmetal Profit and Loss Information.

Learning outcomes

At the end of this chapter, you will be able to:

- Explore the issues around raw materials and their connection t environmental impact
- Consider better methods of production linked to material sourcing and the alternatives
- Evaluate the opportunities for circular models in the fashion supply chain

SDG GOAL(S) – THIS CHAPTER LINKS TO:

6 Clean Water and Sanitation

12 Responsible Consumption and Production

13 Climate Action

14 Life Below Water

15 Life on Land

Right now, sustainability claims are like the wild west, so the EU is trying to regulate that. It creates complexities for brands who want to enter these markets. But the general idea is to prevent unverified, untrustworthy sustainability claims. The SAC taking on the MSI and opening it up to the industry is precisely why we exist: To reduce duplicity and reduce the work to make it easier for brands to make better decision-making and better outcomes.

– Jeremy Lardeau, Sustainable Apparel Coalition

In cases of sustainability, retail brands are often called out for greenwashing and defending false claims of sustainability can be very damaging. It would be good to follow the example of the fashion brand Ganni who has clearly stated, since its conception in 2010, that they do not want to claim to be a sustainable brand and they offer three reasons for this. First, Ganni cited that fashion encourages newness; second, if Ganni stated its brand was sustainable, it said it was afraid of being called out for greenwashing; and third, Ganni explained that it is on a never-ending journey to minimise its impact. The brand has made a clear decision about not promoting sustainability claims because it believes that all fashion brands in the future will have to be sustainable through either legislation or by consumer behaviour, which puts pressure on the brands to improve their business model (Ganni 2021).

Focussing on the issues in the textile and clothing sector in the UK has led to the creation of Textiles 2030 linked to SCAP 2020, the Sustainable Clothing Action Plan, part of WRAP, the Waste and Resources Action Plan, which has started Textiles 2030 and its environmental targets are to:

- Cut carbon by 50%, sufficient to put the UK textiles sector on a path consistent with limiting global warming to 1.5°C, which is in line with the Paris Agreement on climate change, and achieving net zero by 2050 at the latest
- Reduce the aggregate water footprint of new products sold by 30% (Wrap 2021)

For this to happen, brands and retailers need to commit to the agreement and follow guidelines and research on informal self-regulation. This is only the beginning of the story about fabric selection and working to achieve goals set out in the Paris Agreement, the United Nations' (UN) Sustainable Development Goals (SDG) and the recent Fashion Industry Charter for Climate Action, which will require support across the whole of businesses and the stakeholders (United Nations 2021). It is also highly likely that textile recycling will be mandatory in the European Union (EU) by 2025.

Raw materials

There is a growing number of global textile fairs that focus on better fibres and products that meet the UN's SDG. This idea has extended to trade shows such as Premiere Vision in Paris, The Sustainable Angle in London, the Global Fashion Summit (Pui-Yan Ho and Choi 2012) and circular production models.

Decision-making around the use of raw materials is a very contentious part of the supply chain; the price factor is very important, but for any designer, Textiles can be the point of difference and this can be attained with the use of raw materials print and colour. In making these decisions, there is a complex set of criteria and arguments remain at the forefront about the selection of sustainable materials. Many would argue for using wool and cotton for slow fashion durable garments, but there are just as many who would argue against using wool and cotton because the sustainable impacts are very high. Research tell us a consumer's main focus is on the most sustainable fibres, yet transparency around this is often missing. A modern myth is that all things natural, including organic cotton, are one of the best materials, but in this chapter, many options will be discussed and this modern myth and its alternatives will be explained. This is by no means a definitive guide to fabric production – the objective is to highlight the current processes and widely used raw materials and offer the better, more commercially viable alternatives.

The way companies, which includes suppliers and retailers, buy and book fabrics related to price often depends on the weight and the construction of the fabric. The amount of yarn and weight of the fabric will significantly affect the price – and this applies to all materials as the weight of the yarn content is key to the price per metre.

Blends

Price is often a key factor in blended fibres. They can be mixed to give a more affordable price as well as performance qualities. A good example of this is the low aftercare (washing) that comes from mixing cotton with polyester for reduced creasing, ironing and drying time in home textiles. Although these properties are desirable, they make recycling the fibres more difficult. When being recycled, the fabrics are sorted into types, which is often a slow and labour intensive process by hand. The process of separating the fibres from a piece of fabric, sometimes called biological recycling, is being developed in laboratories and is a chemically intensive process that uses acids and alkali to produces new polyester and microcrystalline cellulose. However, this is not being used on a large scale yet. The lifecycle and environmental impact of these processes need to be assessed if they are to be increased in scale commercially (Subramanian et al. 2020). This lifecycle assessment includes the production stage as well as the usage stage; consumers can keep products in use for much longer if durable fabrics are used.

Another significant blend is elastane, commonly known as Lycra, which is mixed with fibres for its inherent performance properties. Its fibre content percentage usually less than 5%.

Jersey knitted fabric has stretch due to the construction of the material and Lycra, a trade name by Dupont, gives mechanical stretch to woven fabrics and has helped the longevity, fit and comfort of numerous garments. Knitted hosiery has been revolutionised by the inclusion of this fibre and shapewear, along with denim and day-to-day workwear in the woven categories. It would be a challenge to produce a close or flexible fitting garment without the stretch qualities and research is underway for a less impactful alternative to Lycra. Much research is being developed on bioplastics that can replicate the stretch of this elastane fibre and will be discussed later in this chapter.

Fibres and textiles are classified by their origin and then by the method of being converted into yarn. Although effectively everything is man-made, the raw material can be natural, synthetic or regenerated, which includes both natural and synthetic sources. A benchmarking table such as the Made-By Environmental Benchmark for Fibres assesses a fibre's relative impact (Common Objective 2021). Within the natural category, there are protein or plant-based fibres. Using the term man-made or hand-made is common but also misleading as most manufacturing is carried out by machine technology. In the development of materials before the second industrial revolution, the wool markets and towns were situated in the east of England and central to the wealth of the area. These were hand-worked fabrics, spun and woven by a hand-worked loom. Although rare in the UK, there are artisan craftspeople who carry on these traditional non-mechanised techniques today. Throughout this chapter, the current view of textile production and the opportunity for new materials and methods will be reviewed. Carbon impacts of the fabric process can be benchmarked against a recognised format such as the "Made-By Benchmark," an non-governmental organization that existed to offer accreditation of fabric and garment sourcing. There are verified measures for environmental impact and source availability, such as the Higg Index and the Materials Sustainability Index (MSI) and wider technical assessment tools through both online applications and a company's own resources. Another example is the Swedish finance application Klarna (Klarna climate footprint dashboard June 2021) that links the carbon footprint of fashion purchases, which it can rate and show comparisons. This makes it effective for affordable brands who link to this payment service. In luxury fashion, Kering has produced the Environmental Profit & Loss report for several years and also now has a smartphone application (Kering 2021), which is available to use on their products. It does require a reasonable amount of sourcing knowledge as to where each component comes from – such as a leather bag with brass fittings made and tanned in France with trims from Chile – and the information is specific to the brands and their sourcing policies.

> *The figures presented to measure the environmental impacts associated with the production of a fashion product from the raw material extraction to the sale to the customer. They are based on economic analysis that estimates the societal cost of the environmental impacts.*
>
> (Kering 2021)

Questioning these metrics with the implications of greenwashing, which may present items in overly favourable light, has grown especially around the use of the Higg Index and its high score for recycled synthetics above conventional wool and cellulose. As regulation for fashion companies does not yet exist, brands can make claims of sustainability with little evidence or promote the more sustainable fibre on a "green label," whether it be a swing ticket, logo on website or section laid out in store (for example, an item with 53% Tencel that claims to be a conscious choice is hiding the 47% cotton from an unknown source). Furthermore, blends exist that show recycled content, i.e., 33% recycled polyester, clouding the impact of the 67% virgin polyester. Brands have been using these blends to support "eco- choices" it is not the reduced environmental impact that they have chosen, but the cost price as the reason the blend exists. Surprisingly, recycled fabrics are more expensive than their virgin material counterparts. This can only change with investment, change in demand and upscaling of the recycling infrastructure.

Court cases are being raised against retail giants as mentioned by The Sustainable Fashion Forum in their article "H&M is Being Sued for 'Misleading' Sustainability Marketing. What Does This Mean for the Future of Greenwashing?" (Sierra 2022).

Legislation begins in France in 2023, and is expected in the EU soon after, that will require every piece of clothing sold in France to have a climate impact label. "The message of the law is clear – it will become obligatory, so brands need to prepare, to make their products traceable" (Autret 2022). Brands will be forced to ensure the data on raw materials will be collated and shared throughout the supply chain and made accessible to consumers.

Animal & protein materials

Leather

This material can come from cattle, sheep, exotic and non-exotic animals and reptiles. For this purpose, it is important to review the most widely used material as being bovine (beef cattle) leather. The Leather Working Group has been instrumental in setting up standards on traceability. (LWG 2021) A UK brand, Owen Barry is known for its leather and sheepskin. The brand clearly shows the source of its farms and that the materials used are a by-product of the meat industry, stating that the skins "would be burnt as waste" if not used to create leather fashion accessories (Owen Barry 2021).

The Leather Working Group has made great strides in managing a very complicated industry where opacity has become the norm; the origin of the animal and the skin's journey through manufacture is hard to trace. The group has set standards to trace the origin back to the slaughterhouse or abattoir. Although the food industry has been able to name the country and farm for its meat supply, it is currently beyond the remit of the leather industry to provide this level of transparency. The issues around animal welfare and the use of highly dangerous substances in the tanning of leather remain as does the subsequent level of risk. In South America, the beef industry is linked to damage to the rainforest by cattle farming for both the food and leather industries.

> Cattle farming activities are socially and politically highly significant and impact on virtually all aspects of the environment. This impact may be direct, for example, through the emission of greenhouse gases, or indirect, for example through expansion of soybean production for feed replacing forests in South America.
>
> (Statham et al. 2017).

A retailer is wise to specify the use of non-hazardous chromium tanning and to join the Leather Working Group to add to their ethical credentials. There are good examples of brands doing this:

> Tanneries from which we source leather must be audited by the Leather Working Group at least once every 18 to 24 months. Additionally, Timberland bans the use of hides from certain countries or regions where we have learned of animal husbandry or animal welfare concerns.
>
> (Timberland 2021)

Fur

There are ethical issues regarding animal welfare and the sustainability of the animals used in fur production and there are a wide variety of opinions on this topic. Key issues include how animal welfare laws, fur farming and illegal hunting are carried out as well as the legality of these actions in each country and its animal welfare policies. Many campaigns have highlighted these issues, notably People for the Ethical Treatment of Animals (PETA 2021).

Customs and Excise in the UK have clear rules on legal and illegal imports and will seize any goods that are not compliant with the laws, particularly around the use of exotic skins and endangered species. This applies in particular to exotic or endangered species even if the material is vintage; proof of this is required transport goods internationally, as stated in the Customs and Excise guidelines: "Endangered animals or plants including live animals, birds and plants, or goods made from them, such as jewellery, shoes, bags and belts, even if they were openly on sale in the countries where you bought them unless you have a valid CITES permit. This also includes caviar, ivory, coral, shells and crocodile, alligator and snakeskin taken from endangered animals, timber products made from endangered trees and cosmetic or medicinal products made from endangered plants" (UK Government publications 2021).

The most important point to recognise is that real fur is often knowingly passed off as fake fur by suppliers and often unknowingly by retailers. The UK government had an investigation into market traders selling real fur products as fake fur after it discovered that the items were indeed real. In the proceedings of the hearing, commentary discussed that the general public and the committee could not believe that real fur could be cheaper than fake fur and cited a lack of consumer awareness. However, the facts proved they were misguided in their assumption. Real fur is much cheaper than fake fur made from acrylic fibres, a man-made synthetic, and there is a profit incentive to pass off the use of real fur, which deceives buyers and consumers and highlights ethical and animal welfare concerns. Noted in the minutes of the response to the enquiry, the investigation states "The Government will, however, commit to keeping evidence of non-compliance with the textile labelling rules under review and remain open to suggestions from businesses, consumers and representative groups about the best way to ensure consumers get the information they need about fur products" (Fur Trade in the UK 2018).

Protein-based natural materials

Wool – from any animal, sheep, camel, angora goat, rabbit, alpaca and more

Merino wool

The fibre from merino sheep requires animal farming, sometimes intensively, and certain conditions to thrive, which might be temperature, specific foods and their cultivation. The carbon impact of the fleece fibres from sheep comes from the farming, feeding, impact of the animals' greenhouse gas (GHG) emissions and using more land for fibre production. These animals also damage the soil through their hooves and overgrazing (Cao 2020). Although the campaign for British Wool is well supported in the UK, the breed of sheep that gives the finest and longest fibre mainly comes from Australia's merino sheep variety. Considering these issues and the additional transport, the fibre wool scores a very low classification of "E." This wool can be recycled mechanically and was known as "shoddy" fabric during the second World War. Recycling wool cannot be an infinite process; the staple length of the fibre and smoothness and lustre will be reduced on each recycling conversion. To upcycle wool and improve its smoothness, there is a need to mix it with new virgin fibre, which is better quality than the recycled fibre (Gullingsrud 2017). Recycled wool is highly rated in Made-By fibre benchmark tool, a significant improvement on the conventionally produced fibre.

The Woolmark company

Woolmark labelling was commonplace to guarantee the origin and quality of virgin wool and this trademark still exists today. Fashion competitions have been organised by the Woolmark company, most famously one in which both Yves Saint Laurent and Karl Lagerfeld won awards back in the 1954s (Conti 2019). Currently, the company is owned in Australia and offer the same types of competitions. They are at the forefront of promoting wool as a sustainable future-proofed fibre and this links very much to the supply of wool coming from the Australasia region.

Additionally, Oritain technology can show the farm origin of specific fibres, shown in Fig 2.1. They have carried out work on the mohair supply chain and, with the ability to identify 50% of the material back to the farm, are protecting the livelihoods of the farmers (Oritain 2021).

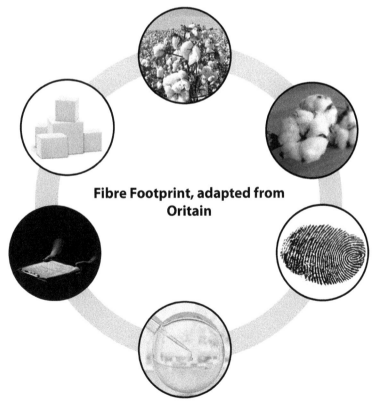

Figure 2.1 *Source:* Alison Johnston

Cotton footprint diagram

Figure 2.2

Harris Tweed fabric Alison Johnston

Harris Tweed

Harris Tweed fits the artisan small producer techniques and now has protected status with the Harris Tweed certification mark.

This yarn from the fleece of Scottish Cheviot and Blackface sheep is a triumph for supply chain transparency. Since 1993 after the Harris Tweed Act, the registered trademark authorised by the Harris Tweed Authority has been synonymous with local artisan producers in the remote Scottish island of Harris in the Outer Hebrides. The Outer Hebrides, also known as the Western Isles, is a chain of islands 30 miles off the west coast of mainland Scotland. The main islands include Lewis, Harris, North and South Uist, Benbecula and Barra (Harris Tweed Authority 2016).

As an export product widely used in accessories, such as Yull shoes, the use of the certification and label requires sheep to be raised on the Harris Islands. The sheep are shorn in June and July each year for the health and well-being of the flock and the eventual woollen yarn is not a by-product of the slaughtering process. Its regulation provides a transparent process (Harris Tweed Authority May 2021). Examples of the Fabric in Fig 2.2.

Silk from silk moths, but also spider silk, wild silk and peace silk

Silk has become an affordable and accessible fibre since the end of the multi-fibre agreement in 2008. It has appeared on high streets and mid-market brands where before it was only available to luxury fashion houses. To cultivate silk from a *Bombyx mori* silk moth requires allowing the moth to live at a high temperature and feed on the leaves of a mulberry tree. This raw material is mainly sourced in larger quantities from India and China and the techniques of manufacturing silk garments are usually close to the supply of the fibre. There was a historic Silk Route that led from China through to Europe and Venice, Italy, which meant there was a large industry for printed silk fabrics around the northern Italian lakes. Although the silk industry in Italy is very limited now in its impact, the design and development of silk prints and fabrics are still one of the strengths of the area. Considering silk as a raw material price is one of the barriers to its use and durability. However, ethical issues around using animal-based protein materials can also be a barrier. There has been some interest in vegan silk, where the moth is allowed to erupt from the cocoon. This causes some damage to the fibres (a shorter filament length with a woodier appearance), but essentially means that no harm is done to the insects in their lifecycle. This is available from some countries such as Madagascar, but it is not widely available. While it produces a less consistent, smooth and lustrous fabric, this technique does meet ethical vegan requirements as the moth is not boiled alive in the process of procuring the yarn.

Innovations in using silk from other insects, such as spiders, have been adopted by some brands. However, there is room for a wide development of this type of product – that is stronger than steel – for the replication of something like a Kevlar vest for technical garments such as skiwear. The brand Spiber has used spider silk with the North Face brand to produce an innovative jacket (Dezeen 2019).

Silk moths live on certain diets (e.g., mulberry leaves) or can only be cultivated in certain countries where the temperature and conditions are perfect. These countries are typically China and India, while small amounts are grown in Thailand and Southeast Asia, notably Myanmar for wild silk.

Natural materials

Plant-based

Global markets show cotton as a very widely used fibre. This is supported by the myth that natural fabrics are, by default, sustainable; however, the farming of this fibre is complex.

There are levels of improvement in supply chains that offer better alternatives to the most widely used fibre, which is conventional cotton. Conventional cotton often uses genetically modified seeds, a high number of insecticides and pesticides and large amounts of land and water in its cultivation. Human rights violations occurred in both Uzbekistan and China with the Uyghur workforce involving forced labour and illness due to the intensity of chemical the process. There is much written about the horrors of cotton farming, as shown in the Environmental Justice Foundation's acclaimed film *White Gold* (Environmental Justice Foundation 2021) in which a broader picture of the issues in Uzbekistan is explored.

Retailers have begun to address the situation with policies and improvements in origin and traceability. These are examined later in the chapter.

Conventional cotton

Less than 1% of the world's cotton is organic cotton (Patagonia 2021). To encourage farmers to use organic methods, fibres are labelled and known as cotton in conversion during the transition until farmers receive certification.

Cotton USA uses "innovative seed varieties, scientifically developed to provide stronger, longer cotton fibres" (Cotton USA 2021).

There is a variety in names among cotton seeds and their qualities that have been branded with their unique names related to their country of origin and the length and smoothness of fibre. These include:

Pima cotton
Supima cotton
Egyptian cotton
Sea Island cotton

All of these are identified by the location in which the fibre was grown, such as Pima cotton from Peru. It is the cotton plant variety that produces a longer, finer, smoother thread to be spun in into a yarn. Historically, these fibres were more expensive and only grown in one location. With agricultural and scientific developments and the cultivation of seeds, the cotton plant can be grown and improved. Issues around genetic modification of the cotton seed and its inflated prices have caused unrest in the industry (De Castro 2021). Monsanto, a seed supplier, protects the development of its cotton seed by patenting it and the resulting future seeds the plants create. This means farmers have to purchase new seeds every year, requiring a larger financial commitment. Consequently, debt and sometimes suicide occur among those farmers caught in this debt-seed spiral.

BCI – the Better Cotton Initiative

A retail claim, often supported by a the BCI logo, made with sustainable cotton can promote the goals of female empowerment through farming in countries such as Pakistan as well as the removal of harmful substances from cotton cultivation.

As the labelling of retailers varies in consistency and clarity, the use of OEKO-TEX's STANDARD 100 helps awareness and avoidance of the negative issues associated with conventional cotton.

> *If a textile article carries the STANDARD 100 label, you can be certain that every component of this article, i.e. every thread, button and other accessories, has been tested for harmful substances and that the article, therefore, is harmless for human health.*
>
> (OEKO-TEX 2021)

This information only applies to the fabric; it would need to have OEKO-TEX's "Made in Green" label to ensure minimal hazards were used in the entire manufacturing process.

This standard 100 applies to fibres other than cotton, and consideration of what types and amount of processes are added to the yarn or fabric is important to fully analyse the environmental impact.

CottonConnect (CottonConnect 2021) is empowering farmers in Pakistan and India to farm with fewer pesticides; in a complex supply chain, it is sharing knowledge with the farmers. Additionally, Oritain (Oritain 2021) technology, which can identify the market and farm for the cotton boll, can give a clearer picture of its source. Science-based traceability is key to the visibility of the whole farm origin and the process of the extraction of raw materials; utilising this service can ensure ethical and environmental compliance. Furthermore, the technology exists to apply this materials science to other raw fibres. It is not enough to assume knowledge – proving the claims of fully traceable products is key.

Historic cultures in South America have been able to produce coloured cotton, which is naturally pigmented. Although limited in supply, the science to cultivate plant fibres in natural shades ranging from white, pink, green and brown is possible and offers potential for further development (Selvedge 2021).

Organic cotton

When it comes to price, a company might sell organic cotton very cheaply, but it will be very lightweight and not very durable. On the other hand, a durable organic cotton t-shirt can cost ten times as much as an entry price model, and if blended with Lycra, becomes harder to recycle.

To gain the Global Organic Textiles Standard (GOTS) accreditation, a supplier of fibre will be thoroughly examined to meet the exacting criteria; and from this, GOTS (2021) provides a useful database of suppliers and processors for cotton garments. This is a valuable tool to find those manufacturers of readymade garments (RMG) who comply with organic and ethical production globally (GOTS 2021). Some brands, notably H&M, have changed their policy from organic cotton to using 100% sustainable cotton by 2020, they missed this target by only 5%, but they have gone further to suggest a more blended offer:

> The commitment to sustainable cotton is part of a larger plan to convert to 100% recycled or sustainable materials across the company's supply chain by 2030.
>
> (H&M 2018)

The organic cotton supply could never match the demand for all the cotton globally and more development of recycled cellulose is important to meet consumers' needs for natural breathable fibres. Land use and water use are still significant factors in the organic production of fibres, especially cotton.

Recycled cotton

Recycled fibres can come from two main sources: Pre-consumer, where the offcuts from bulk manufacturing of RMG can be collected and sent to a fibre converter, or post-consumer, where household or charity garment collections and waste garments are used.

Using pre- or post-consumer fabrics to produce new fibre is becoming more commonplace, but it is worth remembering that, unlike synthetic fibres, there is a limit to how many times this natural material can be recycled as the hand-feel and quality deteriorates with continuous processing.

The Textile Exchange is a global authority on the development of new models in the procurement and recycling of fibres, cotton in particular. Its sustainable cotton report showing the research and development into the multitude of methods and processes developed by textile companies to reuse materials is impressive and covers some of the following textile Standards and accreditations link to chapter 5 brands (Textile Exchange 2020):

Recycled claim standard (RCS)
Global recycled standard (GRS)

Infinited fibre, which has been heavily invested in by H&M, offers a fibre using old garments such as denim processed with International Textile Machinery Association technology; compared with cotton, there is a 20% cost savings, improved dye uptake and significantly less water use (Selvedge 2021). This has great potential for circular textiles, but is important to consider the societal impacts on the 300 million people that currently work in the cotton industry. Other notable regenerated cellulose fibres competing with infinited fibre are listed later in the chapter in the section titled "New Cellulose Fibre Developments." This could hold more power for brands and consumers as the backlash against plastic pollution and synthetic fibres wages and the need for cool breathable fabrics increases, as an alternative to conventional cotton. A brand they are currently developing is Infinna™, being used by the fashion brand Ganni (Infinted fibre 2022)

Tencel/Lyocell

This fibre has become much more available to consumers, but little is known about the history or development of this beneficial fibre that came to market more than 25 years ago in the 1990s. Tencel was and can be used in mid-market fashion products from jeans to dresses. The material is a pulp created from eucalyptus trees, which grow quickly without pesticides or high-water use. In the conversion to yarn, the water is recycled and the solvents are removed in a closed-loop process. More impressively, the hand feel, durability and breathability of the finished fabric is as comfortable as cotton and as smooth as silk. The barrier to using this more often is the price. Sadly, blending this for price benefits reduces the recycling options.

Ecovero™

Ecovero™ branded fibre, a viscose option under the Lenzing™ brand, uses sustainable wood sourcing that has a 50% lower carbon footprint and water use than conventional Viscose (Ecovero 2021).

Acetate

Acetate fibre is commonly used in lining. Although not very durable, it carries about 13% of the man-made cellulosic mix in usage terms. It has been replaced by polyester linings due to its price and durability, the fabric does not wash well and the lined garments generally require dry cleaning. Acetate is dissolved in Acetone, which is used in nail polish remover.

Viscose/Rayon™

Viscose/Rayon™ is a man-made cellulosic category and is the most widely used fibre with 79% of the regenerated cellulose market mix; however, due to its chemical-intensive process this is the least sustainable option (Palmer 2021).

Viscose is widely criticised for causing deforestation as well as its high chemical impact during fibre conversion, which is harmful to both the environment and the workers involved during the process. The fabric itself is extensively used for light-weight dresses and blouses. It also has poor durability in wear, is weak, creases very badly and is often disappointing to consumers who want a product to be of reasonable quality.

Forest Stewardship Council (FSC)-certified viscose offers a better alternative to conventional viscose. Choosing a product that has FSC certification ensures the product has minimal impact on woodlands and forests and that trees are replaced sustainably. This is considered as helping meet the goal of SDG 15, Life on Land.

Bamboo

Bamboo is a very fast-growing invasive crop that grows well without chemical intervention. The resulting fibre is breathable and generally biodegradable if the material in the dyeing and finishing processes does not compromise this. In the conversion to fibre, the chemical retting process is widely used and the chemically rich wastewater requires treatment before being released into the environment. The process of natural retting is long, as the stems of bamboo are hard to break down naturally.

Cupro and modal

Both of these fabrics use regenerated cellulose fibres to produce a light and soft fabric. Cupro is a closed-loop cellulose fibre made of a cotton linter that makes up only 1% of the market. Alongside this, modal is a closed-loop cellulose fibre commonly made of beech wood that makes up 2.8% of the market (Palmer 2021).

The important certifications to look for in man-made cellulosic are FSC, Programme for the Endorsement of Forest Certification (PEFC), Bluesign and Zero Discharge of Hazardous Chemicals (ZDHC), which support goals SDG 15, Life on Land, SDG 13, Climate Action, and SDG 6, Clean Water and Sanitation.

New cellulose fibre developments

These innovations cover reverse logistics in fibre supply and this is a fast-changing area of new development, offering solutions to the impacts of cotton's use of water and chemicals and identifying waste streams with a keen motive of circularity. The field of cellulose and waste products is evolving; while not an exhaustive list, the fibres discussed next offer the least environmental impacts.

Spinnova is a new method for transforming cellulose pulp into textile fibre without using harmful chemicals and it has the potential to use both consumer waste and waste from agricultural settings. This technology can use FSC-certified wood pulp, straw and leather waste to produce new fibre. With a hand-feel like cotton or linen, and using much less water, okthis fabric also can be recycled without affecting the quality. The brand Arket has used Spinnova as 18% of a shirt jacket for men, mixing it with better cotton (Spinnova 2022).

Infinited fibre can use both textile waste and paper and agricultural waste streams. It begins with mechanical shredding and technology that can remove blended polyester from the mixture. This again is a good cellulose or cotton replacement and there is a good indication that this will replace traditional Viscose manufacturing in the same facilities' factories (FAB 2022). Infinted fibre also list Ioncell, which uses wood pulp and no further chemicals, as having been used for clothig by Marimekko. Further developments include Metsa fibre using paper pulp, which is both biodegradable and recyclable, Bio2, which uses agricultural waste and Biocelsol, which uses both textile waste and wood pulp. These innovations are being scaled and, with investment, can offer the solutions to waste in clothing, forestry and farming.

Other notable innovations are listed next.

Re:NewCell uses textile waste and some chemicals to produce new fibre and the base material must be at least 90% cotton to achieve the hand-feel desired (Forbes 2022). This has been supported by Levi's, H&M and Inditex for closed-loop textiles. They appear to be providing the feedstock and using up to 300 million T-shirts per year to make the cellulose fibre (Drapers 2022).

Evrnu has produced NuCycl, another lyocell fibre that is both recyclable and uses textile waste (Evrnu 2021).

Agraloop cellulose and Agraloop BioFibre have developed a circular method and address waste from rice straw, oil seed, hemp, banana, cane and pineapple to create a fibre similar to cotton (Circular Systems 2022). The innovations are being brought to market swiftly and the emphasis has moved from the circular method to a larger consideration of the method's impact with full transparency about chemical use and ongoing recyclability.

Of all the notable mentions here, many are likely to be brought to market with the manufacturing capabilities situated in Europe and the desire for cellulose and cotton-like hand-feel. These raw materials encompass the need for more natural materials that are cool and breathable whilst giving the opportunity to use natural waste streams in new ways, with no impact on non-renewable resources and less pollution and energy use than the conventional alternatives. Using waste materials and achieving more circular production goes a long way to meeting goal SDG 13, Climate Action, and the intention to avoid the pollution and land use associated with virgin materials. These new cellulose fibres should be considered as the alternative to blends for price or hand-feel and as much as possible should only be blended if that still allows satisfactory recycling.

Linen

Linen is an ancient fibre grown from flaxseed with minimal chemical and water use. The resulting fibre and fabric is durable and can be used in light and heavier weights for summer clothing. It will grow in poorer soils and the fabric in naturally moth resistant. It also works well in blends with cotton for a lower price point and with wool for durability and a warmer hand-feel. It can be organically grown and it takes on colour and dyes well. There is a growing market for organically grown and dyed linen. Projects in the UK, such as Fibreshed in Blackburn, grow flax for linen use in projects and clothing that allows newer seed stock and enable regenerative agriculture in a former wasteland (Northwest England Fibre Shed 2021).

Hemp

Hemp is another ancient fibre, which has some connotations to the illegal drug trade; however, this fibre has been used in domestic carpeting and its loose fibre is a great sustainable alternative in packaging. A company known as The Hemp Trading Company (THTC 2021) has grown its business using this fibre. Although it is rough to wear, it is very durable. The Hemp Trading Company runs a business-to-business (B2B) private label to bring this fibre to customers.

Agraloop cellulose & Agraloop BioFibre

Although this fibre is in development, the commerciality and opportunity are swiftly being taken up by fashion brands. The company Circular Systems is looking at a zero-impact fibre using agricultural waste that would otherwise have been burnt. Using residues, low-cost food stock and bioenergy for production as well as the upcycling of all water used, the only impact is needing to add organic soil improvements to go back to the farm. (Textile exchange 2020).

Man-made synthetic fabrics – chemical & oil based

The fibres listed next in this section use oil and are chemically intensive in their virgin material state.

Polyester

This fibre is cheap, easy to manufacture and is currently the most widely used textile fibre globally, although cotton comes a close second. Polyester's raw material is made of oil, a non-renewable resource, which various estimates suggest will run out in as much as 50 years (EarthBuddies). An estimated 56.8 million tonnes of the fibre are produced each year (Palmer 2021).

The benefits of polyester include its easy recyclability from fibre to fibre and its use of plastic source material to be recycled into new yarn. However, there are some questions on how much carbon is produced in chemical recycling and mechanical shredding has proven to be less impactful (Wrap 2018). Conventional recycled polyester uses PET plastic bottles, making them into virgin polyester fibre. However, this is not true circularity, which should be plastic to plastic, instead of downcycling plastic to synthetic fibres.

Newer methods are being developed around enzyme recycling by Caribos, a French company (Carbios 2021). It is investing in plastic bottle recycling (PET) in a plant in Lyon, France.

I am very proud that we successfully transformed polyester textile waste into clear bottles, which have identical properties as those made from virgin PET. This major innovation allows us to expand our sources of supply which, until now, consisted primarily of PET plastic waste.

Professor Alain Marty, Chief Scientific Officer of Carbios

This technology can work both in upcycling and downstream, with the polyester garments being recycled into plastics and the more common PET into polyester fibre. Although this would not solve some of the concerns, a report by the Clean Clothes Campaign states that this is not true circularity. Fibre-to-fibre recycling or bioplastics are more innovative and may curb the ever-increasing consumption of polyester and synthetic fibres (Fossil Fashion July 2021).

Another impact of polyester fibre is that it breaks down into micro-fibres in production and laundry and leaches into water supplies. Currently, research is being conducted on impacts of these micro-plastics on aquatic life and on goals SDG 6, Clean Water and Sanitation and SDG 14, Life Below Water to gauge this potential threat. The biggest issue with man-made synthetics is they do not biodegrade – garments can be rescued from landfills in perfect condition even if they are 30 years old.

Of course, in the consumer use phase, using less power to launder and dry garments is very beneficial and contributes to making this a durable fibre along with the possibility of re-cycling it many times. It is difficult to tell any difference in hand-feel or quality between recycled synthetic material and the original virgin fibre; this is a positive attribute and might outweigh some of the wider issues around synthetics. It is worth noting that, currently, recycled polyester yarns are a 30% higher cost price than virgin materials, which is a notable barrier to increased use of sustainable materials. The price needs to be financially viable and monitored once this is commercially available (Wrap 2021).

Nylon

An invention before the second World War, nylon can be used in a wide variety of products from toothbrushes to backpacks to hosiery, but it is not biodegradable. Nylon is fast and cheap to produce, is durable, has the same impacts of micro-fibre release as polyester and, in its virgin state, uses oil, which is not a finite resource. There is an added complication as this fibre creates nitrous oxide in its production. This is the greenhouse gas that is 310 times more potent than CO_2 (Climate News 2019).

Lycra

This elastane fibre has transformed the hosiery and shapewear industry and is more commonly known by Dupont's tradename, Lycra. Many products have been improved in terms of stretch and, more importantly, recovery by the inclusion of this elastic fibre, with typical composition of up to 5%. In denim, plain woollen fabrics and cotton jersey, this addition will give longevity and shape retention, but it cannot be recycled; even a 1% inclusion of Lycra makes this difficult to separate from the majority fibre. Elastane does not biodegrade, therefore, innovations are being developed. One example is Roica V550 Eco-Smart yarn, which was awarded the Synthetic Fiber prize in 2021 and also uses 50% pre-consumer recycled content. Lycra has also invented a bio-based product of which 70% is made from natural corn, the Lycra T400 EcoMade fibre. Although Lycra uses waste fibres from manufacturing, they also blend these with virgin fibres, which increases the environmental impact (Fisher 2021).

Acrylic

Acrylic fibre easily replicates wool at a fraction of the cost and, therefore, is used in winter-weight garments. Its uses are often in blends to increase the warm hand-feel of fabrics or to make a bulked, fluffy appearance. Like other man-made synthetics, is does not biodegrade and can shed fibres. It is less durable than high tensile synthetics and is used more in the value fashion market.

Polyvinylchloride

There are several iterations of synthetic resin materials normally used to coat a woven or non-woven layer base fabric, this can replicate leather and become faux leather. There is an opportunity to add stretch to the base fabric in jersey construction, but can also be used in multiple products. Clothing, bags and shoes are commonly made from polyvinylchloride (PVC) and they are often offered in vegan product lines. Like the other man-made synthetics, oil is PVC's source material and its decomposition and chemical intensity is very high. It counts as the most environmentally damaging plastic there is because during its lifecycle in production, it releases toxic chlorine-based chemicals (De Castro 2020).

Neoprene

Neoprene is a petroleum-based foam used to coat wetsuits for outdoor sports. It is often replicated as "scuba fabric," a densely knitted jersey fabric made from polyester or nylon. The impacts of neoprene are very high, and closed-loop methods are being worked on. A better choice is a plant-based natural rubber alternative such as Yulex (Yulex 2021).

Coatings

PVC and neoprene are coatings, but the application of numerous materials can be applied to a woven or knitted base. Examples of these include metals, glitter, resin, performance finishes, scents and well-being surfaces such as micro-encapsulation of scent, raised areas and burnt-out holes. The list is infinite and needs to be considered along with micro-encapsulation, such as perfume and moisturisers, in the spinning of the fibre.

Innovative materials

Thankfully, this area of research and development is moving swiftly to solve the textile resource and waste crisis and exploring new manufacturing methods and processes. Some of the materials included here have wider commercial acceptance and scalability, but this is not true of every new invention, which may require more industry investment and traceability. Because of the fast pace of development, the carbon impact information of new materials may not yet be available and the general view is to ask the difficult questions around energy, land and water use, transportation, chemical use and the health and wages of the workers involved. Arguably, this is a great deal to consider, but if the solutions are opaque, then some of these choices should be considered carefully.

Econyl

Econyl was developed by the Italian company Aquafil (Aquafil 2021). Made from regenerated waste, such as carpets and fishing nets, Econyl is used a great deal in swimwear and can easily be recycled. Aquafil is planning to use post-consumer waste to make new fabrics, but have scaled Econyl to a point where it is being used quite extensively.

SCS Global Services

Recycled content certification comes from SCS Global Services and this accreditation is worth seeking out to prove the origin of the raw material and avoid unscrupulous passing off of virgin material as recycled.

There has been a lot of interest in biomaterials that may replicate leather or can be grown in lab conditions from simple organisms. It is important to evaluate each material for its strengths and benefits, particularly if resins are used to stabilise the base material as these may be more toxic than the material on its own. In terms of scalability, of a lot of these materials have issues with larger quantities and accessing the supply in larger quantities, including pineapple leather.

Pinatex

This faux leather material uses waste from pineapple farming to produce a material suitable for shoes and handbags. Pinatex includes coloured and metallic finishes and uses a synthetic resin in its process. It is considerably more expensive than real bovine leather, at approximately twice the price of leather.

Mylo

Mylo is a mushroom leather developed by Bolt Threads and is being used by Stella McCartney, Adidas and Lululemon. This innovative leather substitute is grown like a fungus and then put through a tanning process, however, the Life-Cycle Assessment (LCA) is a work in progress and Bolt Threads states, "While Mylo material is not currently plastic-free, it is not petroleum-based" (Bolt Threads 2021).

Banana fibre

Bananatex is a sustainable innovation with great advantages as a new material. Abaca, the name of the banana plant grown in the Philippines, can be composted and is grown without the use of pesticides or extra water. Furthermore, it has received OEKO-TEX STANDARD 100 certifications for its yarn dyeing method, has a low-impact water-repellent coating and a natural wax finish (The Sustainable Angle 2020).

Dyestuffs – colour & use application

When choosing a base fabric, it will, of course, undergo processing to achieve the colour required or to soften the hand-feel. There are dyeing and printing processes that can be chemically intensive and performance finishes for water repellence, minimum iron use and many more finishes. Technology around micro-encapsulation develops swiftly so that anti-bacterial properties using silver and embedding scent are available. It might be using cooling and warming elements to add a point of difference to a planned range, such as Tencel, in bedsheets, or thermal underwear. With this in mind, the processes by which fabrics can be treated are endless. The table here has been created to show the positives and negatives of the main treatments; none of these is without some hazard to the environment, linking to goal SDG 6, Clean Water and Sanitation.

It is important to review the impact of each process on the raw material that has been chosen. Materials science is a vast topic and the chemistry used to produce colour has developed over hundreds of years to a complicated mixture of novel, innovative and historic methods that add colour to fibres and fabrics. It is worth remembering "20% of Global Industrial water is attributed to the dyeing and treatment of textiles" (Stylus How to Source 2020 July; Ellen Macarthur Foundation 2017).

Dyeing

Usually, the process of dyeing happens in the yarn stage, but it can also be the whole piece of fabric (piece dyed) or, lastly, garment dyed. At each stage of dyeing, the time to a finished garment is shortened. The phrase "green is the new black" links to the fashion industry efforts to predict colour by season. Now more adopted as a sustainable slogan, it was first used to indicate the industry's attempt to predict a colour theme for an upcoming season. Decision-making around colour is subjective and based on sales history and season; however, black as a range colour is a key staple and has less risk for fashion retailers.

Much is written about colour forecasting, but with shortened lead times and data crawling technology, often a quick response is needed to react to current colour trends. This also requires a fast method to achieve colour with the least impact on the environment and goal SDG 13, Climate Action.

For seasonal colour predictions, data retrieval from the initial interest within a colour range can offer the opportunity to forecast more accurately. But buyers beware: Trends can change quickly and being left with a stock of cerulean blue can be a costly problem. Therefore, making colour decisions as close to the critical path deadline as possible can improve the accuracy of these choices. The stages of making these colour choices can be added as listed below:

Fibre dye
Yarn dye
Piece dye
Garment dye

Almost all dyes and printing methods use dangerous substances and many of these are prohibited under ZDHC legislation, along with chromium tanning of leather

Information: In manufacture of the fibre	Leather	Wool	Plant Based Linen and Cotton	Synthetics
Availability	GOOD	BEST	GOOD	BETTER
Length of lifecycle	BETTER	BEST	BEST	BETTER
Recyclable	BETTER	POOR	BETTER	BETTER
Biodegrades	POOR	GOOD	BEST	EXCESSIVE
Impacts of the production				
Energy	POOR	POOR	EXCESSIVE	VERY POOR
Resources	VERY POOR	EXCESSIVE	EXCESSIVE	POOR
Pollution	GOOD	VERY POOR	VERY POOR	POOR
Waste	POOR	POOR	EXCESSIVE	POOR

Figure 2.3

Table information on impacts of fibres through growth and manufacture

and azo dyes. At this point, it is recommended that full textile testing is carried out for performance testing and chemical properties by an authorised test house, such as Intertek's Textiles and Apparel testing service (Intertek 2021).

There is a case for natural dyes, but the scalability and consistency of quality would again be a risk for larger production orders as these still require a mordant to fix the colour, which is a salt or acid mixture. A table reviewing the impacts of materials at various stages, with a colour coded key is shown in Fig 2.3.

Colour & print application

Printing transfer

From a paper image, heat is applied to transfer the image to the garment or fabric, which can result in a resin-like hand-feel to the printed image.

Screen printing

These techniques started with the original hand-drawn silkscreens on wooden frames, creating printed layers that build to the final image. Screen printing is also copied mechanically, but it is still a slow and expensive process and requires the garment design to fit into the confines of the printed area. This has moved onto rotary printing, requiring engraved rollers to apply the colour in stages; a large order volume is needed to setup the engraving.

Digital printing

Digital printing is more sustainable with ever faster and cheaper printers. Short runs of fabric can be processed through a digital printer, much like a home desktop printer but on a much larger scale, which has revolutionised placement printing designs and the accuracy, speed and quality of printed fabrics. Technology moves quickly and early adopters of new methods can have a competitive advantage and save on waste. A notable entrant into super-fast printing is Kornit digital:

> Kornit's products meet the highest sustainability standards with zero wastewater and a low carbon footprint, enabling on-demand printing that fits today's consumer culture.
>
> (Kornit 2021)

Newer printing techniques now enable direct-to-garment printing. Although screen-printed finished t-shirts have been around for a long time, this technology allows pre-printed garment parts for a wealth of product types, cutting down waste and allowing quick response production runs.

> Kornit has found the sweet spot with the Vulcan for screen printers challenged with small and medium print runs that require speed to market.
>
> Scott Valancy, COO, T-Shirt Central

Denim & finishes

Denim fabric dominates many fashion categories, the industry is set to grow further with an expected value for denim fabric to be $87.4 billion by 2023 according to Statista (Statista 2021). The dyeing and washing of denim is a great concern due to the extensive chemicals, water and energy it takes to make a pair of denim jeans. The fabric itself in its raw state has much less impact, but the special characteristics of many denim washes create a negative impact.

As mentioned previously, denim factories have a very different setup from other woven sewing factories and there has been extensive investment in automatic machinery that can reduce energy and achieve these finishes and washes with fewer environmental impacts. These new wash technologies can achieve the same look and innovation in this area for manufacturers to recover their investment costs is important. It is hoped that brands will continue to put pressure on manufacturers to improve the environmental impacts of the fabric around dyeing, washing and finishing.

Raw denim has gained a renaissance amongst connoisseurs of denim production, particularly with denim sourced from Japan. Selvedge denim, which has not gone through the washes and finishes of most commercial denim, has become more popular. The weights and durability of unprocessed denim means that its lifecycle and durability are extensive. However, fashion demands new washes and colourways and the fit aspects of denim require elastane or Lycra to sculpt the human body, which has resulted in myriad fits and finishes for denim brands and it is replicated at all levels of the fashion hierarchy.

In denim washes, brands have historically used potassium manganite and bleaching agents such as hypochlorous acid and sodium hypochlorite, which are potentially being replaced with ozone powder, a is chlorine- and potassium-free way to apply chemicals as a foam to reduce water and energy use. It first needs to comply with ZDHC and third-party accreditation such as Bluesign. Further low-impact finishes are being developed to meet the growing demand for ethical products.

Stonewashing has distressed fabrics for many years, and washing as well is one of the systems used to distress fabrics. New methods are being developed to achieve this finish. New stones even are being made from recycled PET plastic, bio-rubber and bio-sponge as an alternative to pumice stone and can be replaced, like a Velcro, that can distress the fabric in a washing drum.

The brand Tommy Hilfiger has partnered with the Ellen MacArthur Foundation for jeans redesign using recycled fabrics in combination with laser machinery and the known denim technologies Jeanoliga and Tonello. Laser finishing has less impact due to the fact it uses heat rather than chemicals to get the required distressed finish.

Ozone finishes and bio-enzymes add to the wealth of innovations, as ozone can replicate bleached effects. The enzyme treatment attacks the fabric structure to create finishes similar to stone-washing and does not use the rare pumice stone in its process (Premiere Vision July 2021a).

Light chemical solutions exist as well that use the less-hazardous hydrogen peroxide, which can achieve very light washes known as a soft oxidant. There are existing ideas around waterless technology that imply less usage of water in the production process of denim, for example, the more innovative nanotechnology that replaces water with air, consuming no water at all.

For precision finishing and feathering on denim, laser finishing has been developed in which a laser can reduce water compared to standard finishing. Archroma, a waterless technology (Archroma 2021), is dyeing technology to achieve an effect via laser that replicates what would be carried out by manual sandblasting. Archroma has gone on to develop indigo techniques with their zero liquid discharge, that can be accredited by Bluesign and GOTS.

There are of course performance finishes added to fabrics that are hazardous in various levels, although developments are being worked on using natural waxes. The list here indicates the most popular finishes:

Non-iron
Crease-resistant
Shower-repellent
Water-repellent

Trims & accessories

Every component of a garment has an impact at some stage, so it is worth considering after the dyeing and finishing steps what components are being added to the garment and what are the potential impacts. Options for newer and innovative materials are prevalent here, too. It is possible to use recycled materials for all types of accessories. The hardware of brass metals and plastics can be reused and packaged from paper and plastics. It is also worth considering bio-polymers, which are alternatives to fossil fuels and replicate synthetic plastic resins (Premiere Vision July 2021b).

Zips

There are various types of zip fasteners that use Nylon and metal for the teeth and Nylon or cotton for the tape. There is a rise in "green" zips, with companies such as YKK developing these novel components.

Thread

Coats, a thread supplier, has invested in a polyester thread from recycled fibres (Coats 2020) and has pledged that all of its premium polyester thread will be from recycled material by 2024.

Brand and composition labels can be made from recycled materials. Metal components, such as rivets on jeans, can be brass or nickel and easily recycled or upcycled.

Trims such as lace, piping and insertions can be made from a recycled or organic fibres.

Buttons

A the cheapest level, these are made from casein, Nylon and plastics, but there is a multitude of alternatives in both natural and renewable materials, such as the corozo nut. The most expensive options from metals, glass or real mother of pearl can be a beautiful choice and, apart from the expense, there are great natural materials using nuts and wood that can be interesting to explore.

Sequins as decoration along with glitter and beads are contentious choices. These can be bio-plastics from PET plastic, but the most common material is plastic from virgin materials.

To conclude, it is important to align the material to sustainable supply chain management.

Green supply chain management

The 5R and 7R Framework

These new frameworks and models are moving on from the traditional 3R model of Reduce, Reuse, Recycle and has evolved to include Reimagine and Redesign (5R) (Pui-Yan Ho and Choi 2012) as well as Restyle and Rewear (7R) (Choi and Cheng 2015).

"Reduce," in its connection to fashion, is associated with minimising over-ordering of fabric supplies and stock, keeping the quantity lean and avoiding surplus product and resulting markdowns. Stock movement, with increasing freight costs and returns, will impact business margins and affect profit. Although the cost focus is an easy win for fashion brands to adopt, reputational risk is gaining importance and is detailed in Chapter 5.

"Reuse" within clothing applies to many old and new business models where clothing has an extended life, whether through rental, resale or repurposing. Upcycling has gained traction through slow fashion brands using discarded garments to be made into new items.

"Recycle" has been successful in packaging, garment hangers and some smaller components. There are even more opportunities linked to take-back schemes to extend this to second-hand garment sales and the recycling of the raw materials. Early adopters of the circular practices are seen in leather production and high-end denim brands.

"Redesign" can include both a business process and the creative means of product design. In process management, common themes are using new simplifying logistics, perhaps using hubs for fulfilment as opposed to a single distribution location. A good example of this has been promoted by ASOS with its "partner fulfils" scheme that is linked with both Adidas and Reebok, where the orders are sent from the collaborator's distributor.

Reimagine" is linked to business innovation, maybe a new way of manufacturing or selling direct to consumer, reducing overheads and associated costs. There are number of near-shore locations that might reduce the logistics impact, consequentially improving time-to-market and quality. This can have a significant competitive advantage where fashion brands seek to acquire market share in a saturated market.

"Rewear" has become more popular and there are now many rental companies using a peer-to-peer or direct-to-consumer platform. This idea has had success with occasion-wear and luxury accessories.

"Restyle" carries the potential to offer services that support the repurposing of garments by the consumer either through visual content of activities around craft and self-expression.

Most research in fashion sustainability has been on the fast fashion market, and there is some information on luxury fashion, too. Many new business models in recent years have adopted a slow fashion concept, keeping clothes in use for longer, designing them for durability and longevity. Kate Fletcher coined the term "slow fashion" – it focusses on classic styles that may repeat seasonally and may only present new collections on the historic "critical path" of two seasons a year (Fletcher 2010). Slow fashion is often characterised by small- and medium-sized enterprises (SMEs) and micro-organizations (Henninger et al. 2017). This incorporates newness at a slower, considered pace, making conscious purchase decisions for both the brand and customer. These products can be offered in new channels with low overhead costs, such as Instagram, as a shoppable platform. Marketing costs are relatively low, procurement and distribution can be through local networks and independent stores, which encourage a growing following of customers. With new payment applications, the ease of path-to-purchase for consumers and businesses alike allow smooth market entry and low stock holding. Manufacturing can be almost bespoke and result in less markdown and cost of carrying stock.

CASE STUDY

Interview – Sarah Yull – Yull Shoes (traceable sourced materials)

Biography: Sarah Watkinson-Yull started Yull in 2011 whilst at university in London. Yull received funding from the Prince's Trust to set up manufacturing for high heels in the UK and is still one of the only independent shoe brands manufacturing high heels in Britain.

Ethical & sustainable values are founded in our roots and always at the centre of what we do.

1. Can you tell me the number and types of raw materials you use in your shoe range currently and what is the most used material?

We use bovine leather from cows and goat leather and for the vegan options PU polyurethane. Then for components, there are heels and heel caps,

Figure 2.4 *Source:* Yull Shoes
Yull Shoes Harris Tweed boot

boxes, tissues and shoe bags, these protect the shoes in transit and enable returns. The leathers in the collection are sourced as a by-product of the food industry.

2. Do you see a high demand for more ethical sources of shoe uppers and if so, how have you addressed this?

We use vegan PU although the impacts of the material are high, it is the ethical choice of the consumer that drives this.

3. You have used some woven fabrics as part of the design of the shoes. Has this been a successful point of difference?

We have success and a point of difference with Harris Tweed, Linton Tweed and woven checks from Abraham Moon, whom all weave the fabric in the UK. Only Harris Tweed sources the fibre and yarn in the UK and they are the most expensive, but they are the best for doing repeat fabrics in season.

4. Working with several suppliers is challenging. What material has the longest lead time?

The UK-based Linton Tweed has a six-month lead time and they cannot repeat in the season due to the variety and complexity of the yarns involved. The printed leather also has a longer lead time.

5. What stock components can you easily get hold of?

As we reuse the same lasts (shoe moulds), we can buy stock of heels and soles very quickly.

6. You work with a global supply base. Can you tell me what the benefits of this mixed supply base are?

**Is it Speed?
Transparency?
Quality?
Price?**

Quality is the most important followed by price, then the transparency of the product, and lastly, the speed of supply. The product development costs are reduced by "moving on styles" and having a good relationship with our suppliers over the years of being in business. But it also depends on the customer requirements – the price can vary by £10, but the customers have been resilient to this, and the broad customer base helps too.

7. You use a model that I would term as "demand-led supply." What are the benefits of this?

As we produce once the orders (B2B) are placed, we can see the most popular styles for the season. We carry limited stock for the online B2C (business-to-consumer) based on the sales information.

8. Are you aware of extended producer responsibility? How that might affect your business?

Essentially, shoes are not a circular product due to the number of components. It would be amazing to work with a "cobbler" or shoe repair service to offer the refurbishment of shoes to customers and I want to look into this. Certainly in men's high-end brands the service is offered. It would extend the life of the shoes; I want customers to keep and love these shoes and have them for a long time.

9. What have been the challenges in a post-Brexit supply base and how have you dealt with these issues?

All of the delivery companies to our customers charged a €7 handling fee per item and then there was 18–20% retail tax in the European country. We had delays of six weeks into Bulgaria, which was the worst case.

10. You operate both a B2C and B2B model. What are the operations that have been impacted by export issues? Does it affect both time and money?

We have lost 60% of our EU business due to Brexit, but the UK sales and customers have been strong. July 2020 was our best month ever, despite the pandemic. Our USA business has been growing and this has been helped by the Wolf & Badger online stores mainly serving the East Coast of the United States.

11. What are the most successful areas of your business that you are most proud of? I am very proud of making shoes in the UK where other large businesses have tried and failed. We have close relationships with our suppliers.

12. What strategies have you changed with your supply base over the years?

We have had to adapt to changes beyond our control, such as the EU movement of workers around Brexit. We have had to accommodate this with new suppliers.

13. Can you give me your final thoughts on managing a complicated product and supply base and any top tips for new businesses?

There is continuous problem solving and ensuring lasting relationships. As we use a just-in-time model and have existing shoe lasts, which we reuse, we can turn around an order within four weeks. We have seen the evolution of a new fashion calendar that does not follow the traditional summer and winter seasons, and we can respond to this speed to market.

Activities & exercises

Discussion of Fibre and Fabric Impacts

1. Take a garment you are wearing and look at the care label and carry out a SWOT analysis.
2. Identify the fibres and the category e.g., synthetic, natural, plant based, protein, recycled.
3. Look at the fabric construction – what might this fabric be called? You can use a piece lens or magnify on your smart phone.

4. How many processes has this fabric been through before being cut into gar-ment pieces?

5. Where is the highest impact of the processes?

6. What could be done to make this less impactful? Think about water, carbon and waste processing.

7. Propose an alternative method for the textile lifecycle of this product.

8. Do you think this product is designed for longevity, circularity or disposal?

9. How can the manufacturing of the product be improved? Location? Equipment?

10. Lastly what are the care instructions and are these appropriate?

Activity: Care Label analysis questions

Activity: SWOT analysis of a composition label

COMPOSTION LABEL – FIBRES	SWOT ANALYSIS
STRENGTHS	WEAKNESSES
OPPORTUNTIES	THREATS

References

Aquafil. (2021). Aquafil.com/sustainability/the-eco-pledge/. Accessed June 2021.

Archroma. (2021). https://www.archroma.com/solutions/coloration-denim-casual-wear. Accessed 16th August 2021.

Autret, E. (July 2022). https://www.rfi.fr/en/france/20220722-french-agency-to-track-impact-of-clothing-industry-on-climate. Accessed 22nd July 2022.

Better Fabrics. Accessed May 2021. Made by https://www.commonobjective.co/article/made-by-environmental-benchmark-for-fibres. Accessed July 2021.

Bolt Threads. (2021). https://boltthreads.com/technology/mylo/. Accessed 16th August 2021.

Cao, H. (2020). "Fibers and Materials: What is Fashion Made of?" in Marcketti, S.B. and Karpova, E.E. (eds.), *The Dangers of Fashion: Towards Ethical and Sustainable Solutions* (pp. 53–70). London: Bloomsbury Publishing.

Carbios. (2021). https://www.carbios.com/en/#. Accessed 16th August 2021.

Choi, T.-M. and Cheng, T.C.E. (2015). *Sustainable Fashion Supply Chain Management from Sourcing to Retailing.* Cham: Springer.

Circular Systems. (2022). https://circularsystems.com/about. Accessed 2022.

Coats. (2020). https://coats.com/en/Sustainability/Sustainable-Products. Accessed May 2021.

Conti, S. (2019). "Woolmark Reveals Names of Latest Advisory Council," *Women's Wear Daily, WWD*, pp. 5.

CottonConnect. (2021). https://www.cottonconnect.org/. Accessed August 2022.

Cotton USA. (2021). https://cottonusa.org/quality. Accessed May 2021.

Customs and Excise. https://assets.publishing.service.gov.uk/government/uploads/system/uploads/attachment_data/file/946504/6.7005__SE_CUS_v3.pdf. Accessed May 2021.

De Castro, O. (2021). *Loved Clothes Last*. London: Penguin Book.

Dezeen. (2019). https://www.dezeen.com/2019/10/24/spiber-moon-parka-spider-silk-the-north-face-japan/. Accessed August 2020.

Drapers. (2022). https://www.drapersonline.com/topics/sustainable-fashion/sustainable-textile-innovation. Accessed April 2022.

Earthbuddies. https://earthbuddies.net/when-will-we-run-out-of-fossil-fuel/

Ecovero. (2021). https://www.ecovero.com/?gclid=EAIaIQobChMI9s2elbO38QIVD7btCh2IuQyREAAYASAAEgIPMfD_BwE. Accessed May 2021.

Ellen Macarthur Foundation Stylus (How to Source 2020 July) Ellen Macarthur Foundation 2017.

Environmental Justice Foundation. (2021). https://ejfoundation.org/films/white-gold-the-true-cost-of-cotton. Accessed May 2021.

Evrnu. https://nucycl.com/. Accessed April 2022.

FAB. (2022). https://www.stjm.fi/fablehti/tulevaisuus/6-textile-fibre-innovations-leading-the-textile-industry-revolution/. Accessed April 2022.

Fisher, G. (2021). https://www.fiberjournal.com/elastane-materials-expand-with-responsible-stretch. Accessed 30th August 2022.

Fletcher, K. (2010). "Slow fashion: An invitation for systems change," *Fashion Practice,* 2(2), 259–265.

Forbes. (2022). https://www.forbes.com/sites/jimvinoski/2022/01/28/abbs-paper-mill-technology-helps-renewcell-turn-old-clothes-into-new-fabrics/?sh=7782802f61e0. Accessed 2022.

Fossil Fashion Changing Markets Foundation. https://changingmarkets.org/portfolio/fossil-fashion/. Accessed 30th August 2022.

Frost, C. How to Source Stylus. https://app.stylus.com/fashion/sustainable-fashion-how-to-source. Accessed 28th June 2022.

Fur Trade in the UK. (2018). https://publications.parliament.uk/pa/cm201719/cmselect/cmenvfru/1675/167502.htm. Accessed May 2021.

Ganni. (June 2021). Accessed Instagram 28th June 2021.

GOTS. https://global-standard.org/find-suppliers-shops-and-inputs/certified-suppliers/database/search. Accessed May 2021.

Gullingsrud, A. (2017). *Fashion Fibers: Designing for Sustainability*. Bloomsbury USA.

H&M. (2018). https://hmgroup.com/sustainability/leading-the-change/goals-and-ambitions/. Accessed December 2018.

Harris Tweed Its There. https://www.harristweed.org/wp-content/uploads/HTA_Labels_Policy_Brand_Use_Rules_Document.pdf. Accessed July 2021.

Hemp T Shirt Company. https://thtc.co.uk/. Accessed August 2019.

Henninger, C.E., Alevizou, P.J., and Oates, C.J. (2017). "IMC, social media and UK fashion micro-organisations," *European Journal of Marketing*.

Infinited Fiber. https://infinitedfiber.com/blog/2022/08/16/ganni-reveals-infinna-tshirt-copenhagen-fashion-week/. Accessed July 2022.

Intertek. (2021). https://www.intertek.com/textiles-apparel/. Accessed 16th August 2021.

Kering Its There. https://www.kering.com/en/sustainability/measuring-our-impact/our-ep-l/app-my-ep-l/. Accessed July 2021.

Klarna. (2021). https://app.klarna.com/climate-footprint/dashboard. Accessed May 2021.

Kornit Digital Printing. (2021). https://www.kornit.com/sustainability/. Accessed May 2021.

https://www.leatherworkinggroup.com/?gclid=Cj0KCQjwvr6EBhDOARIsAPpqUP
HbbGPzDRJNORqNqnWZzRFYMMjmNYTwD9TNYFJn_4iqElhr3jTdSWcaAo
ygEALw_wcB. Accessed June 2021.

Northwest England Fibre Shed. (2021). www.northwestenglandfibreshed.org/home-
spun-homegrown-sowing-aregenerative-future-for-fashion. Accessed July 2021.

Oekotex. (2021). Standard 100. https://www.oeko-tex.com/en/our-standards/standard-
100-by-oeko-tex?gclid=CjwKCAjw1uiEBhBzEiwAO9B_HcqrdI1_-
nyvTzCnyM4PCXsdSTVVIfbAK0E-iOra2U1hg9g74nrpVhoCj3oQAvD_BwE.
Accessed May 2021.

ORITAIN. (2021). https://oritain.com/industries/fibre/https://oritain.com/partners/
mohair-south-africa/. Accessed May 2021.

Owen Barry. (2021). https://www.owenbarry.com/materials. Accessed August 2021.

Palmer H. (2021a). Polyester the Push to Circular. Asential WGSN 25/01/21.

Palmer H. (2021b). Cellulosics from Forest to Fashion. WGSN Accessed 26/5/21.

Patagonia. https://eu.patagonia.com/gb/en/our-footprint/organic-cotton.html. Accessed
May 2021.

Peta. (2021). https://www.peta.org.uk/issues/animals-not-wear/leather/. Accessed May
2021.

Premiere Vision. (2021a). https://www.premierevision.com/en/magazine/denim-know-
how-finishes-with-a-reduced-impact/?utm_medium=email&utm_
source=pco2021c16&utm_campaign=pco. Accessed July 2021.

Premiere Vision. (2021b). https://www.premierevision.com/en/magazine/savoir-faire-
accessoires-les-solutions-eco-responsables/?utm_medium=email&utm_
source=pco2021c16&utm_campaign=pco. Accessed July 2021.

Pui-Yan Ho, H. and Choi, T.-M. (2012). "A Five-R analysis for sustainable fashion supply chain management in Hong Kong: A case analysis," *Journal of Fashion Marketing and
Management*. [Online] 16(2), 161–175.

SAC. https://apparelcoalition.org/an-open-conversation-on-materials-in-fashion-key-take-
aways-and-learnings-from-thought-leaders-and-industry-experts/. Accessed May 2021.

Selvedge. (2012). https://web.b.ebscohost.com/ehost/pdfviewer/pdfviewer?vid=2&sid=
00ec992a-a5aa-4871-a9e3-52ccb8cb8c3f%40pdc-v-sessmgr03. Accessed June 2021.

Sierra, B. (2012). https://www.thesustainablefashionforum.com/pages/hm-is-being-
sued-for-misleading-sustainability-marketing-what-does-this-mean-for-the-future-
of-greenwashing#:~:text=In%20the%20lawsuit%20filed%20against,cases%2C%20
were%20allegedly%20completely%20untrue. Accessed 18th August 2022.

Spinnova. (2022). https://spinnova.com/collaboration/arket/. Accessed April 2022.

Statham, J., Green, M., Husband, J., and Huxley, J. (2017). "Climate change and cattle
farming," *In Practice*, 39(1), 10.

Statista. (2021). https://www-statista-com.uow.idm.oclc.org/statistics/734419/global-
denim-jeans-market-retail-sales-value/. Accessed July 2021.

Subramanian, K., Chopra, S.S., Cakin, E., Li, X., and Lin, C.S.K. (2020). "Environmental
life cycle assessment of textile bio-recycling – valorizing cotton-polyester textile waste
to pet fiber and glucose syrup," *Resources, Conservation and Recycling*, 161, 104989.

Textile Exchange. (2020). https://textileexchange.org/wp-content/uploads/2020/06/2025_
Sustainable-Cotton-Challenge-Report_20201.pdf.

The Sustainable Angle. (2020). https://thesustainableangle.org/banana-fibre-bananatex-
qwstion-an-interview-with-hannes-schoenegger/. Accessed July 2021.

THTC. (2021). www.thtc.co.uk. Accessed July 2021.

Timberland. (2021). https://www.timberland.com/responsibility/product/materials-
policy-statements/leather-processing.html. Accessed July 2021.

UK Government Publications. https://www.gov.uk/guidance/cites-imports-and-exports.
Accessed July 2021.

United Nations Foundation Fashion Climate Charter. https://unfccc.int/climate-action/sectoral-engagement/global-climate-action-in-fashion/about-the-fashion-industry-charter-for-climate-action. Accessed July 2021.

United Nations (UN). (2021). https://unfoundation.org/what-we-do/issues/sustainable-development-goals/. Accessed July 2021.

World Trade Organisation. (2005). WTO Website. [Online]. Available: www.wto.org (August 2005). WTO. 2001. Comprehensive Report to the Council for Trade in Goods on the Implementation of the Agreement on Textiles and Clothing During the Second Stage of the Integration Process, Textiles Monitoring Body, 31 July 2001. Geneva: WTO.

Wrap. (2018). https://wrap.org.uk/taking-action/textiles/initiatives/textiles-2030. Accessed July 2021.

Wrap. (2021). https://wrap.org.uk/taking-action/textiles/initiatives/textiles-2030. Accessed July 2021.

Yulex. (2021). https://yulex.com/lexcell-oc-open-cell-foam-rubber/. Accessed May 2021.

CHAPTER 3

Relationships in supply chains

Overview and context

Summary

This chapter will cover the varied context of relationships in fashion supply chains, identifying best practices and how relationships may impact sourcing and manufacturing of apparel, including the inherent power struggles between retailers, buyers and manufacturers throughout the chain. The area of non-governmental organizations (NGOs) and other pressure groups as well as the environmental impact of fashion supply chains will be investigated in depth to identify their influence on retailers and their manufacturing processes.

This chapter focuses on the different types of relationships and introduces concepts such as "co-opetition" corporate social responsibility (CSR) and how it relates to fashion supply chain relationships. Sustainability in the fashion supply chain starts with the relationships and networks built, for example with the suppliers, and these should be integrated into the supply chain as if they are your own business.

Learning outcomes

At the end of this chapter, you will be able to:

- Understand how supply chain relationships are interconnected and the different types of relationships that exist between suppliers' manufacturer brands

- Clarify the importance of collaboration and integration of relationships to form successful networks and shared information in the fashion supply chain to support sustainability

- Evaluate the concept of corporate social responsibility (CSR), different elements of sustainability (economic, environmental and social) and how and why the Triple Bottom Line (TBL) is important to measure success and the overall performance of a fashion business and the supply chain

- Appreciate the role of non-governmental organizations (NGOs) in a fashion supply chain and the importance of working with such organisations for a fashion brand

- Appreciate that accreditation such as B-Corporation is desirable for a sustainable fashion brand supply chain and why such relationships matter

SDG GOAL(S) – THIS CHAPTER LINKS TO:

1 No Poverty

2 Zero Hunger

3 Good Health and Well-Being

4 Quality Education

5 Gender Equality

7 Affordable and Clean Energy

8 Decent Work and Economic Growth

16 Peace, Justice and Strong Institutions

17 Partnerships for the Goals

Relationships in fashion supply chains

In the context of fashion supply chains, relationships with suppliers – from raw material supply to logistics and delivery – have become more complex as a direct result of global sourcing. The fast fashion revolution created a complex ecosystem in the fashion industry and collaboration emerged as a key theme in creation of sustainable fashion supply chains (Fernie and Sparks 2019; Perry and Wood 2019; Choi 2018). In the extant supply chain literature, the Japanese were at the forefront of innovation in the creation of supply chains with the rebuilding of the automobile industry after World War II. The Japanese developed techniques that are still used in all types of manufacturing today, such as total quality management (TQM) and just-in-time (JIT)manufacturing, a concept that was used to build fast fashion supply chains and is discussed in Chapter 1. The Japanese concept of *Keiretsu* is worth a specific mention here. This is a concept was used historically to build business networks and supply chains and relies on cooperation, coordination and the network's joint ownership and control amongst those in the network, as many in the network own equity and interests in each business (Cooper and Ellram 1993). It has also influenced the design of other supply chains, for example Uniqlo has a version of *keiretsu* in place in its highly successful clothing brand using a network of connected businesses with close-knit relationships as their supply chain.

- Arms-length – these tend to be adversarial – cost

- Small account – unique product/service

- National account – serving multiples

- Strategic alliance – collaborative, long-term, typical of supply chain

- JV – two organisations invest

- Vertical integration – unusual these days – LUXURY

- N.B SCM using outsourcing as a process is different, an alternative to verticality

Figure 3.1

Different types of relationships – Cooper & Gardener 1993

Quick response used to build relationships

Close collaboration is an ideal situation in the fashion supply chain because of its complexity. The idea behind quick response (QR) was for manufacturers to become more competitive through greater efficiency and speed, developing collaborative relationships between suppliers and retailers, which ultimately led to the development of fast fashion (Perry and Wood 2019). Traditionally, relationships in fashion supply chains have tended to be adversarial and largely cost-based (Barnes and Lea-Greenwood 2006).

Fundamentally, enhancing global sourcing collaboration by building in elements of transparency, long-term commitment and trust with supply partners is essential to supply chain management (SCM). Competition in global fashion markets is intense, so companies need to decide which business activities should be kept in-house, which they need to outsource and where to invest in the relationship building (Garcia-Marquez 2014).

This decision adds to the need to focus on relationships and ensures these relationships are managed with care in fashion supply chains. However, as fashion supply chains became fragmented and outsourcing became the norm, the power shifted towards the brand rather than the supplier, especially noted in the case of large-scale global brands and mass-market retailers (Gereffi et al. 2005). These include large conglomerates in the fashion sphere such as Walmart and other "supermarket" retailers, but also large-scale groups of brands like Vanity Fair, Gap and H&M.

If a relationship is strategic, it is reliant on sharing data and technology to pass information in both directions up and down the chain, including techniques placing the supplier in control. This is known as category management and often these manufacturers are lead suppliers known as full-service vendors (FSVs). This process works well for large-scale brands and suppliers, but in the case of small- and medium-sized enterprises (SMEs), such as those often found in the UK, these tend to be more adversarial and cost-based relationships (Froud et al. 2017).

Good examples of FSV manufacturers can be found in Sri Lanka supplying mass market retailers in the United States and the UK such as Next, Marks & Spencer, Abercrombie & Fitch, Victoria's Secret and Tommy Hilfiger. Sharing strategic plans with suppliers and moving away from purely transactional cost-based relationships can lead to longer-term sustainable partnerships across the fashion supply chain. Trust levels are paramount to make these work.

Corporate social responsibility (CSR) and relationships

The entire area of relationships in fashion supply chains has been positively impacted by corporate social responsibility (CSR), a concept that has grown in importance in the fashion industry, directly linked to the area of sustainability and ethics in SCM. CSR has been described by many as an umbrella term for sustainability issues in the fashion business (Thorisdottir and Johannesdottir 2020), but there is a real need to ensure CSR is embedded into the entire fashion supply chain to manage environmental and social responsibility.

CSR has been partly fuelled by growing public interest in issues like CSR and sustainability, as problems like climate change are given public focus by media and science. The impact of the fashion industry is significant on greenhouse gas (GHG) emissions and is well documented (Haunschild et al. 2019). In 2020, McKinsey research showed that the fashion industry was responsible for some 2.1 billion metric tonnes of GHG emissions in 2018, about 4% of the global total. The fashion industry emits about the same quantity of GHGs per year as the entire economies of France, Germany, and the UK combined; the supply chain is the root of the problem.

Smaller fashion suppliers

It is more difficult for smaller suppliers in fashion supply chains to wield any power as they can be pressured by their large retailer and brand customers. There is significant risk for the supplier in these situations as they can be coerced into cutting corners and may face retailers applying power in the relationship (Maglaras, Bourlakis and Fotopoulos 2015; Cox, Chicksand and Palmer 2007; Casciaro and Piskorski 2005). However, it is mutually beneficial for retailers and suppliers to develop effective committed relationships as this is how trust is built: through positive influencing, sharing information and following best practices on production and quality.

All of this can have a positive impact on CSR and sustainability, creating a win–win situation in the overall fashion supply chain. However, even collaborative relationships can be largely transactional with low levels of commitment on both sides.

A recent McKinsey (2020) survey revealed that fashion retailers are likely to consider further consolidation of their supply base in the future to minimise risk and sustainability will continue to become an increasingly important role in the way apparel companies select their suppliers (see Chapter 5 for more on risk). Environmental and social sustainability performance is likely to become the point of differentiation for suppliers and will be applied to improve sustainability, efficiency, digitization, speed and transparency in fashion supply chains (McKinsey 2020). An overall supply chain focus on relationships can lead to the following three key areas of sustainability:

1. **Economic sustainability:** An example of economic sustainability includes the smaller fashion suppliers who have developed their own design and product development skills to meet the retailer's economic sustainability requirements. These suppliers can also act as a type of innovation hub, offering new designs and, importantly, production techniques to larger fashion retail customers, which in turn creates cost effectiveness and increases profitability (Talay, Oxborrow and Brindley 2020).

2. **Environmental sustainability:** Collaboration by fashion suppliers and adoption of many policies in production processes can support overcoming the environmental concerns of retail buyers within fashion supply chains. Such collaborations may lead to more energy-efficient systems in manufacturing, elimination of chemical processes and reduction of waste, leading to greater circularity in the entire supply chain. Another area is joint training of employees and certification to become compliant – this can create transparent engagement throughout the processes in manufacturing and procurement of raw materials.

3. **Social sustainability:** Many suppliers gain a good reputation and strengthen their competitive advantage through demonstrating ethical credentials in the way they treat their workers and by acknowledging the impact that unethical practices may have on a fashion brand reputation and relationship with customers. Ethics are an important element of brand equity. The investment in training employees and the negative consequences if problems arise are recognised by suppliers as part of establishing effective positive transparent working relationships with retail clients (Talay, Oxborrow and Brindley 2020).

The Triple Bottom Line (TBL)

The theory underpinning supply chain relationships includes the TBL model, a framework originally developed by John Elkington (1998), which exemplifies three areas of social environmental and economic sustainability and measures performance and the impact a fashion company has on the environment and people in the supply chain. Many public companies including Patagonia, DHL, Marks & Spencer and the Kering group use this model.

Another way that collaboration and co-ordination in fashion supply chain relationships can be evidenced is through the third-party involvement of other organisations such as NGOs. These often include self-auditing measures such as those seen with the Higg Index. This is a suite of tools for the standardised measurement of value chain sustainability, and it is central to the Sustainable Apparel Coalition (SAC) mission to transform businesses for exponential impact (Sustainable Apparel Coalition 2021). The integration of tools by the supplier and brand can help to create overall supply chain standardisation. In fact, much more objective standardisation of environmental and social audits should be applied to supply necessary information to consumers on transparency and circularity in the entire fashion supply chain.

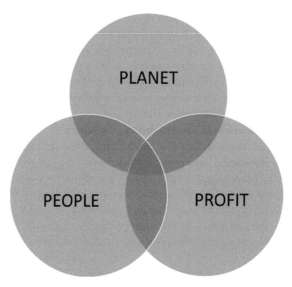

Figure 3.2

Triple Bottom Line John Elkington 1989 – Cannibals with Forks **(Elkington, 1998)**

Ethics and sourcing

Relationships and trust with suppliers is important, but most of the implementation of the joint systems and integration process is led by social and environmental audits. If a brand setting up their supply chain focuses on relationship building from the outset, it is far easier to implement best practices and ensure that they are compliant with legislation. For example, there is much policy surrounding the issue of modern-day slavery in the UK and its relationship to business in the UK and USA (www.gov.uk and www.state.gov).

Auditing and relationships

Many brands building a relationship set up audits and agree on key performance indicators (KPIs) for the manufacturer based upon being compliant. However, such audits are expensive, each one can be upward of £2000, and they do not always reveal the fundamental issues that exist through non-compliance.

Having people on the ground in the region, for example Bangladesh or Vietnam, wherever the manufacturing is located is equally important to provide local knowledge. Employing local experts can help highlight any local risks and support the essential due diligence before setting up a manufacturer as a supplier. Modern-day slavery, child labour and lesser issues surrounding excessive overtime can easily be avoided if brands ensure that checks are made that focus on building partnerships with suppliers. Merely carrying out an audit alone is insufficient to build a relationship. Such issues are often well hidden by manufacturers and this is where mutual trust is crucial to these relationships in fashion supply chains (see Chapter 5 for more on auditing and risk).

B Corp certification as part of sustainable relationships

B certified companies, or B Corps, are a model of companies that meet the highest standards of social and environmental performance, public transparency and corporate responsibility to balance profit and purpose. The certification indicates that Certified B Corporations are ventures that have chosen to embrace third-party voluntary, social and environmental audits conducted by an entrepreneurial non-profit enterprise called B Lab. The B Corp certification not only accredits in which areas a company excels, but also ensures its commitment to consider all stakeholders in decision-making now and in the future by incorporating it into the company's legal governance structure (Branzei et al. 2018). Examples of certified B Corp in fashion include Patagonia, TOMS, Stella McCartney and Eileen Fisher. The B Corp organisation states that the certification separates good companies from those that just have good marketing and public relations. To become registered as a B Corp, there is an impact assessment tool that scores the company in five key areas:

- Governance
- Workers
- Community
- Environment
- Customers

The report must be posted in the public domain and, additionally, the company must include positive stakeholder impact into the organisation. Certification only lasts three years. It is such a rigorous certification that it is unlikely a fashion company would put themselves through this unless they are serious about holistically embedding sustainability into their business.

> *"... B Corps are now in the spotlight because they are the epitome of sustainability... they have become and are becoming a phenomena in fashion..."*
> Federica Levato - Bain & CO

Figure 3.3

Bain & Co

Esquel, Vice-Chairman, Teresa Yang, McKinsey (2020)

"We actively respond to the environmental challenges in relation to energy, water, air quality, chemicals, and waste by optimizing our process management. Through better forecast and resource planning, we reduce waste along our supply chain with a focus on minimizing defects and overproduction, which in turn reduce inventory and extra processing. We also look for innovative ways to weave available technology into our operations to reduce environmental impact from resource consumption and wastewater."

Figure 3.4

McKinsey

Sustainability and relationships

The dependence on outsourcing in fashion supply chains can result in retailers and brands pressuring their suppliers, which can lead to critical social and environmental issues. Risk can be seen in the form of the excessive overtime and poor working conditions. Examples of major catastrophes in fashion supply chains have included: the 2013 Rana Plaza factory collapse in Bangladesh, forced labour in Myanmar and chemical spills in rivers in China – all of which indicate a need for the closer building of sustainable relationships (Brun, Karaosman and Barresi 2020). Prevalent issues have persisted in fashion supply chains surrounding subcontracting, excess sales volume and loss of transparency due to an almost total focus on cost and speed to market, which breaks down existing relationships and collaboration in the supply chain.

Collaborative relationships really can support minimising risks in the fashion supply chain and an investment in training and education by the retailer or brand to support a sustainable approach to business will encourage shared values. Compliance in auditing requires trust and high levels of shared commitment to create a robust supply chain.

The role of NGOs

Fashion Revolution, Labour Behind the Label, the Common Objective and the Sustainable Apparel Coalition are all examples of fashion-focussed NGOs. All of these have been instrumental in creating change in fashion supply chain in collaboration with local governments, trades unions and the support of volunteers in partnership with key brands (Thorisdottir and Johannsdottir 2020). The Fashion

Revolution organisation has been particularly influential to drive fashion companies to obtain and disclose information about their supply chains. Supply chain visibility and stronger partnerships are required to overcome problems relating to supply chain complexity on the way towards transparency. Results suggest that supply chain engagement is fundamental for supply chain transparency, and NGOs can play a pivotal role to enhance transparency through knowledge sharing and awareness building. The results provide numerous implications that can help industrial practice and improve the status quo (Brun, Karaosman, and Barresi 2020).

The circular economy and supply chain relationships

As defined by Jacometti (2019), the circular economy (CE) is a holistic process requiring the ecosystem of brands who invest in global sourcing to collaborate and embed transparency and traceability in their supply chain to measure their impact. The European Union's Circular Economy Action Plan defines this as an economy "where the value of products, materials and resources is maintained in the economy for as long as possible, and the generation of waste minimised" (European Commission 2015). The CE model proposes prolonged use of what is taken from nature to reduce future access to primary resources and reduce waste production (Murray et al. 2017)

There is a push in the fashion industry to make each phase of production sustainable ideally with a transition to a circular economy.

This requirement is further underlined by the United Nations 2030 Agenda for Sustainable Development and the Sustainable Development Goals (SDGs), which means that it is now essential (UN Agenda 2020) to ensure that economic growth and development are accompanied along the whole garment supply chain by social justice, job protection and reduction of environmental impacts through an efficient use of resources and sustainable production and consumption models in the perspective of a CE. This includes due diligence and obligations measures to strengthen supply chain transparency and traceability (Jacometti 2019).

The tangled web of global sourcing makes this a complex process, but implementation of a CE also can support the creation of social welfare and minimize the destruction of social value by decreasing waste, reducing using natural resources, preventing unhealthy working conditions in the extraction of raw materials and reuse (Hofstra and Huisingh 2014). Hence, the CE contributes sustainable development by creating linkages between social, environmental and economic activities. None of this is possible without positive working relationships across the supply chain where brands share best practices with suppliers and embed similar principles.

The environment and supply chain relationships

Collaboration in the supply chains

Fashion retailers have long recognised a greater need for collaborating with competitors in upstream supply chain activities, despite competing against each other downstream in the marketplace. Key relationships with long-term suppliers who work closely with their customers are important for efficiency and can lead to co-operation and collaboration. This evolving area in fashion supply chains is often referred to as "co-opetition" (Rafi-Ul-Shan, Grant, and Perry 2020).

Coopetition in fashion supply chains

This is a relatively new concept in the relationships visible in fashion supply chains and the terminology "co-opetitive" was first used by Brandenburger and Nalebuff (1996) to describe the way that co-operation and competition could be a part of one relationship. However, co-operation is commonly referred to as the joint pursuit of common goals, whereas competition is a fight for scarce resources among structurally equivalent actors (Rafi-Ul-Shan, Grant, and Perry 2020). Capacity sharing, communication, and information sharing, building relationships and partnerships such as joint ventures (JVs) have emerged as motives for co-opetition and are seen as a joint approach to a landscape that includes pressure from retailers and the rest of the fashion supply chain. Although there are risks of opportunism, coopetition has been found to be a useful supply chain strategy and highly influential for creating and maintaining a competitive advantage and sustainability in the volatile and dynamic fashion industry (Rafi-Ul-Shan, Grant and Perry 2020). Some retailers and manufacturers are developing trading partnerships that sit between collaboration and competition as this co-opetitive approach might achieve competitive and sustainability goals better than a singular approach.

For example, in fashion, The Sustainable Apparel Coalition was formed in 2010 as an industry-wide alliance of competing brand retailers and manufacturers committed to improving performance, measurement and the aforementioned Higg Index (www.higg.com; https://www.ethicaltrade.org). The first and most frequent type of co-operation is sub-contracting, where prime contractors (luxury brands) outsource part of their activity to one or several suppliers. A second type of co-operation that has been debated in the supply chain for fashion and conceptualized as co-opetition is licensing (Keller 2009).

Licensing was widely used in previous decades as a technique to grow business, especially globally, but has become less frequent as luxury conglomerates have ended many agreements to maintain control of their brands. Whilst brands like Chanel, Prada and Valentino, for example, have kept their licensing agreements with Luxottica, the leader in the eyewear sector, Kering, on the contrary, decided in 2014 to develop internal expertise for the entire value chain of eyewear products, including the luxury, premium and sport segments. For example, Chanel bought their knitwear supplier Barrie in Scotland and Louis Vuitton has a JV with Marcolin, an eyewear supplier in Switzerland (WWD 2021).

Integrated relationships in fashion supply chains

Technological advances have supported collaboration and integration with suppliers and in fact support sustainability through integrated technology systems. These are sometimes deployed through sophisticated collaborative planning forecasting and replenishment systems (CPFR), sometimes referred to as vendor managed inventory (VMI), to create visibility across supply chains by sharing data and using digital systems such as a blockchain (Rokonuzzaman, 2018).

The fashion market has many technology and software tools available to help fashion businesses coordinate with various suppliers in their supply chain that deserve a mention here – some of these are especially useful to small brands:

- **Zedonk:** A tool that can benefit small- and medium-sized fashion designers and brands looking to produce a variety of apparel. It is online-based, so can be accessed anywhere, and allows the user to clearly define raw materials sourcing and use information to create purchase orders for manufacturing partners. This tool also allows a fashion brand to track delivery logistics and manage and create line sheets and sales reports. www.zedonk.co.uk

- **Accellar:** A support that is for use with cut-and-sew manufacturers based in Asia. The fashion brand can use the tool to track manufacturer waste, monitor cycle times and plan a critical path. http://fortudex.co/accellar/

- **Indigo8:** Small or large fashion businesses with existing fashion supplier relationships can take advantage of the capabilities of Indigo8 and is integrated with existing partnerships like Shopify (www.shopify.co.uk). It is a cloud-based tool where a fashion business can coordinate details of tech packs, sample management, suppliers and sales. https://www.indigo8-solutions.com/

- **Makers Valley:** Makers Valley differs from the aforementioned tools as it enables project management for small and large fashion businesses working exclusively with Italian manufacturers. Fashion brands can build and coordinate their tech packs, source factory designs, evaluate manufacturers, find direct materials sourcing, manage invoices and deadlines and manage quality control and warehouse or store delivery. www.makersvalley.net

Conclusions

This chapter has explained the important area of relationships in SCM and how these different externalized interactions are of acute relevance when planning a fashion supply chain. These include CSR and implementation of sustainable SCM with partners and the ability to "do the right thing" in the fashion supply chain. Fashion businesses working together to produce finished goods have such an overall impact on the people and the environment as well as profitability and cost. Sustainable relationships are a crucial part of the important principle Rs of contemporary SCM as cited by Martin Christopher in Chapter 1 (1998), as they touch every part of the fashion supply chain.

CASE STUDY

Interview – Ilishio Lovejoy – ESG Manager

1. Please can you tell us a little about some of the types of organisations you have worked with previously?

My career started in design and production management before moving to focus on transforming supply chains.

I first worked in costume departments for films, managing design, sourcing and bespoke workrooms in the UK. As my understanding of global supply chains grew, and I realised how much harm the clothing industry was perpetuating, my love of the design process was overtaken with a desire to improve the industry. So, I joined the Ethical Fashion Forum – which is now known as Common Objective – to help build a global movement working towards a fairer, safer and less extractive industry.

I went from having a design perspective to understanding a lot of the sustainability issues, but I wanted to work more directly with the companies that really make up the supply chain such as the farmers, mills and manufacturers. This took me to Ghana, where I managed production for a SME brand called Osei-Duro (https://oseiduro.com). After a few years in Ghana, with Osei-Duro, I moved back to the UK and then became the Sustainability Manager at Katharine Hamnett (www.katharinehamnett.com), a luxury brand with sustainability at its core. They produced mostly in Europe, which broadened my experience working with the supply chain there. I had been supporting the NGO Fashion Revolution in various capacities since its inception in 2013

and in 2018, I joined the UK team full time. I managed several projects working within the Policy and Research team but most notably the Fashion Transparency Index.

In 2021, my ongoing desire to shine a light on and engage the supply chain led me to join Simple Approach, a multinational apparel supplier, as their ESG Manager.

2. In the context of supply chain relationships from the manufacturer perspective, what have been the key changes over the last 5–10 years?

I have worked with several different supply chains, and I now work for an apparel supplier, but I have never worked directly for a manufacturer, so I can only share what I have heard.

I hear that brand expectations have continued to increase whilst prices have dropped. Brands ask for more and more from suppliers and manufacturers, but for less and less money. They are asking for faster times to market (turnaround), better compliance, sustainable materials and processes, and higher spec facilities, services and outcomes. Most of these requests are positive steps forward for the industry, but the catch is that they want all of this in parallel to paying less and less for the product. This creates a disconnect between what the brand wants and what its business model facilitates, and from what I hear, that's the root cause of a lot of manufacturers' challenges.

There is increasing pressure on the supply chain as prices have continued to drop. This can have a compounding effect and price deflation in the market has continued to dominate the supply chain. Previously, there were more vertical business models – which means that a brand owns part or all of the supply chain. Naturally, this would facilitate a lot more accountability. It's rare to hear of this model now and it means there is a lot of push and pull regarding sharing of risks. For example, who pays the upfront costs of materials and production, who pays for the all the improvements and who takes responsibility when something doesn't go to plan? Brands can use outsourcing production as a risk reduction tactic. In recent years, there has been a trend towards one-sided power dynamics between the brand or retailer and the rest of the fashion supply chain.

3. CSR is now discussed as an important pillar of supply chain management. How do you see this linking with relationships in fashion supply chains?

Simply put, corporate social responsibility (CSR) refers to businesses' responsibility to respect the people and resources its supply chain relies upon. The fashion industries create clothes, which use a lot of planetary resources, and the current business model relies on many individuals who farm, weave, and make the clothes the companies sell. CSR is a framework for a company to take responsibility for its impacts throughout its supply chain. It's about a company's relationship with the people who work within their supply chain, the communities their operations impact, and the resources and environments they rely upon to maintain their business model. When we talk about a company's responsibility, the larger a company is, the more responsibility they should take. They must protect resources, communities and people within their supply chain. So, relationships are at the heart of CSR.

It's important to note, though, that there is no global definition of what a CSR strategy covers, and some brands may focus more on some areas of impact than others. CSR in one company versus CSR in another company can mean two completely different things and so there is still no baseline of what these terms mean within companies. More recently, environmental social and governance (ESG) strategies are replacing CSR efforts. But these terms are used interchangeably, along with sustainability. What that means will differ from brand to brand, which can be quite confusing for everyone – especially consumers. It is all largely dictated on a brand-by-brand basis, but this may change with increasing legislative developments, which will likely standardise brands' efforts and reporting.

These strategies inherently impact the brands' relationship with their supply chain, as it is often within the supply chain that most of a brand's impacts occur. And without working in partnership with their suppliers and vendors, a brand cannot understand their impacts or effectively remediate them.

4. When problems arise in fashion SCM (supply chain management), how can effective relationships help to resolve them? Could you provide any examples?

There are many different types of relationships, and they can create issues or facilitate solutions.

To discuss a few common relationship types:

> There is the seller-customer relationship that is purely financially driven. In these relationships, the customer tends to be king. If there is enough competition in the market, this can create uneven power dynamics where the customer can dictate the terms of business because they can switch from supplier to supplier, continually driving their demands. However, when a customer is committed to a supplier (this could be through sourcing commitments or shared assets), the relationship changes, giving the supplier more say. In this instance, committing to a relationship in the long term can facilitate more equal power dynamics and allow both sides to be more transparent about their needs, so benefits for both sides can be created.

> The worst kind of relationship, and one to avoid, is an adversarial relationship – a negative type of relationship where, potentially, the supplier can feel as though their hands are tied. This can lead to decisions that adversely impact their business, employees and their suppliers. This is an exploitative relationship where the weaker party is not able to stand up for themselves and which has negative ripple effects for both sides eventually.

The best type of partnership is a balanced one. These partnerships are mutually beneficial and both parties can achieve a win-win. These relationships are based on making open and honest conversations possible. They can clearly be negotiated from both sides, but this is only possible when the power dynamic is equal. However, they may both have very different gains, and what a brand may call a partnership is sometimes actually better described as a collaboration because the power dynamics can still be a bit uneven.

It's important to understand the dynamics of the relationships you are in and seek relationships that are fair and mutually beneficial. Relationships are not always an equal 50–50 split or even a 30–70 split; if it is a longer-term relationship, it may be possible to negotiate this. The best relationship is the one in which you can more effectively understand and remediate challenges when they occur, and the better a partnership works, the more both sides are likely to gain in the long term. Uneven relationships may bring large benefits for one partner in the short term, but will not be sustainable in the long term. More equal relationships will balance the benefits for each side and be much more likely to be sustainable in the long term.

To provide an example, during the height of the COVID-19 pandemic, brands cancelled their orders and many collaborations or partnerships quickly turned into the adversarial type of relationship because brands pulled orders and production commitments, crippling suppliers' businesses. This resulted in suppliers struggling to stay afloat and employees going without housing and food. With better partnerships, the worst impacts could have been avoided and remediated.

I have heard of strong relationships where brands and suppliers worked together when the pandemic hit and said, "Okay, this is happening, how do we manage this together?" They worked to resolve the situation by taking shared responsibility and accountability. Both parties lost, but the shared responsibility meant that the loss was more manageable and both companies were able to weather the storm. These companies were the quickest to bounce back and are now showing the healthiest growth. This attitude of shared responsibility can really strengthen a relationship in the fashion supply chain.

Achieving balance and integrity in the way you handle relationships is crucial in such circumstances. Integrity and CSR responsibility are also crucial if you rely on a supplier for your products and services, as you simply won't be able to function without good suppliers. Brands have a responsibility – to the future of their business and to the well-being of everyone working within their supply chain – to maintain a good supply chain partnership that can deliver.

Effective working relationships in the fashion supply industry are advantageous for both sides. They can deliver competitive outcomes and protect the longevity and durability of those businesses involved.

5. How would you guide a fashion brand that is looking to set up a long-term relationship with a manufacturer? What are the important areas to look out for and avoid?

Getting started

Focusing on a specific product area or product type and seeking out specialist manufacturers that work in that area can be a great place to start when setting up a fashion brand.

Here are some other tips:

Do your homework

I suggest taking some time to get to know your suppliers. Try to understand their strengths and weaknesses and how you can complement one another. Finding out the brands they already work with can give an indication of quality and practices and can allow for wider collaboration on pre-competitive issues, such as social and environmental investments and improvements. Additionally, I would advise checking a supplier's length of relationships with their customers, since it may give you some valuable information.

You can also try to understand how long their employees have worked with them. If several employees have been there for many years or, conversely, if you find out there is a very high turnover of customers or employees, that may be an important indication of the culture and how that supplier conducts relationships.

Assessing third-party audits and certifications can also provide valuable information and indications. Getting to know a supplier and making a self-assessment is important, but it can be equally important to seek third-party audits and evaluate what third-party certification the supplier holds. Audit findings are not always conclusive but can give a good indication of what is happening within the factory.

Finding out about a supplier's clients and working practices is important, and does not have to be an invasive process, but it is crucial for the success of your business. Basing a decision to work with a supplier on their quality and sustainability practices is paramount now. So, my advice would be to take your time. Understand a supplier's quality, relationships, values and ways of working before you commit to that relationship.

Building the relationship

Once you start a new relationship, try to build a genuine two-way relationship from day one. Setting and aiming for a long-term relationship at the onset will set the tone for the relationship and the way business will be conducted. Be certain to evaluate if communication appears honest, open and clear and make sure to visit all manufacturing sites throughout the relationship, not just at the start. Getting to know partners in person brings so many benefits.

Grow together

I have seen great examples of smaller brands working with relatively small suppliers. In this situation, both parties can grow together. In one case, a supplier initially had 100 machinists and was subsequently able to grow to 500 by working closely with a brand, who also grew their sales with the additional manufacturing support. Growing together provides benefits for both parties and can facilitate a strong relationship, which makes innovation and change so much easier to navigate.

Value your suppliers

It's important that you value your suppliers – and that they know that. I've seen suppliers move mountains for the brands with which they have the best relationships, knowing that they will be looked after in return.

Relationships are one of the key pillars of sustainability, because without a strong relationship, the rest of the work will be so much harder and the outcomes won't be sustainable. Building a good relationship with a supplier is fundamental to the business and can enable everything else. This type of collaborative approach will then enable solutions to be found when required.

Find a balance

It is essential to try to strike a balance with suppliers, especially on costings, as even in the value sector there is a fine line between the lowest price and below cost. These are two very different prices and it's important to understand and look out for them.

Lowest price: When the true cost of the garment is accounted for to the best extent possible. Each partner should be able to cover operational costs like decent wages and product costs such as the cost of materials and machinery. They should also be able to earn some profit.

Below cost: When the price is driven so low that the brand is paying less for the product than it costs to make. In this scenario, someone is making a loss or exploiting a situation or person to make an item at that price. So, your gain is at someone else's expense. When negotiating cost, try to understand the current price averages of materials, components and labour to ensure that you are not driving the price below the lowest cost.

Avoid greenwashing

Be sure to ask for certificates and evidence of any social and environmental claims, as some businesses are more talk than action. Be aware of and avoid being complicit in greenwashing when collecting and sharing social and environmental claims. For example, if suppliers say they are saving or reusing water, find out how this works and be sure to see the evidence. Sustainability is increasingly being used as a marketing tactic, but it is also increasingly being cracked down on by authorities. By obtaining clear details, you can ensure that you can act in a transparent manner and be totally authentic with your customers about information provided.

And remember, it's about honesty, not about being perfect. Customers want to buy from genuine people that are working to improve over brands that claim they are doing more than they are.

Ending a relationship

Sometimes despite your best efforts, a relationship will come to an end – strategic directions change, suppliers' performance dwindles, or you must look at ending a relationship for another reason. This should be a last resort, but ending a relationship with a supplier is sometimes the right thing to do. Before you start commercial relationships, it's important to define your exit strategy so both parties are aware of what it will entail, the procedure that should be followed from both sides, and what to expect when the time comes.

Having a clear exit strategy and proving ample time for the supplier to fill their capacity at the end of a relationship can help ensure that you don't contribute to unintended harms caused by sudden changes to a supplier's income, such as worker layoffs and other cost-saving activities.

6. What is the best way to work with NGOs?

(Examples of NGOs include Fashion Revolution, the Ethical Trading Initiative and Common Objective)

There are two main ways to engage with NGOs:

1. **Engagement for learning and awareness**
NGOs can be a great source of information and learning. They are often able to shed light on issues and potential solutions. Engaging with NGOs specific to your sector, and the issue you want to address, can provide you with information to help you understand your risks, and how to respond to them. NGOs can also support you in finding likeminded people and groups to work with.

Most NGOs are very approachable (if you are willing to do the work of improving) and I would recommend that you research and engage with a range of NGOs in the beginning, as it's important to understand multiple perspectives and approaches to change. You can sign up for newsletters, follow them across their channels, read reports and attend webinars. If there are organizations that particularly resonate with you, try reaching out to see if they have time for a conversation. It's a great way to enhance your risk assessment and response.

2. **Engagement for support**
Many NGOs also offer free or paid-for support with risk understanding, strategies, project design and implementation, and community engagement. When engaging NGOs on this deeper level, it's important to clearly understand your goals from the start. This way, you can make sure you engage with an NGO who has experience with the issue you are trying to address. Some NGOs can support with knowledge and research, whilst others can help assess and respond to supply chain social and environmental issues such as solar energy or gender rights.

However, there are countless NGOs, and it is impossible to engage with all of them. I would advise creating a checklist to evaluate which one(s) will align best with your goals and strategy, or who might help with building these out if they are not yet in place. If, for example, you want to support gender equity or better improve water use and effluent, this can help narrow the decision-making process. Some NGOs may not have worked in the supply chain or in the area you are seeking help, and this can make them overly ambitious in their goal setting and not proactive in supporting implementation. In other words, some NGOs may be more about ideas whilst others focus on helping you design and implement change. In my experience, engaging with a great NGO can support a brand to move in an aspirational direction, some with a light touch while others can hand hold you through processes of change.

It is vital to note here that working with an NGO is not a "one size fits all" process. Ultimately, it comes back to relationships again. Seek out NGOs with which you feel you can build a trusting and supporting relationship. Ideally, this can lead to being challenged and supported to build the best company you can. But also keep in mind that being a member of too many NGOs can mean too much time is spent trying to deliver all their expectations, resulting in a loss of direction and focus.

When working with NGOs consider the impacts for your partners, too. Many manufacturers are asked to engage with different pilot projects by all their brands. This can be overloading; it might be a good idea to understand which NGOs your suppliers are already engaged with and learn how you can further support progress already under way. There are many approaches to most social and environmental issues, and sometimes a group effort can be more effective in yielding results than a supplier spread thin trying to respond to more than it can handle.

Another piece of advice is to acknowledge that not everything can be done immediately and prioritization by taking things step-by-step is the best approach. A final point is to acknowledge that sustainability is a journey and we are not there yet – we are all on the journey together. If everyone in the fashion industry knew how to fix everything, the industry would be perfect, but everyone is still learning. It's about looking at what you are doing now and working to improve with integrity and transparency throughout your journey.

7. Can you give us an example of a good NGO/ certifying body to work with?

B Corporations seem to be gaining in popularity. They can support rigorous self-evaluation and improvements across multiple governance, social and environmental indicators. There are legal requirements attached to the membership of a B Corp (www.bcorporation.co.uk), and registration and membership of B Corp goes beyond social and environmental programs (as with other NGO memberships) and requires a company to commit to considering how its decisions will impact people and the planet in the long run. However, I would like to add that there are many other NGOs and organizations that may be helpful to work with such as the Ethical Trading Initative (ETI) and Fair Wear Foundation.

8. The area of compliance and the different types of audits for manufacturers, from social to environmental, are complex. Can you advise anyone wishing to choose a manufacturer to work closely with?

I would recommend that you start by defining your company social and environmental standards and policies. There are several guidelines in this area but a good place to start is the United Nation's guiding principles on business and human rights (https://sdgs.un.org/goals).

Additionally, there is the OECD (www.oecd.org) website, which provides specific due diligence and guidance for the fashion and textiles sector, which I would also highly recommend. Current best practice is to take a due diligence approach, which the OECD describes as an approach to be used by enterprises to avoid and address adverse impacts in their operations, supply chains and business.

The ETI and Fair Wear Foundation have template code of conduct clauses and can support you with establishing policies and audit programmes.

Once you have your policies and procedures established, you can work with auditing companies and NGOs to assess adherence with your policies, prevent risks and remediate issues found. It is important to make sure that you find NGOs and auditors who understand the local context, with employees who have cultural understanding and speak the local language. When looking for an auditing partner, I also advise vetting them to understand their track record and reputation within the industry. NGOs may be able to support with the vetting process.

At the moment, I think the Social & Labor Convergence Program (SLCP) is an interesting choice as it is attempting to harmonize auditing frameworks and reduce multiplication for suppliers, so more resources and funding can go towards addressing audit findings with long-term solutions (www.slconvergence.org).

My understanding of SLCP is that it is trying to synchronize and decrease auditing duplication. Sedex is another example that can provide auditing support. It has worked within the fashion and textile industry to reduce audit fatigue and help companies assess and respond to human rights issues for many years now (www.sedex.com).

9. In your experience, what type of problems are most common when working with a global supply chain?

This is a difficult question as it really varies from brand to brand and from country to country. But one major issue that still needs attention is a lack of visibility. Without transparency, it just isn't possible to identify risks and opportunities and react to them. The supply chain is such a complex environment that there will always be issues, and you need to ensure you have a due diligence process in place to identify, respond to and remediate issues based on their scale and severity. If there is a lack of visibility and a lack of an effective relationship, this can become extremely challenging to do.

Human rights and environmental issues are getting broader as they are better understood and they can differ greatly depending on the country, company, and context. But the ETI base code responds to some of the most prevalent social issues for address (https://www.ethicaltrade.org/eti-base-code).

Forced labour is an issue gaining renewed traction within the industry due to major forced labour violations withing the cotton industry of China. Again, this is contextual; if you use cotton, you should address this risk. If you don't, you should be looking at what the major risks are within your specific product supply chains. The biggest problems might vary and are usually country specific. For example, in Bangladesh, a key area to look out for is building safety after the Rana Plaza disaster in 2013. Bangladesh is also known for issues with overtime. In Italy, transparency and traceability is crucial as outsourcing is still quite prevalent. But the list really can go on and on, so I would really encourage everyone to take a contextual approach.

Conclusions

To recap, relationship building begins with strong company values that support relationships based on integrity, honesty and mutual benefit. It may sound obvious, but it is so important. This will support you in making the best product you can, whilst also enabling you to understand your supply chain and respond to contextual risks and opportunities.

Human rights and environmental protection are no longer a "nice to have." You must address this issue from the start and you can begin by finding NGOs and networks to support you. In my career, I have encountered many brands that have multiple sustainability efforts in place, but remain unclear about why they are focusing on a particular area. Make sure your efforts in these areas respond to your supply chain and your values. It can be "easier" when working with a single type of product or a single type of fibre. For example, if you are a knitwear or a sportswear specialist, it is likely you will need a smaller number of materials and suppliers and that network can be tight, which can aid transparency and improvements.

Good luck!

Activities & exercises

1. **The ETHICAL TRADING INITIATIVE (ETI) BASE CODE:** The ETI Base Code is an internationally recognised set of labour standards based on International Labour Organisation conventions. It is used by ETI members and others to drive improvements in working conditions around the world (ETI 2022).

   1. Employment is freely chosen
   2. Freedom of association
   3. Working conditions are safe and hygienic
   4. Child labour shall not be used
   5. Living wages are paid
   6. Working hours are not excessive
   7. No discrimination is practised
   8. Regular employment is provided
   9. No harsh or inhumane treatment is allowed

   Investigate each element of the above ETI Base Code and find out if and where legislation or guidance exists to support brands setting up new suppliers in fashion supply chains.

2. **Why is it important to fashion brands to incorporate this ETI Base Code into fashion supply chain relationships?**

3. **Investigate some fashion brands in different market sectors to find out what type of supplier codes of conduct they use when setting up contracts with suppliers and try to identify what guidelines (if any) these are based on.**

References

Barnes, L. and Lea-Greenwood, G. (2006). "Fast fashioning the supply chain: Shaping the research agenda," *Journal of Fashion Marketing and Management*, 10(3), 259–271. https://doi.org/10.1108/13612020610679259

Brandenburger, A. and Nalebuff, B. (1996). *Co-opetition*, 2nd Edition. New York: Doubleday.

Branzei, O., Parker, S.C., Moroz, P.W., and Gamble, E. (2018). "Going pro-social: Extending the individual-venture nexus to the collective level," *Journal of Business Venturing*, 33(5), 551–565. https://doi.org/10.1016/j.jbusvent.2018.06.007

Brun, A., Karaosman, H., and Barresi, T. (2020). "Supply chain collaboration for transparency," *Sustainability*, 12(11), 1–21. http://dx.doi.org/10.3390/su12114429

Carroll, A.B. (2016). "Carroll's pyramid of CSR: Taking another look," *International Journal of Corporate Social Responsibility*, 1, 1–8.

Carroll, A.B. and Shabana, K.M. (2010). "The business case for corporate social responsibility: A review of concepts, research and practice," *International Journal of Management Reviews* 12, 85–105.

Casciaro, T. and Piskorski, M.J. (2005). "Power imbalance, mutual dependence, and constraint absorption: A closer look at resource dependence theory," *Administrative Science Quarterly*, 50(2), 167–199.

Choi, D.D. and Hwang, T. (2018). "The impact of green supply chain management practices on firm performance: The role of collaborative capability," *Operations Management Research*, 8, 69–83.

Cooper, M.C. and Ellram, L.M. (1993). "Characteristics of supply chain management and the implications for purchasing and logistics strategy," *The International Journal of Logistics Management*, 4(2), 13–24. https://doi.org/10.1108/09574099310804957

Cox, A., Chicksand, D., and Palmer, M. (2007). "Stairways to heaven or treadmills to oblivion?" *British Food Journal*, 109(9), 689–720. http://dx.doi.org/10.1108/00070700710780689

Elkington, J. (1998). *Cannibals with Forks: The Triple Bottom Line of 21st Century Business*. Gabriola Island, BC; Stony Creek, CT: New Society Publishers.

European Commission. (2015). Communication "Closing the Loop—An EU Action Plan for the Circular Economy COM 614." Brussels: European Commission.

Fernie, J. and Sparksm, L. (2019). "Logistics and retail management: Emerging issues and new challenges in the retail supply chain," in Fernie, J. and Sparks, L. (eds.). Fifth edition. London: Kogan Page.

Froud, J., Hayes, S., Wei, H., and Williams, K. (2017). Coming Back? Capability and precarity in UK textiles and apparel [Online] https://foundationaleconomycom.files.wordpress.com/2017/02/coming-backcapability-and-precarity-in-uk-textiles-and-apparel-march-2017

Garcia-Marquez, F.P. (2014). *Application of Decision Science in Business Management*. https://dx.doi.org/10.5772/Intechopen.83336

Gardner, J.T. and Cooper, M.C. (2003). "Strategic supply chain mapping approaches," *Journal of Business Logistics*, 24, 37–64. https://doi.org/10.1002/j.2158-1592.2003.tb00045.x

Gereffi, G., Humphrey, J., and Sturgeon, T. (2005). "The governance of global value chains," *Review of International Political Economy*, 12(1), 78–104. http://www.jstor.org/stable/25124009

Greenpeace. (2011). Dirty Laundry 2: Hung Out to Dry, Greenpeace International: Amsterdam, The Netherlands.

Hofstra, N. and Huisingh, D. (2014). "Eco-innovations characterized: A taxonomic classification of relationships between humans and nature," *Journal of Cleaner Production* 66, 459–468. https://doi.org/10.1016/j.jclepro.2013.11.036

Hudnurkar, M. and Rathod, U. (2017). "Collaborative practices with suppliers in Indian manufacturing multinationals," *Journal of Global Operations and Strategic Sourcing*, 10 (2), 206–231. https://doi.org/10.1108/JGOSS-07-2016-0022

Jacometti, V. (2019) "Circular Economy and Waste in the Fashion Industry," *Laws*, MDPI AG, 8(4), 27. doi: 10.3390/laws8040027

Keller, K. L. (2009). "Building strong brands in a modern marketing communications environment," *Journal of Marketing Communications*, 15(2–3), 139–155. https://doi.org/10.1080/13527260902757530

Maglaras, G., Bourlakis, M., and Fotopoulos, C. (2015). "Power-imbalanced relationships in the dyadic food chain: An empirical investigation of retailers' commercial practices with suppliers," *Industrial Marketing Management* 48, 187–201.

Masieri, C. (2018). "L'economia circolare nelle fonti europee e il possibile cambiamento di paradigma nell'ambitodei rifiuti," in Bini, V., Dal Borgo, A., and Fiamingo, C. (eds.), *Città Sostenibili* (pp. 173–186). Campospinoso: Altravista.

McKinsey. (2020). https://www.mckinsey.com/~/media/McKinsey/Featured%20Insights/The%20Next%20Normal/The-Next-Normal-The-future-of-fashion. Accessed July 2021.

Moroz, P.W., Branzei, O., Parker, S.C., and Gamble, E.N. (2018). "Imprinting with purpose: Prosocial opportunities and B Corp certification," *Journal of Business Venturing*, 33(2), 117–129. doi: 10.1016/j.jbusvent.2018.01.003

Moulds, J. (2015). Child Labour in the Fashion Supply Chain. *The Guardian*. Available online: http://labs.theguardian.com/unicef-child-labour/

Murray, A., Skene, K., and Haynes, K. (2017). "The circular economy: An interdisciplinary exploration of the concept and application in a global context," *Journal of Business Ethics*, 140, 369–80.

Perry, P. and Wood, S. (2019). "Exploring the international fashion supply chain and corporate social responsibility: Cost, responsiveness and ethical implications," in Fernie, J. and Sparks, L. (eds.), *Logistics and Retail Management*, 5th Edition, Kogan Page.

Rafi-Ul-Shan, P.M., Grant, D.B., and Perry, P. (2020). "Are fashion supply chains capable of coopetition? An exploratory study in the UK," *International Journal of Logistics Research and Applications*. https://doi.org/10.1080/13675567.2020.1784118

Rafi-Ul-Shan, P.M., Grant, D.B., Perry, P., and Ahmed, S. (2018). "Relationship between sustainability and risk management in fashion supply chains: A systematic literature review," *International Journal of Retail & Distribution Management*, 46(5), 466–486. https://doi.org/10.1108/IJRDM-04-2017-0092

Rokonuzzaman, M. (2018). "The integration of extended supply chain with sales and operation planning: A conceptual framework," *Logistics*, 2(2), 8.

Sustainable Apparel Coalition. (2021). https://apparelcoalition.org/the-higg-index/

Talay, C., Oxborrow, L., and Brindley, C. (2020). "How small suppliers deal with the buyer power in asymmetric relationships within the sustainable fashion supply chain," *Journal of Business Research*, 117, 604–614. https://doi.org/10.1016/j.jbusres.2018.08.034

Thorisdottir, T.S. and Johannsdottir, L. (2019). "Sustainability within fashion business models: A systematic literature review," *Sustainability*, 11, 2233. https://doi.org/10.3390/su11082233

Thorisdottir, T.S. and Johannsdottir, L. (2020). "Corporate social responsibility influencing sustainability within the fashion industry: A systematic review," *Sustainability*, 12(21), 9167. http://dx.doi.org/10.3390/su12219167

UN Agenda. (2020). Sustainable Agenda 2030. https://www.un.org/sustainable development/development-agenda/

WWD. (2021). https://wwd.com/business-news/mergers-acquisitions/lvmh-marcolin-joint-venture-10773251/

CHAPTER 4

Fashion logistics and reverse logistics

Summary

This area was once the "Cinderella" function area of the supply chain and has evolved to become a key success factor. The "fast fashion" businesses have applied and embedded logistics to create fashion retail success. The entire area of logistics became more significant as international sourcing and manufacturing gained traction. Logistics is a crucial element of supply chain management, and the highly volatile nature of the fashion business means that a quick response linked to order processing, forecasting and replenishment as well as "lean and agile" supply chains have been supported to an extent through the efficiencies of the logistics function. Flexibility in the fashion supply chain and the agility of suppliers throughout the entire chain, including techniques such as drop shipping and fulfilment will be discussed.

This chapter focuses on an introduction to fashion logistics and reverse logistics linked to sustainable supply chain management, defines the main areas of significance to fashion supply chains and outlines the current challenges for logistics in the fashion supply chain.

Case study: TU PACK LOGISTICS – HENRY HALES

Learning outcomes

At the end of this chapter, you will be able to:

- Outline the key stages of the logistics mix and role of third-party logistics (3PL) providers

- Understand the concept of reverse logistics and how it is applied in fashion supply chains with relevance to sustainable fashion supply chain management (SCM)

- Discuss the importance in fashion supply chains and logistics of green SCM linked to logistics

- Understand the 7R framework of reuse and waste management and the importance of these options in fashion SCM

DOI: 10.4324/9781003145783-4

SDG GOALS – THIS CHAPTER LINKS TO: **13 Climate Action**

7 Affordable and Clean Energy   **14 Life Below Water**

8 Decent Work and Economic Growth   **15 Life on Land**

12 Responsible Consumption and Production

Introduction

In simple terms, logistics management is the use of:

- Technology
- Data analysis
- Project planning
- General management

Logistics management uses these four areas to enable the efficient movement from raw materials to distribution to end consumer and it is a key factor in the procurement of price, product and service coupled with the fact that the fashion industry is geographically interspersed across the globe. Areas in fashion logistics such as fulfilment and returns (bearing in mind that the customer is part of the process) have evolved in importance. Logistics can also enable retailers to fully respond using a push-versus-pull strategy in logistics. In recent years, there have really been two key drivers of fashion logistics: e-commerce and the intense need to respond to customers who are effectively switched on 24 hours a day (DHL 2020). One area of fashion logistics that many brands are investigating to make the supply chain more sustainable and transport greener is the area of carbon emission reduction. At the same time, brands must also ensure on-time deliveries and packaging reduction in addition to the security of delivery and prevention of trucks and courier services adding to traffic issues as online retail continues to grow (the last mile of delivery to the end customer can often be the most problematic). Third-party logistics (3PL) providers can support fashion retailers in achieving their sustainability targets in the supply chain and minimise their carbon footprint through collaboration. From here, the area of reverse logistics has gathered in importance as a sustainability factor in the supply chain (Pietro, Lodovic, and Thomas 2018).

Reverse logistics is an element of fashion logistics and is a concept that maximizes the utility of a product after its end-of-life or end-of use. There are many ways to utilize this concept in sustainability, including: reuse, repair, recycle and remanufacture. Incineration and landfilling are not sustainable and have led to bad publicity for those involved. Many countries where Western brands have shipped their unwanted clothing are now rejecting this due to the negative impacts. Unwanted clothes do not have to go to a landfill and the second-hand market has grown, whilst 30% of transactions take place within friends and family. Several new start-ups (Thredup, The RealReal, and Vinted) have created platforms and formalised this market. More consumers are seeing the benefit of second-hand clothing as they seek out unique and sustainable alternatives – not necessarily always cheaper. Even luxury brands such as Burberry are embracing this trend. Zalando, Europe's largest fashion online retailer, just launched a used business model on their platform where consumers can buy and trade-in clothes. Reverse logistics can support this type of recycling in the fashion supply chain and manage the products consumers returned for recycling or reuse. Many of the aspects of reverse logistics in the fashion industry include decision-making along the value chain to include collection, sorting, reprocessing and upcycling (Nayak 2021).

Many charitable organizations can also support the reverse value chain of fashion products though collaboration. The process of up-cycling is increasing in popularity and the maximum value of the materials used and the product lifecycle can be gained. Overconsumption of fashion at a lower cost, usually driven by ultra-fast fashion (see Chapter 1) brands such as ASOS, Boohoo, Misguided, Little Thing and, recently, Shein, can create barriers to reverse logistics in the fashion industry due to the excessive use of polyester and continual production of new products sold at low cost, thus encouraging overconsumption (Camargo, Pereira and Scarpin 2020).

E-commerce and fashion logistics

According to a recent white paper between DHL and the British Fashion Council (BFC), fashion e-commerce sales now total £1.9 trillion worldwide and online shopping is responsible for transforming fashion and the distribution model of stores on the high street has shifted over the last decade to 24/7 e-commerce, which has radically changed how people consume fashion. This is why the logistics function and overall impact of items travelling to and from delivery centres to customers' homes can add significantly to the carbon footprint of clothing (www.britishfashioncouncil. co.uk). The footprint of clothing spans the entire global supply chain and the increase of on-demand fashion through e-commerce motivates brands to stock by consumer demand, therefore producing apparel only as needed, largely using "just-in-time" manufacturing techniques (Barnes and Lea Greenwood 2006; see Chapter 1).

In very simple terms, logistics has been defined as "the process of strategically managing the acquisition movement and storage of materials and finished goods through an organisation and marketing channels so current and future profitability is maximised through the cost- effective fulfilment of orders" (Xiang 2014). In the

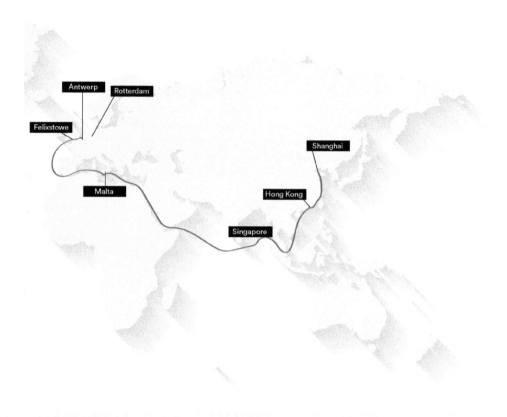

Figure 4.1

Map global sourcing

fashion business, the entire area of logistics has the potential to create success or failure and one of the key areas in fashion is now e-commerce (Oláh et al. 2019; Qin, Liu and Tian 2020). The main shipping locations for the fashion industry are reflected in the map above.

Logistics and sourcing in the fashion supply chain

Global sourcing of fashion supply chains is dependent on a web of logistics and creates a complex layer of lead time of anything from 7–28 days on top of the finished orders from leaving the factory. There has been much interest recently in on-shoring or re-shoring in the case of the UK and the US markets, and according to Clothesource (2021), 80% of sourcing managers in fashion expect most manufacturing to be fully automated and on-shored by 2025–2030. However, on-shoring is most suited to the following types of brands, including these UK examples:

Country	% since 2019	% since 2010
CHINA	30%	32%
BANGLADESH	8.8%	223%
VIETNAM	6.3%	274%
TURKEY	3.8%	31%
INDIA	3.3%	52%
CAMBODIA	2.5%	151%
INDONESIA	1.6%	48%
SRI LANKA	1.4%	110%
PAKISTAN	1.3%	80%
MEXICO	0.8%	17%

Figure 4.2

Major sourcing locations EU (www.clothesource.com)

- Luxury brands with a UK heritage and smaller production runs with a need for customisation. For example, Burberry, Mulberry, Barbour, John Smedley, and those brands who want a very fast turnaround time.

- Small, high-end designer labels for example, Victoria Beckham or Erdem. This would be the best choice for start-up brands and a good choice for automated production such as Snag hosiery (see Chapter 7), but not suitable as the main source for mass market brands or for large designer brands.

It should be noted here that Burberry's UK factory only accounts for 9% of its world-wide workforce; sourcing locations can be a moving target, as discussed in Chapter 2 and many predictions have been made about "new" locations to replace China, such as Africa, but this prediction has not yet materialised. Figure 4.2 shows the growth in some locations for clothing manufacture, highlighting China as very steady growth and "new" locations such as Burma and emerging markets.

For this to happen, technology needs to be in place in the supply chain to support it. Examples are shown in Figure 4.3.

The fashion supply chain creates a relationship between order and supply, and something called the "decoupling point" is where an order becomes very specific to a customer. The decoupling point depends on the type of contract agreed upon between the supplier and the brand placing the order (Christopher 2000). The positioning inventory diagram above shows the point at which inventory passes from the supplier to the customer or retailer and ownership is shifted.

The contract will define if it is a cost price including freight (CIF), which has been replaced by landed duty paid (LDP), if it is a freight on board (FOB) price or if this is a factory gate price (FGP). That point where demand meets the inventory is called the decoupling point and the inventory positioning often includes different geographic locations (Aftab, Qin and Kabir 2017). The decoupling point is when and where the order belongs to a specific customer or retailer. There are many leading logistics

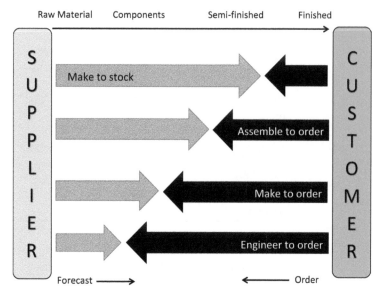

Figure 4.3

Positioning inventory in the supply chain

suppliers that are an important part of many major fashion supply chains. The big 3PL logistics who collect from the factory and manage the shipping and distribution are:

- UPS: www.ups.com
- DHL: www.dhl.com
- FedEx: www.fedex.com

DHL is well known for working closely with the fashion industry and ran an exclusive collaboration with Vetements in 2017. This was run as a pop-up event in China the following day. The Kai Tak Cruise Terminal, the luxury cruise ship terminal at the dock of the former Kai Tak Airport runway, became Hong Kong's most sought-after venue, and DHL functioned as the official partner for this event, whilst the limited Vetement capsule collection was sold to the public directly through DHL trucks that turned into market stalls.

This was modelled on the famous Hong Kong ladies market site and featured were Vetements' collaborative fashion items from DHL, Tommy Hilfiger, Umbro and Reebok. These were globally exclusive ready-to-wear items, including limited sneakers, raincoats, jackets, T-shirts and socks. DHL has conducted much research with the fashion industry (DHL 2020) and recently developed research in collaboration with the BFC provides measures and indications for sustainable logistics for the fashion industry (DHL 2017; Lee and Shen 2020).

The logistics mix diagram above highlights all the key areas within logistics that need to work together to create successful delivery of fashion products, from raw materials transportation to finished products to the customers. In fact, in relationships (see Chapter3, one aspect of the supply chain which is of strategic importance and can support value creation is customer satisfaction – these relationships can build

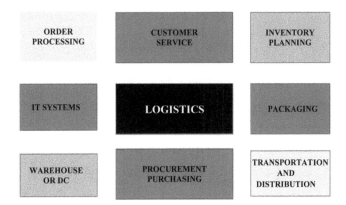

Figure 4.4

Logistics Mix

loyalty and satisfaction. The area of logistics in the supply chain and fulfilment of orders is an important element that supports customer service.

A resilient supply networks includes four levels (Siagian, Tarigan, and Jie 2021):

- Reactive management of the supply chain
- Integration of the internal supply chain
- Collaboration across the extended supply networks
- Flexibility of the supply chain

The important last mile of logistics

All this integration and collaboration in the fashion supply chain involves moving raw materials stock and a product including "last mile" logistics to the door of the end consumer. However, this can be a complex process. The "last mile" delivery, which can create brand loyalty, is something customers want fast and free and, particularly in the fashion industry, customers want easy to use return shipping (McKinsey 2020). The end customer is the final delivery point and often creates one of the largest challenges for fashion retailers to achieve an acceptable and profitable balance between customer service, warehousing or distribution center (DC) cost and security. Most customers would prefer fast deliveries at a precise time with 100% reliability, but the reality is this is NOT cost-effective for most brands

Innovations in the last mile in terms of local deliveries include the use of collection and delivery points (CDPs) – local convenience stores offering pick-up and drop-off points and secure lockers. wwwdeloitte.com. Logistics in fashion is mainly about the fulfilment of orders, which is closely linked to brand loyalty and service. This means many fashion brands have stock held in their own warehouse or DC so the digital e-commerce platforms can meet their delivery times. The result can be large inventories, hence many brands will no longer rely solely on marketplace fulfilment, but will set up their own logistics. For example, SIRPLUS, a UK-based brand selling menswear, has their own logistics provision called Tu Pack and they are now performing a warehouse and delivery operation for other fashion brands in the UK (Tu Pack 2021; see case study in this chapter for more information).

Very large logistics providers can be cost prohibitive for small- and medium-sized enterprises (SME) brands and retailers. At the same time, the focus on sustainability in the supply chain and increase in fashion e-commerce growth is increasingly of interest to customers, and sustainable business practices can offer genuine added value that can set brands apart from the competition. Tu Pack offer sustainable packaging that is recyclable and they are working toward "B Corporation accreditation" (see Chapter 3).

Fulfilment of the orders and logistics

The fulfilment of orders is a much-discussed activity in fashion e-commerce and can act as a success factor and create a brand competitive advantage. This highly specialised service is often provided by a 3PL supplier on behalf of the seller.

Fulfilment usually involves a warehouse or DC, and the process begins when the receipt of goods arrives in the warehouse from the supplier to an online store.

The operators in the warehouse (or robots) prepare and complete the picking and packing of the orders, preparing all the documentation and including any marketing materials such as brochures, adverts or free samples. They will also deal with returns to an extent; using a fulfilment service means the online shop owners can concentrate on product promotion and sales. The 3PL fulfilment warehouse has the responsibility for managing the fluctuation in demand in terms of space in the warehouse and staffing (Jain and Sundström 2021).

The other components of fulfilment services are as follows (Alfieri, De Marco and Pastore 2019):

- Order fulfilment status management
- Inventory management
- Visibility
- Tracking
- Planning
- Postponement services
- Ticketing and labelling
- Commercial documents
- Integration of the IT system with courier systems to clients
- Comprehensive services dedicated to returns from the clients
- Quality control (QC) of returns
- Reprocessing of the value of returned goods

Challenges for fulfilment include the hours of taking orders from customers. Many fashion online shops require fulfilment service providers to accept orders later and to process them within the same working day; in the 24/7 switched-on fashion industry, speed and efficiency of orders are crucial to success. On the other hand, many online fashion brands use "just-in-time" manufacturing methods (Barnes and Lea-Greenwood 2006; see Chapter 1), which, in practice, can mean that brands advertise products that they are not holding in stock. In this case, interest levels are monitored online and as orders arrive, the customer will receive an e-mail saying, "We will let you know when this item is in stock in your size" or similar message, whilst producing the stock to meet the orders (McKinsey 2021). Although highly efficient and lean, this is a high-risk process for a brand, especially when demand is high, as it is dependent upon a flexible supply chain with quick access to raw materials.

Examples of fashion logistics

Some well-known designer fashion platforms including YOOX Net-a-Porter have same-day delivery services that allow customers to try on items at home. This same-day delivery service offers customers a service in the comfort of their home, whilst a personal shopper waits. Anything to be returned can be collected immediately. The services are only available to VIP customers, often referred to as Extremely Important People (EIPs) or, available in London, New York, Hong Kong and Los Angeles. Additionally, their service includes "Net-A-Porter at Home" and "Mr Porter at Home," a highly personalized service of one-on-one consultations available on request. After consultation with a personal shopper, customers receive a curated selection of products and are invoiced only for the items they choose to keep (Berezhna 2019). To maintain such services, luxury platforms require highly sophisticated tailored logistics services. Many use data-collection services to provide what is often described as a "white glove" service in the field of luxury fashion logistics. Third-party logistics providers such as DHL are used by brands to forecast demand and plan production. In fact, these are also used to optimise production routes and determine the most efficient routes, size and type of transport.

The drop-shipping model – online fashion retail logistics

An area of fashion e-commerce known as drop shipping has become an important element of retail fulfilment and logistics that online stores use to sell without having to hold any stock or inventory. It is often regarded as an "easy" method for a small brand to set up, but there are advantages and disadvantages. Equally, many well-known fashion platforms use this method to keep down costs of storage and delivery of goods to the final customer.

A definition of drop shipping is "A retail fulfilment method in which an online store does not keep goods in stock but sells a product by shipping it directly from a third-party supplier to customer" (Khouja 2001).

When orders are placed, the online retailer buys the product from a third party and ships directly to its customer. The fashion retailer is making money without the up-front investment in products, and this can significantly reduce up-front costs, as a fashion brand does not have to deal with packing, shipping or handling returns. There are, of course, disadvantages when multiple purchases are made by a customer. For example separate shipping costs may occur for each item as it is not always possible to pass shipping costs onto the buyer (Jain and Sundström 2021).

How Drop Shipping Works

Figure 4.5

Drop Ship Model

Drop shipping is an entrepreneurial way to start a business without the need of warehousing and holding stock, and it can allow a brand to learn how to select products and test the market while completely avoiding the need for 3PL logistics providers. The drop ship diagram above illustrates this process. With drop shipping, the brands do not have to manage or pay for their own warehouse and pack-and-ship orders, nor do they need to track inventory or handle returns and inbound shipments whilst having to continually order products and manage stock. Additionally, there are low start-up costs and a business can be based from just a laptop and a flexible location that is set up to easily communicate with suppliers and customers. The product ranges do not have to be pre-purchased, so a wide range of fashionable products can easily be displayed, and trial products are often an effective way to "test" the market with new or different ranges in different categories, such as beauty accessories or homewares, with relatively low commitment levels. However, one of the biggest disadvantages of drop shipping are its very low margins; it is a highly competitive area because it is relatively straightforward and the overhead cost is low. There can be inventory problems due to sourcing from multiple warehouses and fulfilling orders for other retailers, hence, items can easily become out of stock and shipping costs and errors can be made by the third party, for which the buyer will be responsible. Additionally, there are limited customisation and branding opportunities due to a lack of control over the product itself. Personalising your brand or any additions to the product will incur minimum order quantities (MOQ) (McKinsey 2020).

Green supply chain management & logistics

Green supply chain management (GSCM) is often defined as an organizational philosophy rather than a theory that integrates the environment into the supply chain and covers all processes involved from procurement of raw materials through manufacturing and, importantly, disposal, recovery and reuse. GSCM is part of sustainable SCM (SSCM) (Vonderembse et al. 2006). Other authors have suggested different supply chain strategies are pursued in different product lifecycle phases and, furthermore, proposed a hybrid supply chain design with an environmental focus as the most appropriate sustainable supply chain strategy. Successful implementation of GSCM needs implementation within the core business strategy and should emanate from the top of the business downward, with leadership and culture crucial to success. One brand example is H&M who has launched a "Conscious" collection – this is a paradox when considering fast fashion practices. This form of incongruous message from fashion brands sends out a "greenwashing" message, which lacks credibility. A more integrated and embedded SSCM strategy that extends throughout the chain would be a better implementation that embraces truly holistic processes (Kim and Hall 2015).

Collaboration between the networks such as suppliers, transporters, 3PL logistics and the end customer requires involvement and buy in. This is where those important links with relationships fit into the fashion supply chain. Collaboration in GSCM can improve sustainability and organizational performance. According to Srivastava(2007), GSCM evolved because of climate change and serious global environmental degradation. Over the last two decades, pollution has exceeded safe levels, threatening dire consequences. The fashion industry has a responsibility, since overconsumption due to fast fashion's globalised supply chains has impacted the situation. Hence, GSCM evolved as an organizational philosophy that can provide a competitive advantage to the organization in terms of high product quality, high service quality, minimum waste, zero pollution, a better image and a high return on investment (Srivastava 2007).

Reverse logistics and closed-loop supply chains are critical elements of sustainable and green supply chain management practices. Mishra et al. (2012) proposed the implementation of a networked approach to the supply chain that would handle recycling and reverse logistics and frameworks for end-of-life recycling. This should be implemented by all fashion brands as an essential element in the supply chain and can be partly achieved by working with logistics providers. The reprocessing of pre-consumer and post-consumer waste can create innovative products used in fashion and other industries and there are some excellent examples of GSCM initiatives merging in fashion logistics. Two of these examples are discussed next:

- Tommy Hilfiger launched an initiative called "Make It Possible," a sustainability programme aiming to create fashion that "wastes nothing and welcomes all." It comprises 24 environmental and social targets, with the main thrust being circularity and inclusivity (Hughes 2020).
- Refashioned Ventures, an early-stage supply chain venture fund, championed companies involved in refashioning their supply chains, with a focus on circular regenerative textiles (Refashioned 2022).

The circular economy and logistics – closing the loop

Following on from GSCM and as discussed in Chapter 1, the circulat economy (CE) is defined as an economic model where resourcing, purchasing, production and reprocessing in the supply chain is designed to consider environmental performance and human well-being (Murray, Skene and Haynes 2017). Waste should be treated as a resource in the green and sustainable supply chain, but a CE does not always mean a recycling economy. Extended producer resource schemes (see Chapter 7) can respect the waste hierarchy and prioritise waste prevention and re-use *first* over recycling.

To truly become circular, brands need to invest (either directly or with partners) in reverse logistics to collect clothing and prevent them from ending up in a landfill. Product lifecycles can be extended by establishing repair services, as

Patagonia and The North Face have done successfully, enabling customers to send in or drop off damaged clothes and have them repaired by experts in days. Ghisellini et al. (2016) argued that the CE has its foundation in industrial ecology and industrial ecosystems and reverse logistics plays an important role in the implementation of closed-loop systems.

Logistics and green shipping

Maersk, one of the largest container shippers, reports that over the past two years, a growing number of fashion companies are investing in sustainable logistics solutions as transparency has improved and clearer standards have emerged. Logistics providers have an important part to play by optimising logistics to enhance sustainability in their activities. Maersk, for instance, has supported a major sporting equipment company by transferring all the cargo from air freight to an intercontinental rail service, which has resulted in reducing CO^2 emissions by 97%. Maersk also has invested in "ECO Delivery," a carbon-neutral ocean transportation service for customers based on using sustainable and certified biofuels; some fast fashion brands are investigating this option. In fact, Maersk has cut their overall CO^2 emissions in half over the past ten years in their shipping container business and aims to decarbonise the entire business by 2050 (Maersk 2022).

Logistics and the digital footprint

Returns can be a lost opportunity in logistics. Some shippers use different transport and logistics providers for their outbound and return flows, and this may negate some of the benefits gained from efforts to create more flexible and faster supply chains that reduce waste. Closer alignment in the supply chain with logistics providers can also strengthen the collaboration of fashion brands with their supply chain provider's longer-term co-operation. Many fashion brands are working in this way to create broader sustainability initiatives. Several global brands, including Nike, have committed to sharing best practices to achieve net zero emissions through Maersk with a joint project called "Transform to Net Zero" initiative (Maersk 2022.

The project is in partnership with the Environmental Defence Fund and BSR, a global non-profit organisation dedicated to sustainable business practices, and runs until 2025. The debate about sustainability versus value is often a trade off, but such initiatives can support both profit and sustainability in this area of the fashion supply chain. The shipping and logistics industry enables global supply chains to keep inventory and raw materials by transporting items sourced by the fashion industry from across the world. It needs to be considered that each journey increases the carbon footprint of a product. DHL, and most of the other 3PL logistics providers, have introduced green vehicles as part of the fleet to reduce the impact of greenhouse gas emissions and air pollution, and many are training relevant staff to become specialists who can help customers assess the environmental impact of their shipping solutions (DHL 2020).

Logistics and freight – One Belt One Road initiatives

DHL recently investigated the use of trains and trucks from China instead of sea freight. The most significant changes in global logistics have been created by the recent One Belt One Road (OBOR) initiative—Chinese investment will have a significant impact on the ability to do this. The Chinese government has invested extensively in road and rail links across China and Asia into Europe, working with other governments to create land routes that form to an extent a more sophisticated version of Marco Polo's original route from Europe to Asia (Lee and Shen 2020).

E-commerce and logistics

Sea freight is preferable to air travel from a sustainability and environmental viewpoint, and this can be supported by detailed data-planning. Obviously, using the most optimum way to reach end customers is essential, but the speed and convenience of the delivery windows now expected by some consumers are unsustainable. Hence, 3PL suppliers usually provide guidelines of how long it should take to receive the goods. Many of these are investigating alternative delivery options such as drop points in a neighbourhood, as this can reduce the delivery destination to one point rather than 50 (McKinsey 2020).

Logistics and packaging

Despite recent improvements and switching to more easily recyclable and compostable packaging, many fashion products worldwide have continued to rely on single-use plastics as part of packaging and wrapping. However, the increasing public awareness of the issues around plastic pollution and climate change has helped put pressure on the industry. The significant waste in packaging according to the Ellen MacArthur Foundation report on the plastics revolution found at least 20% of plastics can be recycled (McKinsey 2020).

Reverse logistics and sustainability in the fashion supply chain

Reverse logistics is a process that can enable fashion brands to minimise impact and create levels of circularity in the supply chain (Hazen et al. 2021; Zhu et al. 2018). There are six critical success factors that can support and influence reverse logistics in the fashion industry.

These critical success factors are:

- Strategic partnership and collaboration
- Design for "second" life consideration

- Optimal recovery processes and channel structure
- Access to information
- Legislative and regulatory instruments
- Consumer relationship management and awareness building

The logistics function has long been associated with levels of recycling and sustainability in the movement of goods area of the fashion supply chain and has begun to attract more attention by researchers into fashion supply chains and in sustainable fashion. It is discussed as reverse logistics and part of a closed-loop system (Yang, Song and Tong 2017).

In the fashion business, the function of reverse logistics has been present for some time and can refer to the process of returning goods or materials, including the packaging. Returned clothing can be re-processed and sold or, in the case of waste or used clothing, may be sold to another market. Increasingly, there is a market for recycled and the re-use of textiles to transform clothing back into raw materials or other products (De Brito and Dekker 2004; Yang, Song and Tong 2017). When used clothing is sent for re-use to third-world countries, it is essential that they are properly sorted to ensure that any low-quality textile (that is essentially waste) is retained by the country it belongs to and, if possible, recycled or properly disposed of.

Unfortunately, some investigations into disposal have revealed that textile export destination countries are burdened with waste. For example, in Ghana, 40% of all textiles sent to the country's second-hand market is waste. The concept of reverse logistics is designed to maximise the use of an item once it is discarded by a customer, and although part of this is recycling, ideally, waste should be minimised throughout the supply chain (Cernansky 2021).

Recycling targets, reuse, and the prevention of waste should be set by fashion brands as well as the minimum criteria for fashion products use and durability. However, this is very difficult without necessary regulation and legislation in the fashion industry.

There are many ways that fashion can be re-used, and the logistics function supports this. There is a framework that can be applied to identify the key areas in the supply chain and forms that this recycling and re-use might take.

The 7R framework includes: recycling, re-using, reducing, redesigning, reimagining, re-wearing and restyling (Srivastava 2014).

- **Recycling** can be shredded and re-used. In the UK, there are initiatives in place such as the Waste and Resources Action Programme (WRAP) that encourage re-use of clothing and work across government local authorities and the public to extend product lifecycles (WRAP 2018).
- **Re-use** focuses on extending a product's useful life by utilising it again in its original form as well as the possible re-use of denim, which is turned back into denim fabric. Brands such MUD Jeans are good examples here (MUD Jeans 2022).
- **Reduce** focuses on limiting the actual waste materials produced, whilst on the other hand refering to the carbon footprint of a piece of clothing. Pattern design and cutting can reduce waste but also "thinking critically about materials." Christopher Raeburn is experimenting in this field with 3-D design and sampling (Sutherland, 2020).

- **Redesign** is linked to what is known as sustainable design in the fashion industry and emphasises the timelessness of a product or garment. Timeless fashion and classic items that can be repaired include Rimowa luggage (Rimowa 2022).

- **Reimagine** links to the production process as a whole and the implementation of new innovative techniques that could enhance the supply chain (Thompson 2012). Examples are seen in Prato, Italy, where many brands (for example in the Kering Group) are working on innovations in the laboratory on site.

- **Reward** focuses on giving a product an extended lifecycle by, for example, encouraging a second-hand culture and the charitable third sector as well as vintage or thrift stores that provide a treasured alternative and can identify one-off pieces for customers (Ho and Choi 2012).

- **Restyle** is an area linked to adding or decorating an item, sometimes referred to as upcycling, which can extend a product lifecycle by creating a one-off piece through tailoring, cutting and sewing into a different item (Ho and Choi 2012).

The 7R framework has many challenges and there are barriers to reuse and the recycling of clothing. Some brands have in fact used incineration and landfills, which are both unnecessary and not at all sustainable. It is important for brands to try to build waste management and levels of reuse and disposal into their supply chain operations by working with logistics partners to create the most sustainable options for the brand (Niinimäki 2019).

Reverse logistics, being an essential part in contemporary efforts toward environmentally friendly closed-loop systems, has in recent years attracted a lot of research attention. Reverse logistics is an important component of modern supply chains (De Brito and Dekker 2004) and it is usually defined as "The process of planning, implementing and controlling flows of raw materials, in process inventory, and finished goods, from a manufacturing, distribution to a point of recovery or disposal" (De Brito and Dekker 2004).

In fact, in the reverse logistics literature, Rogers and Tibben-Lembke (2001) introduced a waste hierarchy model to clarify how resource efficient different reverse processes are, i.e. what environmental value the different processes bring. The article discusses that, except for resource reduction in a traditional "forward" supply chain, all businesses should attempt to maximise re-use activities, including recycling activities. The last resort should be disposal with energy recovery or landfill. In the waste hierarchy, there is consideration for how much economic value could be created in the reverse clothing supply chain (Choi and Li 2015). According to Choi, the main elements of reverse logistics are:

- Efficient collection
- Transportation
- Recovery
- Proper disposal

Finally, it is important to consider the redistribution of products coming back from consumers to maximize economic and environmental value at minimum cost (Krikke 1998).

Logistics and reprocessing of returns

There is a further dimension to returns that is linked with an increasing quantity of goods bought online, which is a sharp increase in the number of returns from customers. The percentage of clothing items returned varies considerably between categories of clothing and country of sale, but ranges from 10% for standard basic clothing (such as white T-shirts) to more than 60% for high fashion goods. There is also evidence of demographic (e.g., gender, age and income) differences (Cullinane and Cullinane 2021).

Logistics and extended producer responsibility

Leading on from reverse logistics and reprocessing but linked to circularity and waste management in the fashion supply chain, is the extended producer responsibility (EPR), (WRAP 2022). This piece of work took place in the European Union (EU) and is being looked at by other countries where targets for collection and re-use of clothing are being set (see Chapter 7). Much of the work to date in the fashion supply chain is largely open-loop recycling, which means waste being turned into rags or other materials, but closed-loop targets are likely to be set, linked to the CE and able to be applied to the design of the clothing in the first place by regarding waste as a resource. Fashion brands may be forced to consider EPR as part of the overall process of production and management of the supply chain to support the environmental impacts of disposable fashion and textiles (WRAP 2022).

At the end of this chapter on logistics, it is worth mentioning again the work of DHL and the BFC white paper report on fashion and sustainability. Three areas where digitalization and e-commerce together have created both challenges and opportunities for fashion supply chains linked to logistics were identified, which led to future of fashion logistics collaborations (DHL 2020).

The first area is "**process ownership**," which involves defining clear and flexible processes that extend from purchase through production to delivery with partners. The importance of aspects such as transparency and sustainability also need to be communicated by fashion brands to their logistics partners and suppliers so that they too can become more transparent and sustainable in their business activities and learn from each other.

The second area is "**relationship building**." The fashion industry has always sustained itself on personal networks and contacts. Since cooperation and sharing of expertise and structures have become increasingly important to sustainable supply chains, the significance of relationships and partnerships, such as logistics providers, has also continued to increase in fashion supply chains and can support sustainable practices on both sides (see Chapter 3).

Brand operations are the third key focus and are linked to the messages that fashion brands wish to convey to their customers. This is of major significance when it comes to working efficiently and giving a consistent image to customers and suppliers. Furthermore, in fashion, the overall supply chain for a fashion product can form an important element of a brand story and, by ensuring a clear and consistent flow of information between suppliers, designers, and customers, fashion brands can ensure efficiency and transparency through their supply chain (DHL 2020).

Conclusion

To conclude this chapter, fashion logistics have evolved from a low skilled labour-intensive activity to one that is now data driven and thrives on strategic real-time information, which can add a competitive advantage to the brand with collaborative vendor relationships. Online fashion retail has created an increase in returns, and DCs and warehouses often store large amounts of stock for fulfilment. Due to the trend toward e-commerce, DCs and smaller units for local deliveries have grown in significance and retailers have had to relocate these centres closer to customers to process the sheer volume of orders and, importantly, re-process their returns. Sourcing and manufacturing of fashion remains globalised, and this trend is likely to continue despite the concerns around the environment and climate change as globalisation continues to impact the sourcing policies of fashion brands (UK Government 2019). However, reverse logistics in the supply chain can be used as an opportunity to implement closed-loop models that regard the use of textile waste as an asset and essential part of the product development phase. Meanwhile, high levels of returns and reprocessing involved in online retailing can also make this a highly unsustainable area of the supply chain and should not be ignored. Sustainability and fast fashion do not sit easily together and availability of fashion at low cost can act as a barrier to the growth of reverse logistics in the fashion industry. But issues of overproduction and overconsumption in the fashion supply chain can be minimised by utilising waste and managing these processes throughout the entire supply chain. A collaborative logistics function can support fashion supply chain sustainability moving to closed-loop systems (De Aguiar, Andreza de Nadae and Da Silva Lima 2021).

CASE STUDY

Interview on logistics – Henry Hales – Tu Pack founder

1. Can you tell us why you decided to set up Tu Pack?

I originally started a clothing brand called SIRPLUS, which uses surplus fabrics to make menswear. We found that as orders grew for SIRPLUS, we needed

a facility that would fulfil stock for us. It was frustrating to find that most 3PLs did not cater for our needs as they:

■ Could not ensure the brand identity and those who did were overpriced

■ Largely had outdated warehouse management systems

■ They were not environmentally conscious

So, with these gaps in the industry in mind, Tu Pack was born.

2. Approximately how big is your operation and where is the warehouse?

Currently, there are 12 full time workers at Tu Pack. We hare handling approximately 2500 orders per month and we are currently renting a 20,000-square-metre warehouse in Coventry.

3. How many brands are you working with now approximately?

Between 20–30 brands are working with us currently.

4. Can you tell us about the packaging used? Is it customised for clients?

Through conducting a survey with clients, we discovered that all our clients wanted us to provide them with packaging too. We even had potential customers ask us to provide the packaging for them to ensure a hassle-free service.

However, a significant amount of our clients wanted similar packaging. So, we found that if we could bulk buy and customise the packaging with tissue paper and stickers, we could save the brands and clients both time and money as well as increasing profit and create pack efficiency for ourselves.

5. Do you transport stock or work with couriers? If so which ones?

We work with the following couriers: DPD and DHL.

6. What level of accuracy in picking stock do you currently have/aim for?

We currency have a stock accuracy of 99.7% but are aiming for 100%.

7. Do you provide a key customer contact for each brand you work with?

The first port of call is our support team and if this does not resolve the issue, then they can escalate to management.

8. Can you tell us how sustainable Tu Pack is and how that manifests itself? For example, do you intend to be a B Corp in the future?

We are currently in the process of becoming a B-Corporation. This is something very important to us. Our mission is to enable retail brands to maintain their identity and differentials across the delivery journey without having to compromise on issues of sustainability, service level and price. Therefore, it is a priority of Tu Pack to obtain the B-Corp accreditation soon as our pledge is to be

net zero by 2022 and become the first B Corp fulfilment company in the UK. In line with our mission statement, we have gone to great lengths to ensure that all our packaging is recyclable and to install solar panels and monitor and record all our carbon emissions. We truly believe we have a duty to adhere to the highest standards of verified social and environmental performance.

9. How important is B Corp accreditation in the fashion industry in your opinion?

Because the fashion industry, with an image and focus on "fast fashion" and consumerism, has a poor history of abusive labour practices and environmental damage, we believe that a B Corp accreditation is of highest importance to tackle such issues. We have also noticed that as transparency and purpose become key values for consumers, these business trends are shifting toward ethical fashion that encompasses transparent supply chains, organic clothes, and focusing on a consume-less ethos that in turn creates brand value.

10. Can you tell us about your interpretation of reverse logistics?

Reverse logistics refers to the type of supply chain management where goods are moved from customers, back to the sellers or manufacturers and the packaging is reused or recycled. Once the customers receive a product, processes such as returns or recycling require reverse logistics. The process of reverse logistics starts at the end consumer, moving backward through the supply chain, eventually to the distributor or from the distributor to the manufacturer.

11. What sort of technology are you using now and how do you see this evolving in the future?

Tu Pack will be 60% automated by the end of 2021. We have invested in robot fleets that will allow our current pickers to focus on packing goods, quality control and replenishment. This will increase our efficiency by 49% and, in turn, this efficiency gain will reduce our costs by requiring fewer workers and less space, boosting our efficiency, accuracy and revenue. We have also designed a hanging rail system to be moved by robots, which will be the first of its kind in the UK.

12. How difficult is it for smaller SMEs to find reliable logistics services such as Tu Pack?

This is obviously relative to the specific firm and industry, but to put it short, this is the reason we started Tu Pack. The alternatives we looked at could not ensure brand identity and those who did were overpriced. Moreover, they had outdated warehouse management systems and weren't environmentally conscious.

13. What are the drawbacks of working with large scale 3PL logistics businesses for an SME?

- Loss of control
- Differentializing
- Business understanding

14. Do you work with overseas shippers to fulfil services for clients?

Yes

15. What is your overall opinion of the importance of accurate reliable logistics in today's fashion industry?

As customers have become much more environmentally aware of how their clothes are produced, the entire supply chain needs to be evaluated and reliable. Furthermore, their increased purchasing power entitles them to pick and choose among thousands of brands. Having a reliable set of logistics is becoming more of a need than a want in today's fashion industry.

Activities & exercises

1. A. Investigate the recycling of fashion and different methods used. What do these look like and what role does a logistics provider play in this? Create visuals/diagrams for the different types of supply chains to reuse textile waste or re-sell and upcycle fashion.
   B. What do these supply chains look like?

2. Much fashion clothing goes to landfill or is shipped to other countries for resale. Investigate the impact of this practice on the environment and local industry where such goods end up.

3. How can the 7R's of recycling support the circular economy in the fashion supply chain? Find brand examples of each one and investigate each one critically.

4. Drop shipping is used by many online platforms working with multiple brands. What are the positives and negatives of this business model in a sustainable fashion supply chain and how can 3PL partners enable these?

5. What are the benefits of reverse logistics for fashion retailers and brands? Discuss these and evaluate the possible impact in the fast fashion market if such processes were implemented.

References

Aftab, M., Qin, Y., and Kabir, N. (2017). "Postponement in the fast fashion supply chain: A review," *International Journal of Business and Management*, 12(7), 115. DOI: 10:5539/ijbm.v12n7p115

Alfieri, A., De Marco, A., and Pastore, E. (2019). "Last mile logistics in fast fashion supply chains: A case study," *IFAC-PapersOnLine*, 52(13), 1693–1698. https://doi.org/10.1016/j.ifacol.2019.11.444

Barnes, L. and Lea-Greenwood, G. (2006). "Fast fashioning the supply chain: Shaping the research agenda," *Journal of Fashion Marketing and Management*, 10(3), 259–271. https://doi.org/10.1108/13612020610679259

Beh, L.-S., Ghobadian, A., He, Q., Gallear, D., and O'Regan, N. (2016). "Second-life retailing: A reverse supply chain perspective," *Journal of Supply Chain Management: An International Journal*, 21, 259–272. DOI: 10.1108/SCM-07-2015-0296

Berezhna, V. (2019). Available from: https://www.businessoffashion.com/articles/luxury/luxury-personal-shopping-net-a-porter-matches-moda-operandi/

Camargo, L.R., Pereira, S.C.F., and Scarpin, M.R.S. (2020). "Fast and ultra-fast fashion supply chain management: An exploratory research," *International Journal of Retail & Distribution Management*, 48(6), 537–553. https://doi.org/10.1108/IJRDM-04-2019-0133

Carter, C.R. and Rogers, D.S. (2008). "A framework of sustainable supply chain management: Moving toward new theory," *International Journal of Physical Distribution & Logistics Management*, 38(5), 360–387. https://doi.org/10.1108/09600030810882816

Cernansky, R. (2021). The ugly side of fashion's take-back programs, *Vogue Business* [ONLINE]. Available at https://www.voguebusiness.com/sustainability/the-ugly-side-of-fashions-take-back-programmes

Choi, T.-M. and Cheng, T.C.E. (2015). "Sustainable fashion supply chain management: From sourcing to retailing." https://doi.org/10.1007/978-3-319-12703-3

Choi, T.-M. and Li, Y. (2015). "Sustainability in fashion business operations," *Sustainability*, 7(11), 15400–15406.

Christopher, C. (2016). *Logistics and Supply Chain Management*. 5th edition. Prentice Hall.

Christopher, M. (2000). "The agile supply chain: Competing in volatile markets," *Industrial Marketing Management*, 29(1), 37–44. https://doi.org/10.1016/S0019-8501(99)00110-8

Christopher, M. and Towill, D. (2001). "An integrated model for the design of agile supply chains," *International Journal of Physical Distribution & Logistics Management*, 31(4), https://doi.org/10.1108/09600030110394914

Clothesource. (2021). https://www.clothesource.net/

Cullinane, S. and Cullinane, K. (2021). "The logistics of online clothing returns in Sweden and how to reduce its environmental impact," *Journal of Service Science and Management*, 14, 72–95. https://doi.org/10.4236/jssm.2021.141006

De Aguiar, H., Andreza de Nadae, J., and da Silva Lima, R. (2021). "Can fashion be circular? A literature review on circular economy barriers, drivers, and practices in the fashion industry's productive chain," *Sustainability* 13(21), 12246. https://doi.org/10.3390/su13211224

De Brito, M.P. and Dekker, R. (2003). "A framework for reverse logistics," ERIM Report Series Research in Management ERS-2003-045-LIS, Erasmus Research Institute of Management (ERIM).

Delai, I. and Takahashi, S. (2013). "Corporate sustainability in emerging markets: Insights from the practices reported by the Brazilian retailers," *Journal of Cleaner Production*, 47(2013), 211–221.

Delgoshaei, A., et al. (2021). "A new model for logistics and transportation of fashion goods in the presence of stochastic market demands considering restricted retailers' capacity," *RAIRO - Operations Research*, 55, S523–S547. http://dx.doi.org/10.1051/ro/2019061

DHL. (2017). Vetements X DHL limited edition pop-up sale in Hong Kong. Available from: https://inmotion.dhl/en/fashion/article/vetements-x-dhl-limited-edition-pop-up-sale-in-hong-kong

DHL. (2020). Available from: https://www.dhl.com/content/dam/dhl/global/dhl-global-forwarding/documents/pdf/dhl-glo-dgf-belt-and-road.pdf

DHL and the British Fashion Council. (2020). Report on Fashion and Sustainability. Available from: https://www.dhl.com/global-en/home/press/press-archive/2019/dhl-and-the-british-fashion-council-publish-white-paper-on-fashion-and-sustainability.html

Dubey R., Gunasekaran, A., Papadopoulos, T., Childe, S.J., Shibin, K.T., and Wamba, S.F. (2016). "Sustainable supply chain management: Framework and further research directions," *Journal of Cleaner Production*, https://doi.org/10.1016/j.jclepro.2016.03.117

Eunomia Research & Consulting. (2018). Policy Toolkit for Carpet Circularity in EU Member States.

Fleischmann, M., Bloemhof-Ruwaard, M., Rommert, D., van der Laan, E., van Nunen, Jo A.E.E., and van Wassenhove, L.N. (1997). "Quantitative models for reverse logistics: A review," *European Journal of Operational Research*, 103(1), 1–17. https://doi.org/10.1016/S0377-2217(97)00230-0

Gaudenzi, B., Mola, L., and Rossignol, C. (2021). "Hitting or missing the target: Resources and capabilities for alternative e-commerce pathways in the fashion industry," *Industrial Marketing Management*, 93(2021), 124–136. https://doi.org/10.1016/j.indmarman.2020.12.016

Ghisellini, P., Cialani, C., and Ulgiati, S. (2016). "A review on circular economy: The expected transition to a balanced interplay of environmental and economic systems," *Journal of Cleaner Production*, 114, 11–32.

Govindan, K., Soleimani, H., and Kannan, D. (2015). "Reverse logistics and closed-loop supply chain: A comprehensive review to explore the future," *European Journal of Operational Research*, 240(3), 603–626. https://doi.org/10.1016/j.ejor.2014.07.012

Hazen, B.T., Russo, I., Confente, I., and Pellathy, D. (2021). "Supply chain management for circular economy: Conceptual framework and research agenda," *The International Journal of Logistics Management*, 32(2), 510–537. https://doi.org/10.1108/IJLM-12-2019-0332

Hinkka, V., Häkkinen, M., Holmström, J., and Främling, K. (2015). "Supply chain typology for configuring cost-efficient tracking in fashion logistics," *The International Journal of Logistics Management*, 26(1), 42–60. https://doi.org/10.1108/IJLM-03-2011-0016

Ho, H. P.-Y. and Choi, T.-M. (2012). "A five-R analysis for sustainable fashion supply chain management in Hong Kong: A case analysis," *Journal of Fashion Marketing*, 16(2), 161–175.

Hughes, H. (2020). Available from: https://fashionunited.uk/news/fashion/tommy-hilfiger-launches-circular-initiative-tommy-for-life/2020100851289

Jain, S. and Sundström, M. (2021). "Toward a conceptualization of personalized services in apparel e-commerce fulfilment," *Research Journal of Textile and Apparel*, 25(4), 414–430. https://doi.org/10.1108/RJTA-06-2020-0066

Kawa, A. (2021). "Fulfilment as logistics support for E-tailers: An empirical studies," *Sustainability*, 13, 5988. https://doi.org/10.3390/su13115988

Khouja, M. (2001). "The evaluation of drop shipping option for e-commerce retailers," *Computers & Industrial Engineering*, 41(2), 109–126. https://doi.org/10.1016/S0360-8352(01)00046-8

Kim, H.S. and Hall, M.L. (2015). "Green brand strategies in the fashion industry: Leveraging connections of the consumer, brand, and environmental sustainability," in Choi, T.M. and Cheng, T. (eds.), *Sustainable Fashion Supply Chain Management*, Springer, Cham, 31–45. https://doi.org/10.1007/978-3-319-12703-3_2

Krikke, H.R. (1998). "Recovery strategies and reverse logistic network design," Doctor of Philosophy, University of Twente.

Krikke, H.R., van Harten, A., and Schuur, P.C. (1998). "On a medium- term product recovery and disposal strategy for durable assembly products," *International Journal of Production Research*, 36(1), 111–140. DOI: 10.1080/002075498193967

Lee, Hau L. and Zuo-Jun Shen. (2020). "Supply chain and logistics innovations with the belt and road initiative," *Journal of Management Science and Engineering*, 5(2), 77–86. https://doi.org/10.1016/j.jmse.2020.05.001

MacArthur. (2020). Designing out plastics. Available from: https://plastics.ellenmacarthurfoundation.org/breaking-the-plastic-wave-perspective

Maersk. (2020). Sustainable style: Fashion supply chains make green gains. Available from: https://www.maersk.com/news/articles/2020/12/08/sustainable-style

Maersk. (2022). Available from: https://www.maersk.com/transportation-services/eco-delivery

McKinsey. (2020). Available from: https://www.mckinsey.com/industries/paper-forest-products-and-packaging/our-insights/the-drive-toward-sustainability-in-packaging-beyond-the-quick-wins

McKinsey. (2021). https://www.mckinsey.com/~/media/mckinsey/industries/retail/our%20insights/state%20of%20fashion/2021/the-state-of-fashion-2021-vf.pdf

Mishra, N., Kumar, V., and Chan, F.T.S. (2012). "A multi-agent architecture for reverse logistics in a green supply chain," *International Journal of Production Research*, 50(9), 2396–2406. https://doi.org/10.1080/00207543.2011.581003

Mud Jeans. (2022). Available from: https://mudjeans.eu/pages/sustainability-fair-production-recover

Murray, A., Skene, K., and Haynes, K. (2017). "The circular economy: An interdisciplinary exploration of the concept and application in a global context," *Journal of Business Ethics*, 140, 369–380. https://doi.org/10.1007/s10551-015-2693-2

Nayak, R. (ed.). (2020). *Supply Chain Management and Logistics in the Global Fashion Sector: The Sustainability Challenge* (1st ed.). London: Routledge. https://doi.org/10.4324/9781003089063

Niinimäki, K. (2019). *Sustainable Fashion in a Circular Economy*. Aalto ARTS Books. ISBN 978-952-60-0090. https://aaltodoc.aalto.fi/handle/123456789/36608

53. Women's Wear Daily. 10/9/2019, p21-21. 1p.

Oláh, J., Kitukutha, N., Haddad, H., Pakurár, M., Máté, D., and Popp, J. (2019). "Achieving sustainable E-commerce in environmental, social and economic dimensions by taking possible trade-offs," *Sustainability*, 11(1), 89. https://doi.org/10.3390/su11010089

Paras, M.K., Curteza, A., and Varshneya, G. (2019). "Identification of best reverse value chain alternatives: A study of Romanian used clothing industry," *Journal of Fashion Marketing and Management*, 23(3), 396–412. https://doi.org/10.1108/JFMM-04-2018-0060

Pietro, E., Lodovic, S., and Thomas, A. (2018). "Environmental sustainability in third-party logistics service providers: A systematic literature review from 2000–2016," *Sustainability*, 10, 1627. DOI: 10.3390/su10051627

Qin, X., Liu, Z., and Tian, L. (2020). "The strategic analysis of logistics service sharing in an e-commerce platform," *Omega*, 92, 102153.

Refashioned. (2022). Available from: https://www.refashiond.com/

Rimowa. (2022). Available from: https://www.rimowa.com/gb/en/repair/repair-services.html

Rogers, D.S. and Tibben-Lembke, R. (2001). "An examination of reverse logistics practices," *Journal of Business Logistics* 22(2), 129–148. DOI: 10.1002/j.2158-1592.2001. tb00007.x

Rokonuzzaman, M. (2018). "The integration of extended supply chain with sales and operation planning: A conceptual framework," *Logistics*, 2(2), 8.

Sandberg, E., Pal, R., and Hemilä, J. (2018). "Exploring value creation and appropriation in the reverse clothing supply chain," *The International Journal of Logistics Management*, 29(1), 90–109. https://doi.org/10.1108/IJLM-10-2016-0241

Shen, B. and Li, Q. (2015). "Impacts of returning unsold products in retail outsourcing fashion supply chain: A sustainability analysis," *Sustainability*, 7, 1172–1185.

Siagian, H., Tarigan, Z.J.H., and Jie, F. (2021). Supply chain integration enables resilience, flexibility, and innovation to improve business performance in COVID-19 era," *Sustainability*, 13, 4669. https://doi.org/10.3390/su13094669

Singh, A. and Trivedi, A. (2016). "Sustainable green supply chain management: Trends and current practices," *Competitiveness Review*, 26(3), 265–288. https://doi.org/10.1108/CR-05-2015-0034

Srivastava, S.K. (2007). "Green supply-chain management: A state-of-the-art literature review," *International Journal of Management Reviews*, 9(1), 53–80. https://doi.org/10.1111/j.1468-2370.2007.00202.x

Sutherland, E. (2020). Raeburn's 'three Rs' of sustainable innovation. Available from: https://www.drapersonline.com/insight/drapers-bespoke/raeburns-three-rs-of-sustainable-innovation

Thompson, H. (2012). The future of design: Craft reimagined. *The Guardian*. Available from: https://www.theguardian.com/education/2020/jan/28/meet-the-makers-how-craft-based-degrees-are-fusing-tradition-with-innovation. Accessed 24 July 2013.

UK Government. (2019). Fixing Fashion Report. Available from: https://publications. parliament.uk/pa/cm201719/cmselect/cmenvaud/1952/report-summary.html

Vonderembse, M., Uppal, H., Huang, S., and Dismukes, J. (2006). "Designing supply chains: Towards theory development," *International Journal of Production Economics*, 100(2), 223–238. DOI: 10.1016/j.ijpe.2004.11.014

WRAP (Waste & Resources Action Programme). (2012). Valuing our clothes: The true cost of how we design, use, and dispose of clothing in the UK, WRAP. Available from: http://www.wrap.org.uk/sites/files/wrap/VoC%20FINAL%20online%20 2012%2007%2011.pdf. Accessed 1 April 2022.

WRAP (Waste & Resources Action Programme). (2018). Newsletter: Re-use, WRAP. http://createsend.com/t/y-D59B8FF7AFD81B2D. Accessed April 11 2022.

WRAP. (2022). https://wrap.org.uk/resources/guide/getting-ready-extended-producer-responsibility

Xiang Li. (2014). "Operations Management of Logistics and Supply Chain: Issues and Directions," *Discrete Dynamics in Nature and Society*, 2014, 701938. https://doi.org/10.1155/2014/701938

Yang, S., Song, Y., and Tong, S. (2017). "Sustainable retailing in the fashion industry: A systematic literature review," *Sustainability*, 9(7), 1266.

Yong, G. and Doberstein, B. (2008). "Developing the circular economy in China: Challenges and opportunities for achieving 'leapfrog development'," *International Journal of Sustainable Development & World Ecology*, 15(3), 231–239. DOI: 10.3843/ SusDev.15.3:6

Zhu, S., Song, J., Hazen, B.T., Lee, K., and Cegielski, C. (2018). "How supply chain analytics enables operational supply chain transparency: An organizational information processing theory perspective," *International Journal of Physical Distribution & Logistics Management*, 48(1), 47–68. https://doi.org/10.1108/IJPDLM-11-2017-0341

CHAPTER 5

Auditing and managing risk in the supply chain

Summary

This chapter addresses the key issues surrounding the ethical and legal requirements of compliance in aspects of manufacturing and logistics. The auditing of suppliers and the approval process of raw materials is explained in the context of fashion products to mitigate risks and benchmark standards. Complex levels of scrutiny are required in the supply chain whilst using current and future-proofed methods of transparency to assess the stakeholders in the critical path, and this chapter will apply the Triple-A supply chain theory – a best practice. Risk management theory is explored and the importance of methods and accreditation are discussed.

Case study:

LMB TEXTILE RECYCLING – ROSS BARRY – COST AND RISK

Learning outcomes

At the end of this chapter, you will be able to:

- Understand the difference between compliance and engagement
- Explore the types of accreditations available and review those that have most significance around product and profit
- Explore ways of promoting better conditions for workers within fashion supply chains

SDG GOAL(S) – THIS CHAPTER LINKS TO:

12 Responsible Consumption and Production

16 Peace, Justice and Strong Institutions

17 Partnerships for the Goals

Cost and risk

"Brands must break down and break through the adversarial bargaining that is focused on the price of finished goods out of the factory," John Thorbeck, chairman of supply chain analytics firm Change Capital told *The Business of Fashion* in September 2020 (P72. 180).

"Most importantly, it means sharing risk, sharing value and sharing upside with suppliers, rather than a total focus on lowest cost," Thorbeck said. "The hard work is to change the culture and that means focusing on supply flexibility more than lowest cost. The required change is to be collaborative, not adversarial; to be relational, not transactional; and to create and share value, not extract it."

In an era when brands have viewed cost efficiency as a priority alongside expanding market share, sourcing unique products and materials and moving closer to sales and manufacturing markets is gaining and near shore location will grow in importance (Caniato et al. 2015). As a result of this expansion, companies have been able to reframe their supply chain to "improve resilience, and re-examine relationships with suppliers in order to reduce systematic risk" (McMaster et al. 2020).

In this chapter, the aim is to explore the current issues associated with auditing and compliance in global supply chains, including the methods and processes involved in gaining accreditations and how to present the information gathered to your suppliers and customers.

Also included is examining the rationale behind ensuring compliance and how to move from compliance to engagement. It is worth noting that these processes are not infallible: "Given the highly complex nature of the fashion supply chain and the high level of outsourcing of manufacture, bureaucratic control mechanisms such as codes of conduct and supplier audits are not infallible" (Perry and Towers 2013).

Historically, the necessity for a purchaser or buyer to set out a clear code of conduct (COC) was optional, as issues developed and companies and brands sourced further afield from their home country, supplier manuals with a higher level of detail became more commonplace.

These supplier manuals set out terms and conditions for working with a retailer. In this, they could specify any number of regulations and the supplier could take these rules and interpret them for their situation. These COCs only more recently covered health and safety and compliance with local laws; historically, they reviewed only hours of work and minimum wage (Bonacich and Applebaum 2000). The monitoring of these codes was often carried out by the brand, but more likely to be carried out by a third-party organisation at a distance. The aim of this monitoring was compliance, but there has been a call for these methods to move from compliance to engagement.

After a customer complaint and injury after finding metal pieces in clothing, a key first initial rule widely adopted was the needle policy, which aimed to prevent any chance of metal pieces and contamination. To ensure this would not happen, the sewing needles for industrial machines are kept in a secure safe. All broken needles are logged and every segment is collected and recorded. This is a standard process now and it is taken further in some cases to enforce metal detectors at the end of the production line to ensure complete safety from the hazards of broken needles. As consumers become more litigious, brands are similarly concerned about the health and safety of products and what that may involve with business liability.

There are quite strict and detailed rules on garment requirements in the UK; this is a legacy issue with certain products and age groups. When many houses had open fires, the rules on nightwear became important due to a large number of accidents and anti-inflammable fabrics were required by law. This label is apparent in children's and adult nightwear, but it does not apply to loungewear. This is a tricky path to navigate and testing houses and compliance are the best way to ensure adherence to regulations. Other legislation applies to children's clothing and accessories with flammability, small parts and the removal of drawstring fastenings for health and safety reasons. It is worth examining the requirements of the market where the products are being sold to meet these specifications and ensure compliance.

The terms that became part of the negotiated contract covers several processes in the supply chain, not solely the manufacture of the garments. The intention here is to provide in this chapter a good overview of the stages of accreditations in all tiers and levels of the supply chain along with new accreditations and awarding bodies that seek to amplify the transparency of suppliers. Overarching risk management theory will underpin the discussion and evaluate the prime operational methods with the aim of transparency and avoiding greenwashing and marketing scandals.

Risk in fashion supply chains

A risk is an unplanned event with negative consequences, and sometimes taking a risk is often necessary to gain a competitive advantage.

As with fashion trends, risk can be a macro- or micro-occurrence. A macro-event, such as the global COVID-19 pandemic was both unpredictable and impacted all global locations. A micro-event, such as minor flooding in part of a country or lack of vehicle drivers, has less impact and is more localised. Risk can also be defined as external risk, which is beyond the control of the company (such as the global pandemic or political instability) or internal risk (usually process or product failures), which can be managed by the company.

Risk can be defined as *Probability × Impact = Risk.*

This can be further explored by examining if the risk is high, medium or low in terms of impact on the business, supply chain or externally. Impact can be defined as high, medium or low as well. You can assess if the likelihood or probability of an event is very likely (high probability), but the impact might be low. This is explored in the activities at the end of this chapter.

The process of risk management can be broken down into four key stages:

1. Identify the business capability to respond should incidents occur.
2. Assess the probability of the most likely and damaging risk, the appetite of the business and the available funds. Some risks are too unlikely and costly to act upon.
3. Review the impact of the risk on the business should that risk occur.
4. Disclose and raise awareness of potential risks and actions to reduce them both internally and externally.

The types of risk and their impact are often caused by working at arms-length with suppliers – often because these are not established relationships (see Chapter 3). It can

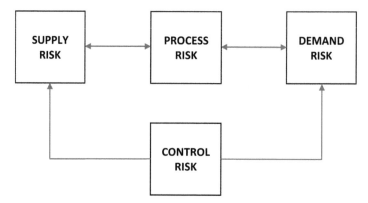

Figure 5.1

Process control diagram

be a key operational area to manage risk in fashion supply chains, although fashion has been very slow to follow the examples of the health and motor industries. Risk is further defined by Martin Christopher as (Christopher et al. 2011). These elements of risk are intertwined as shown in Fig. 5.1.

1.   Process risk
2.   Control risk
3.   Demand risk
4.   Supply risk
5.   Environmental risk

Areas of process and control risk are internal factors to the organisation, the demand and supply risk are internal to the supply chain but external to the organisation, and environmental risk is external to both the organisation and the supply chain. Internal and process examples can be affected by global markets and trading, particularly currency variations. Over the past few years, the political and economic landscape has caused volatile currency because of Brexit and government elections, causing peaks and troughs in the value of the UK pound sterling (BBC News 2019).

Process risk

A Mckinsey supply chain report discusses American Eagle Outfitters, which has been revolutionised with a full-service model to support consumers and offer solutions to demand fluctuations. They have risked their in-store fulfilment to prioritise online orders from stores and distribution centres. They have turned the old model around by creating hubs of supply with quicker response. This had significant process risk, as stores may not have had full availability of a product, but it met the needs of the increase in online orders and the desire to meet the newly increased demand (Mckinsey Report 2021).

The networks involved in global fashion supply chains expose companies to levels of risk that were previously managed with local supply networks. Increasingly, sourcing garments has been a "race to the bottom" in terms of price, but global sourcing in many countries also can have benefits of supply flexibility, better quality and access to new markets. Unfortunately, in recent years, terrorism, diseases and natural disasters have been risks arising from global sourcing (Peck and Juttner 2002; Christopher and Peck 2004).

The bullwhip effect is an influence on demand quantity, causing overinflation of volume and affecting markdown and excess stock (Nguyen, Adulyasak, and Landry 2021).

It is often made worse by unpredictable demand and stakeholders not communicating effectively; if real-time information is shared, then this risk can be minimised, according to Sarkar and Kumar (2015). Additionally, the ripple effect as noted by Ivanov, Dolgui and Sokolov (2019), can be reduced by applying technologies such as data crawling and radio-frequency identification (RFID) technologies to repurpose resources during this business recovery stage, linked to the global pandemic and resilience. The ripple effect during the pandemic caused disruptions throughout the supply chain and led to long-term impacts and disruptions on both supply and demand.

Demand risk

Fashion has a non-essential element to align with – wants rather than needs – and this paradox can lead to unpredictable demand, which will ripple both up and downstream. These fashion products can be categorised into functional clothing with more reliable demand and innovative garments that have more highly volatile demand (McMaster et al. 2020).

This is then linked to the ideas around complex global supply chains. In fashion, the demand for products has been, and is likely to continue to be, unpredictable. Brands and the competition amongst them in business, especially in online and small- and medium-sized enterprises (SMEs), is greater now than it has been previously. Lean and agile models of supply are now normal, increasing the speed-to-market of trends. Some fashion brands have become specialists in unique products, ensuring they have greater market share. Outsourcing operations with suppliers may increase the lack of visibility in the supply chain, e.g. sub-contracting, and therefore expose the company to **reputational risk**. This issue has been widely shown in manufacturing in Bangladesh where there are 7000 clothing factories but only 4000 are registered (Labowitz and Baumann-Pauly 2015). Unfortunately, this has not been limited just to overseas suppliers, but is also prevalent in the UK in Leicester as mentioned in Chapter 6.

Traidcraft is petitioning for a UK fashion watchdog to prevent "problematic purchasing practices" and ensure that buying is carried out fairly both in the UK and globally. Examples of where this has not happened are the Rana Plaza disaster discussed in previous chapters. The reaction to the global pandemic – cancelling orders and retrospective discounts – have been common ways of doing business combined with the excessive financial strain on small businesses with punitive payment terms. The Groceries Code Adjudicator (GCA), "is the independent regulator whose mission is to ensure that regulated retailers treat their direct suppliers lawfully and fairly" (GCA 2021) and Traidcraft wants the same board to ensure decent and working conditions in the garment industry.

Supplier integration and flexibility is key to overcoming these challenges and is often better managed by online retailers, such as ASOS in the UK, who quickly switched production to suit the rise in demand for loungewear during the pandemic (ASOS 2020). Managing unpredictable demand can be lessened by creating a buffer stock of essential materials or trims (essentially postponement, mentioned earlier) and delaying the production of specific goods when demand is less easy to predict.

Supply risk

Supply risk could be endless and can be any number of these challenges:

■ Increased costs
■ Factory unable to make the product as planned
■ Competitor uses the same product
■ Poor quality, which is usually linked to price
■ Ethical issues
■ Unreliable deliveries

A perfect storm of both demand and supply factors was highlighted by a report in *The Guardian* (2021) as business came out of the pandemic restrictions and lockdown was lifted, the unpredictable demand was also hit by supply issues. The Office of National Statistics said 6.5% of businesses could not get the necessary goods or services in August 2021. The fall in retail sales had contracted for four months and matched the lowest fall in retail sales since 1996. With demand falling and a move to online, the proportion of online sales before the pandemic had been 19.7% and rose to 27.7% in August 2021. These issues were further compounded by post-Brexit supply chain disruptions and vehicle driver recruitment. With an increase in UK inflation and personal taxation, they predicted that consumer demand would recover to its pre-pandemic peak by the third quarter of 2022 (Partington 2021). Added to this, the UK ports became overloaded. The British Retail Consortium (BRC) said, "further disruption to supply chains may be unavoidable after Maersk, the world's largest container shipping company, said that it was directing big vessels away because main UK ports are chock-a-block" (Bancroft 2021).

ASOS had reported in August 2021 great results despite the pandemic, fuelled by the rise in online shopping; they predicted inflation impacting on profit due to supply chain disruptions and longer lead times from third party brands. These issues impacted promotions such as Black Friday and meeting the full Christmas sales potential. Several solutions were offered to improve the impact of these issues, such as American Eagle Outfitters (demonstrated in Fig. 5.2), mentioned previously, adopting a fulfilment platform to minimise the risk and allow customers to access stock from distribution centres globally. A competing fulfilment model from Next retail looking at collaboration known as 'partner fulfilment' allowed other brands to use its distribution centres, which provided improvements until supply chain disruptions calmed down (Collins 2021).

Possible solutions to avoid sea container delays would be to offer sea/road, where the shipment is split by more than one transportation method, as H&M has used, and the potential to avoid air and sea freight with the One Belt One Road initiative (see Chapter 3) invested in by the Chinese government that follows a rail route from China to Europe, along the ancient Silk Route.

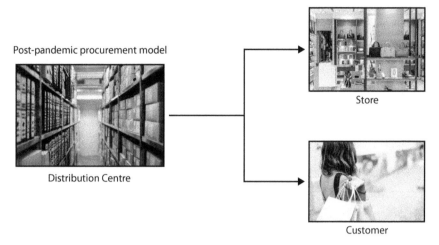

Figure 5.2

Old and new procurement models

The Mckinsey report discusses changes in structure and process to minimise risk can "bend the cost curve" and implement methods to capture consumer interest with stock flexibility and meet the orders in a timely and cost-effective manner (Mckinsey Report 2021).

In an article for *I* news, Cahal Milmo stated the global shipping crisis was causing shortages and shutdowns, since the container ship Ever Given was stuck in the Suez Canal back in August 2021. A backlog was created that could last as long as nine months and would affect Christmas deliveries as vessels queued at congested ports. This has been seen as a global perfect storm with labour shortages caused by COVID-19 and a shortage of warehouse space affecting supply chains in South Asia, China and many ships anchored off the United States' west coast.

In Europe, both Rotterdam and Antwerp were overloaded with vessels, although the British Ports Authority (BPA) said there was plenty of capacity in the UK and much less congestion. However, the news of shortages and missing out on goods has caused panic buying as seen in the examples of toilet rolls and petrol during and after the pandemic in 2020–21 (Milmo 2021).

In addition to the recent news, there are always these factors to manage such as:

- Bad weather
- Delays: Customs/paperwork
- Administration errors
- Theft
- Incorrect amounts
- Fire
- Floods
- Snow

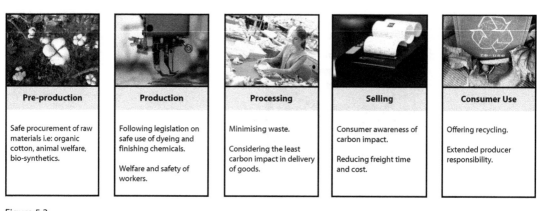

Pre-production	Production	Processing	Selling	Consumer Use
Safe procurement of raw materials i.e: organic cotton, animal welfare, bio-synthetics.	Following legislation on safe use of dyeing and finishing chemicals. Welfare and safety of workers.	Minimising waste. Considering the least carbon impact in delivery of goods.	Consumer awareness of carbon impact. Reducing freight time and cost.	Offering recycling. Extended producer responsibility.

Figure 5.3

Risk framework in the fashion value chain

With the new post–Brexit regulations and climate, both delays in paperwork through customs and the examples of forest fires are both evidence of the impact of supply disruption. In Chapter 2, Sarah Yull spoke about the disruption to deliveries into the European Union (EU) post-Brexit – with delays of up to eight weeks to clear customs paperwork. The environmental risk framework shown in Fig. 5.3.

Risk framework

Ethical issues and environmental risk

"The issue of labour exploitation, non-payment of the minimum wage and poor working conditions in UK-based garment factories, as demonstrated by recent reports coming out of Leicester (but by no means limited to that location), continue to persist." Written evidence during UK Gov. 2021 (Labour Behind the Label (LBL) 2021). "Due to fashion's global importance in terms of export volumes and number of employees, its **environmental** impact is significant" (Caniato et al. 2011).

In managing environmental risk, firstly consider the support of the workforce to improve and maintain good working conditions and create a COC for suppliers and ensure compliance. In this area, non-governmental organisations (NGOs), especially the Ethical Trade Initiative benchmark, are essential accreditations. Although the pressure of shareholders and other stakeholders can enforce this to an extent, a good example is a group like PETA buying shares to encourage accountability (Glover 2021). Secondly, consider the welfare of animals through maintenance of better farming, shearing and traceable materials. The Leather Working Group and Responsible Down Standard are good examples of this.

Sustainability issues are endemic in fast fashion systems in particular, due to the pressure on reducing cost and lead time, which can lead to unsustainable production practices, including labour exploitation and environmental pollution from production and distribution activities (Turker and Altuntas 2014).

Cotton supply in Bangladesh over many years has been severely affected by changes in the climate, causing flooding and damage to the cotton harvest. While there is a monsoon most years, changes to its timing, increased rainfall and alterations to the average temperature affects both the output of cotton and the price. Farmers and buyers have to be resilient to these adverse impacts during procurement and production (Nadiruzzaman et al. 2021). As an internal risk for buyers, planning the cotton supply or switching to replacements such as Viscose can help with price volatility or restrictions in supply due to weather factors, but are done more to ensure less reliance on this thirsty crop and to see more sustainable alternatives are available.

Reputational risk through supply is highlighted in Chapter 2 around the mis-selling of fur, which has resulted in brands clearly defining the identification of real fur for both customers and the buying teams.

The announcement from the CEO of the Kering group that they will no longer use animal fur in their products from 2022 made headlines. It is a bold departure for the luxury industry and in some markets, it has been widely used and preferred. They consider their use of leather as a by-product of the meat industry and this stance has been further enhanced with their Environmental Profit & Loss report and application (Pinault 2021). This has been applauded since Gucci went fur-free in 2016 and certainly sets this luxury house apart from its competitors. The risk is traceability of all the materials, but in contrast to this, Kering is heavily investing in new developments such as mushroom leather (Glover 2021).

Other risks to consider are:

Financial: Product obsolescence, markdowns

Chaos risks: Second-guessing, overreactions, unnecessary interventions, mistrust between supply chain partners and distorted information. i.e., the bull-whip effect

Market risks: Failure to identify market signals and not reacting quickly enough to meet these can be linked to poor communication

There are also business and brand reputation, visibility, control, disruptions, ethical, environmental and complexity risks in fashion supply chains (Christopher and Peck 2004; Christopher and Lee 2004; Masson et al. 2007; Caniato et al. 2011).

Triple-A supply chains

Professor H. Lau developed the idea of the Triple-A supply chain – agile, adaptable and aligned – in 2004, which connects to the "leagile" term coined by Martin Christopher. Since this concept in Christopher and Lee (2004), sourcing locations have widened and new entrants to the market have shaped a new fashion landscape. Notably, the retailer Zara has been working on demand-led supply from near-shore sources, which has reduced their inventory and increased their assortment of on-trend fast fashion. But the longer-term reaction to this has been the scrutiny of the waste and water consumption of these products and the term "planned obsolescence" (Jackson and Shaw 2009).

The **agile** supply chain needs to address the issues of carbon footprint and sourcing standards with quick response to market factors, and these multiple challenges need new and complex solutions.

Furthermore, being able to **adapt** to sudden changes on demand requires allowing for flexibility in sourcing locations as supply chains are more global; the risk associated with this is that some of this visibility can be lost.

Lastly, **alignment**, is having a shared vision for the products, which might be through sharing data, knowledge and goals. Along with linking all aspects together in offering a transparent flexible sourcing strategy, the challenge is in knowing the real-time information for all the stakeholders in the supply chain.

The lean supply chain, which has links to just-in-time manufacturing, is at risk from global disruptions and low inventory levels, which impact the fulfilment of orders. Supply chain managers should look at diversification of the manufacturing base to avoid single-source or location dependence (McMaster et al. 2020).

Performance testing

Mitigating risk and supplier auditing

Overarching government laws and policies are a huge influence and impact businesses – and these international policies do not stand still. The United Nation's Global Sustainable Development Goals (SDGs) remain a driver for new and future legislation. To manage the supplier base in line with new regulations, whether they are formal or informal, is known as compliance or the corporate social responsibility (CSR) function in head office. These roles vary among brands and the level of scrutiny can vary widely. It is good to review what the best examples of this strategy involve and whether it is "in house" or carried out by a third party or member of an accredited NGO. Although many argue that CSR is not a department but a way of doing business, which should involve all aspects of the retail head office.

A job role of vendor performance analysis is common in a retail head office and supply planner roles can include these tasks also looking at capacity challenges.

Collaboration is highly important and effective communication between merchandising, sourcing and demand planning is equally effective. In turn, managing the data around forecasting and improving the analysis of data management is a required skill. Looking at systems applications and products (SAP) through remote monitoring and management is embedded in the role of supply chain planning. It is useful to have systems knowledge and possibly the advantage of speaking another language, especially with near-shore producers. Product lifecycle management (PLM) and blockchain technologies can enhance real-time data retrieval and analysis if the businesses are willing and able to collaborate in this way. A high level of investment and training to use these technologies is required. PLM software has been available for some years from many software providers. It was adopted by Marks & Spencer and Debenhams department stores, and the most successful adoption of this has been in Burberry's head office in the UK. This mitigates the risk of tiers of supply.

> *A historic over-reliance on one sourcing location such as China, which the fashion industry depends on, it is worth noting that 70% of woven fabrics used in Bangladesh come from China and a vast 90% of fabrics used in Myanmar ready-made garments industry. The ripple effect of one market affecting the next is concerning and would need to be managed carefully.*
>
> (McMaster et al. 2020)

Although many retailers have published these Tier 1 supplier lists and this has become more commonplace, Mango, the Spanish retailer, has gone further publishing their Tier 2 suppliers. In an agreement with trade unions in Spain in 2018, the *Comisiones Obreras* has the intention of improving working conditions in its supply chains. It noted that as a caveat, that it does not own any of the factories and intends to keep the list of suppliers updated every six months and disclose Tier 3 suppliers in the future (Remington 2021).

Historically, brands had thought publishing supplier lists would give away the competitive advantage, but with more collaboration and cooperation, this has been unfounded and adds to more layers of transparency through the tiers of supply.

Codes of conduct and corporate social responsibility

Once a member of Sedex for either an auditor, buyer or supplier, there is a choice to carry out a Sedex Members Ethical Trade Audit (SMETA). The novelty of this system is the ability to share audit reports across many brands to avoid duplication. The inspectors consist of an opening meeting, a paperwork review, a tour of the factory site and interviews carried out with management. Finally, workers provide a final Corrective Action Plan Review (Sedex 2021). The audits protect brands and suppliers and minimise the risk of any unethical practices in the factories, with labour rights and regulations being a priority. However, this audit also covers raw materials and technology, such as Intertek Inlight (Intertek 2021), and can link to textile testing reports for performance and dangerous substances as mentioned in Chapter 2.

Bluesign technology allows members to keep up to date with new chemical regulations and keep vendors in the know about new environmental laws (Quinn 2015).

As mentioned in Chapter 3, the profit for the business model of the B Corporation has been adopted by some forward-thinking brands and businesses. This creates both social and environmental value throughout the organisation. The audit is not based on financial performance alone and allows for review of the positive impacts on the community and the environment, too (Chouinard and Stanley 2012). The UK-based brand Baukjen, who has gone through the B Corporation accreditation process, won the "Best for the World" accolade at the UN Climate Change Conference, COP26, in 2021. Baukjen has made improvements in "Climate Neutral Now," category saving on water use and CO_2 in both materials and logistics in the supply of garments (Fibre2fashion 2021).

Product authenticity

Much has been written about the counterfeit market for Fashion goods. This has impacted brands especially at the Accessible Luxury level, where goods have been copied and passed off as authentic products. Although good technology helps the manufacture of counterfeit goods (Phau and Teah 2009; Eisend and Schuchert-Guler 2006; Penz and Stottinger 2005), it can also help customers know if they are buying the original item with the use of QR codes in labelling. This has become more important than ever as the luxury product resale market is growing, i.e., the Vestiaire Collective.

Counterfeiting has many reasons for a potential impact on brand reputation. Often, a consignment of goods is lost in transit, more commonly at the customer delivery stage, and single items can go missing, now known as "pavement piracy." With better technology in containers and shipping, it is less likely that a whole shipment of a product would go missing. It is lucrative for manufactures to copy original products and while there is a market for this, there is also an awareness by global customs and excise departments in the value of this hidden market. Fake goods were seized in Hong Kong in 2006 heading for an Internet auction worth $700,000 HK (Chow 2006). These fakes can appear on sites like eBay for a fraction of the retail price. Another shipment had 20 cases of counterfeit goods heading for auction sites worth nearly $2 million HK and 24 people were arrested. A job role that has grown from this is that of an authenticator, particularly on luxury resale platforms, to avoid the sale of counterfeit merchandise.

Methods of mitigating risk

The first method to mitigate risk is to ensure the stock level commitment is adapted for different types of stock, possibly using a collaborative planning forecasting and replenishment system for core products that always need to be available. Hosiery is a good example of this as it needs to be replenished on an ongoing basis and working with key suppliers in a connected manner can facilitate this. Secondly, relationships built over a long period with key suppliers is another way to work with less risk and encourage reliability. Thirdly, visibility in the supply chain can be linked to the use of technology.

Looking at the political situation when choosing a location for manufacturing is a way to assess risk, and it would be best to avoid a country that has domestic political issues, although minor complications do exist within most countries. Political instability in governments carries a high risk for disruption such as civil wars occurring in many clothing manufacturing areas in the past and currently. A network of local suppliers is an advantage. A review of existing competitors and their collaboration when using these suppliers, and then combining this with a blend of near-shore and far-shore suppliers, can reduce the impact of supply chain delivery issues. There are certainly benefits to long-term contracts with key manufacturers, which might enable booking factory space in advance and facilitating "postponement" (see Chapter 3) of the decision on what the final garment might look like. All of these factors can be built up over time and culminate in trusted relationships.

As mentioned, collaboration and shared technology in the digital era can support real-time data, further supporting critical path management and monitoring. Some of the currently used technologies are listed here and those that have potential to improve authenticity and transparency.

RFID   Radio Frequency Identification
PLM   Product Lifecycle Management
SAP   Systems Applications and Products
Blockchain

This can also be as simple as a shared spreadsheet on a cloud server, but it requires engagement from all parties and dedication to adhering to the process management. In sharing information, it is paramount that there is trust between all key stakeholders.

Summary

Using technology can address the issues with geographically complex and fragmented manufacturing locations and allow products to arrive on time with minimum inventory and support at the sales window for a fashion trend-led product (Rafi-Ul-Shan et al. 2018).

Risk can be minimised if the owner of the business is committed to sustainability (Walker and Jones 2012), and this can avoid the bad press associated with product recalls, especially in the health and safety of garments, pollutants and chemical use.

Managing these risks will support the development of the business and its ongoing resilience, avoiding delayed shipments, which can lead to reduced costs. With better technology, there can be better visibility and improved relationships between many tiers of manufacture, which then should avoid major and minor operational disruptions (Rafi-Ul-Shan et al. 2018).

Although levels of risk can be managed with good frameworks and contingency planning, the exercises in this chapter are organised to help evaluate risk and the likelihood of these events. Also, assessing the impact of these scenarios and remembering that people are always involved in the decision-making process, can affect workers and the environment.

CASE STUDY

LMB Textiles Recycling – interview with Ross Barry

Biography: With 20 years of experience in the textile re-use and recycling sector, Ross is passionate about developing more effective re-use systems that divert our clothing from landfill and into the hands of the people who will value them the most.

Ross is actively involved in the development of emergent recycling solutions to enable the UK to transition to a more sustainable circular economy.

Keeping its roots in East London, LMB set up a headquarters in a large warehouse in Canning Town where all the clothes, shoes and textiles are taken to be sorted, baled and loaded onto containers. A subsidiary company, the Britannia Wiper Company, was also formed to recycle clothes that couldn't be used by cutting them into industrial wiping cloths, used by various industry sectors.

On an average week, LMB now collects 170–200 tonnes of textiles, clothing and shoes of which 80% will be sorted and exported for re-use, 10% that isn't fit for re-use will be cut into wiping cloths, 5% will be sent for flocking and felting, leaving a minimal 5% waste, incorporating household rubbish, hangers and single shoes.

LMB has recently been involved in various new initiatives encouraging the younger generation to recycle and re-use. Its Shoe Friend and Clothes

Collectors schemes work in schools across the Southeast, educating primary school children of the need to recycle paired shoes and clothes. Soon to be launched is "Reskinned," an innovation in repurposing customers' old items, through the retail brand and LMB in a profit-sharing business model.

1. Are you aware of extended producer responsibility (EPR) and how that might affect your business?

Yes, of course. It is a voluntary basis with retail, but the value of the product is very low and can cost more to transport than it is worth.

2. You are a member of Sustainable Clothing Action Plan (SCAP) now moving to Textiles 2030, how does this support your business?

This has helped with noting that the charity sector is overloaded and we have seen a rise in retailer responsibility and consumer recycling rates being higher in the UK. We still have a very linear model and a unique charity sector to deal with this.

3. The figure produced by the Ellen MacArthur Foundation quotes that only 1% of textiles are recycled into new fibres and fabrics. Do you think this is improving four years after the report was published?

Because of the linear nature of clothing disposal, we expect to have about 5% by 2026. This is what we have that ends up being recycled into new fibres. Companies like Re:NewCell and Sodra use cotton fibre like paper recycling.

4. Where does the largest number of garments donated come from and how many different sources do you have?

The breakdown of what clothing we process is 50% from charity shops, 40% from clothing banks and 10% is EPR, also known as take-back schemes. Reskinned, our new project, is working with Finisterre and Sweaty Betty on the take-back and resale scheme through their platforms, and we would process that.

5. Do you define the goods received by material type or quality or both?

This is more by quality – the ability to resell the clothing product. What has no value will be shredded for insulation, cut up for cleaning cloths, wool cladding or, lastly, incinerated if it has no other viable use.

6. Can new technology and investment help your business to grow?

Through SCAP, we purchased a small handheld fibre scanner to identify material content. Eventually, with joined-up thinking, RFID and QR codes could aid this process. Also, this can help authenticate products for re-sale. This needs universal encrypted information across brands to work within our organisation. The scanner can help to support closed-loop recycling with technologies like Worn Again.

7. What are the routes for recycling garment waste?

Recycled, sold, destroyed. It is resold and shipped overseas at about 50–60% and then sold in the UK. A small amount is destroyed by incineration.

8. What can improve the amount of waste product being recycled?

There is a need to raise consumer awareness and offer easy ways to recycle. Not many local authorities can process textiles in recycling facilities if they are mixed with other items. The clothing banks started in 1990 work well for convenience in supermarket carparks, but can result in fly-tipping in a street scenario.

9. What have been the challenges in your current business?

There are some long-standing relationships with waste collectors and local authorities and changes are slow. There was a real turning point with the "Blue Planet" moment when awareness of waste in the supply chain and households encouraged better recycling rates in the UK.

10. Do you think countries in the EU have better models for handling garment waste?

In the Nordic countries, they burn quite a lot of clothing waste. Germany has better and consistent recycling through their local authorities and although France has an EPR scheme, there are only two recyclers, so it is unclear where this textile waste ends up. The COVID-19 pandemic could have resulted in market failure, but Africa and Chile were still able to accept clothing bales. With a rise in charity shop sales, the donations have been slower post the second lockdown, when everyone had their clear-out of old clothes.

11. The third retail sector (charity shops), historically, were where waste garments ended their life. What has changed in consumer behaviour to require your business to evolve?

Charity shops are moving away from towns to retail parks to make consumer donations easier and more is going onto online platforms like Depop and eBay. It is a great time to launch Reskinned with the brand partners to allow them to control re-sale of second-life garments – we can reprocess this in house, sanitise, photograph and send out. The couriers can pick up the product from the customer at the same time as delivering, it saves an empty trip. The sales are handled on the retailers' platform.

12. And finally, do you see huge opportunities for growth in this sector?

The Reskinned business is a profit share with brands such as Finisterre and Sweaty Betty. It will add even more credibility to these pioneering brands in terms of environmental impact.

Activities & exercises

1. Role play
2. Risk quiz

Activity 1 Coats disaster – top stories: panel debate (1 hour)

Learning objectives:

- To explore and evaluate the relationships between players involved in supply chains and the complexities of those connections.
- To encourage students to consider the issues from a number of different viewpoints.

What you do:

1. Read the news article to the group.
2. Explain that everyone is going to take Part I and compose a reaction to the story. A quick response is vital as there are social media channels picking up on the content and NGOs are getting involved.

3. Divide the class into groups of four to represent D'Jan Fashions: the owner of the factory; the factory employees; a group of activists/journalists and the retailer Daxon. Each is given a role card to read.

4. Divide into groups and allow 20 minutes for groups to discuss their standpoint.

5. After 20 minutes, have a discussion and allow each stakeholder to share their concerns from the pressure groups: Daxon Coats, D'Jan Ltd. and the employees of the factory

6. Get feedback from the group, using the discussion questions below as a starting point.
   - What are the main issues?
   - Who might be to blame?
   - How can this issue be resolved?
   - What could have been done in hindsight?

As a follow-up from this activity, students could look at real supply chain stories to understand how this occurred and how these incidents could be avoided.

Fire destroys coat factory

Monday 30th April 2022

A suspicious fire wiped out a key supplier of a High Street coat brand this weekend. Thankfully, no workers were onsite at the time of the blaze.

D'Jan Ltd. had supplied the British High Street for a number of years with classic coats, which were successful and popular amongst its social media following – pre-orders inspired by the influencer "Kat Loves Coats" were at 10,000 pieces per week. The factory was destroyed, along with masses of clothing, 125 sewing machines and specialist factory equipment. Inspectors from the fire department assessed the damage and a full report is due at the end of the month. No workers were injured in the fire, but there are strong concerns that the fire was started deliberately as the business had been struggling financially and workers were on a "go-slow."

Workers are concerned that they will lose their jobs because the fire destroyed all the raw materials in the factory. Workers had furthermore not been paid their full wages for the previous month and worried that these would not be paid.

The factory was producing export goods for a number of brands including, Daxon Coats, and supplied other European department stores.

Role Play Cards – print and cut these out for each group.

Daxon Coats – The Brand

The last report from the factory shows that equipment was old. However, this is not unusual and local health and safety certificates were fine, so the factory was passed.

It is important to make a statement on your website to acknowledge the disaster. However, you do not want to pay for stock you have note received.

You are aware this is an old-fashioned factory, but you relied on their own due diligence to ensure safe working conditions.

As a company, consider what you can do to avoid a reputational disaster but also to appease your Finance Director who controls the budgets. Discuss this as a retail head-office team and then decide collectively what you would do and say.

Mr. D'Jan, Factory Managing Director

Daxon Coats was a great customer, however, they changed their payment terms from 30 days to 90 days. This meant that you had to pay for fabric long before receiving payment for the finished goods.

You have passed all the building inspections, but some machines had been left on over the weekend, including the boiler for the steam presses. A lot of fabric scraps and waste had not been collected and this is potentially where the fire started.

The brand was putting a lot of pressure on you to fulfil lots of special orders on a quick turnaround, and you think this issue was partly their responsibility.

You are owed money by Daxon Coats and they need to pay up. This would allow you to pay your wage and fabric bills.

As a group, spend some time discussing your situation. Come up with a strategy for the statement to the fire department and the press.

The Workers

You are angry and worried. You suspect that Mr. D'Jan will become insolvent and not pay the outstanding pay you are owed.

The cost-of-living crisis has been very real and you have worked to-rule because of missing overtime payments. There might have been financial struggles for the owner, but you will have to find other work to support your family. You really enjoy your work, but there are few sewing jobs locally and D'Jan was a big local employer. As an ageing workforce, it is unlikely you would want to retrain.

Journalists/NGO

As pressure groups and activists, the story has been widely spread on social media channels. Can you find out the truth? You have strong suspicions this was an attempt at an insurance claim and that Mr. D'Jan deliberately started the fire to get compensation.

Who is to blame? What questions would you ask and who would you ask them to?

What else can you do to improve the situation?

The rules (30 minutes)

Learning objective:

■ To help students consider employment rights and health and safety issues in garment production factories.

■ To give students the opportunity to explore the factory relationships, with a particular emphasis on health and safety and workers' rights.

Background Information: Explain what a code of conduct is. Talk about supplier engagement and compliance. What are basic health and safety standards? What are workers' rights and expectations, especially around hourly pay and remuneration?

What you do:

1. Ask participants to idea storm some issues for garment workers. What are the difficulties for a worker? Would you say that some of the situations they face are unfair?

2. Explore the issues of minimum wage, living wage and incentives in factories.

3. Explain about factory inspections and accreditation such as the Ethical Trade Initiative.

4. Give groups 10 minutes to discuss this.

    Some things to consider:

    ◼ How to ensure a safe and healthy working environment.
    ◼ How to ensure that workers are not victims of modern slavery.
    ◼ How to ensure hours/days of work and overtime conditions are not excessive.
    ◼ How to monitor the legal rights to work of the workforce.
    ◼ How to ensure workers have a way to express complaints about their work.

    Report as a whole group what was discussed. Explore corporate social responsibility reports as group (they are published online by public brands). Come up with ideas to set up some rules for retailers and suppliers to follow.

5. Get groups to consider what steps need to be taken by brands, factory managers, consumers and others to ensure their rules are adhered to.
6. Report on ideas.

Additional activity:

Think of other clothing categories produced in other countries and examine the standards and wages that exist in each sector. In doing this, explore the contrast between working hours, minimum wage and the living wage. There are many instances of outsourcing and how this occurs – what are the pressures and risks of this type of manufacture?

Activity 2 Allow students to score each statement on Probability & Impact – 2 scores per statement

Supply Chain Risk Quiz

Score each statement out of 1–5 for both Probability & Impact, 5 being the highest.

PROBABILITY VERSUS IMPACT – SCENARIOS

QUESTIONS	
1.	River close to factory is polluted by dyestuffs.
2.	Factory producing core lines burns down – workers are killed.
3.	The cost of high-volume raw materials, e.g., cotton, increases by 15%.
4.	Deliveries maybe late and you discover that some work is subcontracted out.
5.	Ethical NGO campaigners publicise your business/supplier as using harmful chemicals in production of textiles.
6.	Quality is poor on 25% of orders.
7.	Beads on a hand-embroidered dress are loose and customers complain/return goods activity.
8.	An Earthquake/Monsoon/Tsunami hits a region adjacent to where you produce 50% of your business.
9.	Children/illegal workers are found working in a factory.
10.	Workers are found sleeping in a factory, working 60+ hours per week and being paid below the minimum wage in that country.
11.	A global pandemic threatens all manufacturing and shipments to all customers.
12.	Marks are found on the cuffs of a white shirt on 10% of an order.

References

ASOS. (2020). Working with our suppliers during Covid-19: May 2020 Update. ASOS PLC. Available online: https://www.asosplc.com/~{}/media/Files/A/Asos-V2/reports-and-presentations/working-with-oursupoursuppliersg-covid-19-May-2020-update.pdf. Accessed 3rd November 2021.

Bancroft, H. (2021). https://www.independent.co.uk/news/business/news/ports-congestion-hgv-drivers-maersk-ships-b1936927.html. Accessed October 2021.

BBC News. (2019). https://www.bbc.co.uk/news/business-46862790. Accessed August 2021.

Bonacich, E. and Applebaum, R. (2000). *Behind the Label: Inequality in the Los Angeles Apparel Industry.* Los Angeles: University of California Press.

Caniato, F., Caridi, M., Castelli, C., and Golini, R. (2011). "Supply chain management in the luxury industry: A first classification of companies and their strategies," *International Journal of Production Economics*, 133, 622–633. Available from: https://www.sciencedirect.com/science/article/pii/S0925527311002118

Chouinard, Y. and Stanley, V. (2012). *The Responsible Company: What We Have Learned from Patagonia's First 40 Years.* California: Patagonia Books.

Chow, V. (2006). Fakes heading for net auction seized pirated goods worth HK$700,000 were made on the mainland. *South China Morning Post,* 06.

Christopher, M. and Lee, H. (2004). "Mitigating supply chain risk through improved confidence," *International Journal of Physical Distribution & Logistics Management*, 34(5), 388–396.

Christopher, M., Mena, C., Khan, O., and Yurt, O. (2011). "Approaches to managing global sourcing risk," *Supply Chain Management: An International Journal*, 1(2), 67–81.

Christopher, M. and Peck, H. (2004). "Building the resilient supply chain," *International Journal of Logistics Management*, 15(2), 1–19.

Collins, C. (2021). https://go.pardot.com/webmail/375052/3891609091/7069a28d3acb971373054c0c2e09f86e80b029ba710a2ba261e6696550b2cf39. Accessed October 2021.

Fibre2fashion. (2021). Available from: https://www.fibre2fashion.com/news/fashion-news/uk-fashion-firm-house-of-baukjen-wins-2021-un-climate-action-award-276794-newsdetails.htm

Glover, S. (October 2021). https://www.ecotextile.com/2020100526773/fashion-retail-news/adidas-kering-and-mccartney-explore-mushroom-leather.html

Groceries Code Adjudicator (GCA). (2021). https://www.gov.uk/government/organisations/groceries-code-adjudicator. Accessed October 2021.

Intertek. (2021). https://www.intertek.com/inlight/

Ivanov, D., Dolgui, A., and Sokolov, B. (2019). "The impact of digital technology and okIndustry 4.0 on the ripple e_ect and supply chain risk analytics," *International Journal of Production Research*, 57, 829–846.

Jackson, T. and Shaw, D. (2009). *Mastering Fashion Marketing.* New York: Palgrave Macmillan.

Labour Behind the Label. (2021). https://labourbehindthelabel.net/wp-content/uploads/2020/06/LBL-Boohoo-WEB.pdf. Accessed August 2021.

Labowitz, S. and Baumann-Pauly, D. (2015). Beyond the tip of the iceberg: Bangladesh's forgotten garment workers. Stern NYU. https://www.stern.nyu.edu/experience-stern/faculty-research/cbhr-bangladesh-mapping-project. Accessed 25th August 2021.

Mckinsey Report. (October 2021). https://documentcloud.adobe.com/link/review?uri=urn:aaid:scds:US:4303e3c3-b54e-4dbb-99ff-1d2642ac8f03

McMaster, M., Nettleton, C., Tom, C., Xu, B., Cao, C., and Qiao, P. (2020). "Risk management: Rethinking fashion supply chain management for multinational corporations in light of the COVID-19 outbreak," *Journal of Risk and Financial Management,* 13(8), 173.

Milmo, C. (October 2021). https://inews.co.uk/author/cahal-milmo

Nadiruzzaman, M., Rahman, M., Pal, U., Croxton, S., Rashid, M.B., Bahadur, A., and Huq, S. (2021). "Impact of climate change on cotton production in Bangladesh," *Sustainability,* [online] 13(2), 574. http://dx.doi.org/10.3390/su13020574

Nguyen, D.T., Adulyasak, Y., Landry, S. (2021). Research manuscript: The Bullwhip Effect in rule-based supply chain planning systems–A case-based simulation at a hard goods retailer. *Omega (Oxford).* 98 102121. Available from the luxury industry: A first classification of companies and their strategies. *International Journal of Production Economics* 133: 622–33.

Niinimäki, K. (2015). "Ethical foundations in sustainable fashion," *Textiles and Clothing Sustainability,* 1(3). https://doi.org/10.1186/s40689-015-0002-1

Partington, P. (2021). "Unexpected drop in August retail sales as supply chain problems weigh on stores," *The Guardian,* London, 18th September 2021.

Peck, H. and Juttner, U. (2002). "Risk management in the supply-chain," *Logistics and Transport Focus,* 4(10), 17–21.

Perry, P. and Towers, N. (2013). "Conceptual framework development: CSR implementation in fashion supply chains," *International Journal of Physical Distribution & Logistics Management,* 43(5/6), 478–501. https://doi.org/10.1108/IJPDLM-03-2012-0107

Phau, I. and Teah, M. (2009). "Devil wears counterfeit Prada a study of antecedents and outcomes of attitudes towards counterfeits of luxury brands," *The Journal of Consumer Marketing,* 26(1), 15–27.

Pinault, F. (September 2021). https://www.businessoffashion.com/articles/sustainability/kering-ceo-says-fur-has-no-place-in-luxury

Quinn, S. (2015). *Sustainable Sourcing: Sustainable Fashion; What's Next?* London: Bloomsbury.

Rafi-Ul-Shan, P.M., Grant, D.B., Perry, P., and Ahmed, S. (2018). "Relationship between sustainability and risk management in fashion supply chains: A systematic literature review," *International Journal of Retail & Distribution Management,* 46(5), 466–486.

Remington, C. (17 December 2021). https://www.ecotextile.com/2021122328776/fashion-retail-news/mango-publishes-list-of-tier-2-suppliers.html

Sarkar, S. and Kumar, S. (2015). "A behavioural experiment on inventory management with supply chain disruption," *International Journal of Production Economics,* 169, 169–178.

Sedex. (2021). https://www.sedex.com/our-services/smeta-audit/. Accessed 25th August 2021.

Turker, D. and Altuntas, C. (2014). "Sustainable supply chain management in the fast fashion industry: An analysis of corporate reports," *European Management Journal,* 32(5), 837–849.

UK Gov. (2021). https://committees.parliament.uk/work/654/fixing-fashion-follow-up/publications/written-evidence/

Walker, H. and Jones, N. (2012). "Sustainable supply chain management across the UK private sector," *Supply Chain Management: An International Journal,* 17(1), 15–28.

CHAPTER 6

Costing in the fashion supply chain

Summary

In this chapter, the methods of acquiring baseline cost information in many countries are explained, which will include the net labour cost and standard minute value. The information around minimum wage, living wage, working hours and incentives is analysed along with health and safety aspects and recent legislation. This enables the assessment of work content, links this to the total cost of the bill of materials (BOM) and considers specific factory requirements to meet cost and efficiency. The theory of cost-versus-volume and how to manage production volumes and price is addressed, whilst covering the variable, additional and hidden costs of manufacturing locations.

Case study: PURSUIT SWIMWEAR – A SINGLE NICHE SUPPLY CHAIN – COSTING AND TRANSPARENCY

Learning outcomes

At the end of this chapter, you should be able to:

- Explain the methods to acquire labour cost and calculate approximate final cost prices
- Evaluate problematic purchasing practices and offer open-book transparent information
- Consider all factors in the calculation of retail baseline costs, which lead to final retail prices

SDG GOAL(S) – THIS CHAPTER LINKS TO:

1 No Poverty

5 Gender Equality

8 Decent Work and Economic Growth

Introduction – cost versus price

At stages of the critical path, the freight on board (FOB) cost price will be determined and agreed upon, but initial costs and a "ballpark" estimate will have been indicated in the "open to buy" plan.

A budget is set for the financial commitment for the fashion range, which would plan the quantity and options within this.

Sampling happens in the development process. If this is being outsourced, samples can arrive with the FOB cost price. Everything needs to be agreed upon at this stage such as fit and fabric, delivery and quantity and, above all, the cost price. There may be many samples reviewed and the first samples often require amendments. It is worth remembering that the more samples requested, the more time it takes to meet the required delivery date.

Critical path timeframes vary from brand to brand depending on the adoption of trends and whether they follow a typical fashion calendar or more of a quick response model or even demand-led supply. At all stages of product development, the cost price will be examined and this will include the cost of samples, which might be for the sales team, the number of amendments to the design and if the price is affected by these changes. The cost will also cover shipping, duty and customs, and any further distribution elements, but not usually e-commerce to the final consumer.

Costing can be described as the process of estimating and then determining the total cost of producing a garment, including the cost of materials and labour and the general expenses of indirect costs (Brown and Rice 2001).

Global wages have been the motivator for sourcing in poorer countries and the "race to the bottom" in terms of cost price. The issues that this magnifies are linked to the United Nation's Sustainable Development Goal (SDG) 1, No Poverty. In negotiating cost prices, fair wages and an end to modern slavery are both goals and ethical requirements for modern manufacturing. This may be resolved with more automation and better jobs, which in turn may allow for improved working conditions. Good jobs and economic growth in poorer countries are an important aspect of the SDGs and these would align with SDGs through safer more automated workspaces.

As such a large number of women are employed in ready-made garment (RMG) manufacturing, SDG 5, Gender Equality could be supported by improved conditions, but this can could also be considered a diverse workforce that provides for LGTBTQ+, and gender discrimination in the workplace can be covered by this.

Sampling & product development costs

Following the critical path from the original design through to the go-ahead for production is a challenging process for a number of reasons. When selecting styles to run and place into production, sales history, current trends and competitive shopping are key to the decision-making process. As the speed to market has shortened and become ever faster, the need to cut down on the number of samples and the time it takes to approve and sign-off on concepts has become more pressurised. Adding to this, the impacts of remote and hybrid working, which evolved since the COVID-19 pandemic, have further affected the costs and time associated with this. To solve these issues, brands have taken a number of measures to ease the path to purchase and keep a keen eye on overheads.

Design-led brands essentially cover the in-house costs of product development by first making a toile garment and pattern. They would approve the initial sample and see a counterpart made by the supplier in the correct base cloth. The base cloth is important for many reasons, as the dimensional stability of the fabric and sizing can be affected by using a substitute base cloth. Having machinists, pattern cutters, procuring the sample fabric and employing a designer would incur the highest degree of in-house overhead costs.

In mixed product development models, some brands have cut the overhead in development costs and now send sketches out to suppliers. This in turn needs additional flat drawings with key measurements added by an in-house product developer. There may have been an initial cost of providing block patterns to the supplier that are in-line with the ideal sample size for the brand and their target customer. There would be costs associated with the buyer/designer to start the process, but are reduced from the higher cost of running a sample room. The brand may have a small sampling section for innovation, but it would not cover all product categories.

In the selection process in this most remote design development process, an initial sample will be made by the supplier and shown to the brand's buying team. Then, alterations are likely to be made for the customer profile and trend information. This is the lowest cost scenario for the retailer, but it is worth remembering that these costs will be passed on in some form by the suppler and this might not be easily identifiable. This links to the theory of hidden cost discussed later in this chapter.

Volume & negotiation

Over recent years, buyers have moved from traditional sourcing methods, where the fabric would be selected and prescribed to the supplier, to what has now become the FOB purchase model widely used across the industry. A final price is agreed upon, with little indication of the content and accuracy of that price. The method associated with price negotiation has become very opaque after this buying shift, as many in-house services were outsourced in the product development stage and this gave more control to the supplier. The traditional critical path has been shortened and heightened, led by the desire for fast affordable trends.

New business models have been developed to counteract this mystery and campaigns such as "Who Made My Clothes?" (Fashion Revolution 2020) have encouraged brands in all manner of transparency, most notably in the Fashion Transparency Index. Nevertheless, some brands are making big strides in publishing supplier lists and going one step further to share their cost prices, known as open-book costing.

Filippa K introduced open costing for all their suppliers. The brand developed an open costing sheet, explained it to all its suppliers and showed transparency about its finances to them (Fairwear Foundation 2019).

Historically, both suppliers and brands have been reluctant to give the true cost price, as there is always a point of negotiation – you made this for $2 – now make it for $1.90 (Miller, 2013). Working as a buyer in the fashion industry requires knowledge and information to negotiate prices fairly and to build a solid relationship with suppliers.

When exploring cost price, it affects the final retail price and if or when a price comparison is carried out across several brands, also known as a competitor shop, it

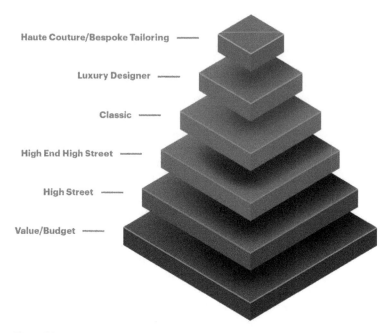

Figure 6.1

Retail hierarchy

is obvious that retail prices can vary significantly for what appears to be an identical product. This can be seen in basics such as a T-shirt or a hoodie, where prices can start as low as £19.99 for a hoodie from Primark and go up to £345 for a version at Stone Island (Mr. Porter 2021). It would be right to ask why and how much the cost prices vary that will influence or decide the retail price. An investigation by the non-governmental organisation (NGO) Public Eye uncovered the true cost of a Zara Hoodie, which had a retail of £22.70, €1.53 went to the factory in Turkey and €1.10 went to the workers, the resulting profit for Zara after VAT was €4.20 (Marriot 2021). This could reflect a typical costing scenario in affordable brand manufacturing in Turkey.

Of course, each brand has its markup or margin and Primark is a good case in point. It works on a margin similar to food sales, selling garments on a commodity basis at a quite low margin. But still, even considering this, it will be a challenge to learn how can a retailer hit those low target cost prices.

Retail prices will vary across market levels, defined by the market segments also known as the retail hierarchy, starting at the bottom with value or budget clothing and ending at luxury and haute couture (Craik 2009). Figure 6.1 further defines the market segment levels.

Women's and men's segments: Retail hierarchy.

Order quantity & pricing

The expected profit margins will vary across brands and so will the order quantity and the minimum order quantity (MOQ), which will also impact the cost price. Core product lines and those that are a top store or exclusive line will have different order sizes. Core lines might be carried forward through seasons and in larger volumes and top store lines might be the trial order of a high-fashion design and therefore a smaller quantity.

It is the delicate management of these variables that help in beneficial price negotiation – the purchaser must understand the breakdown of the garment cost and the supplier must appreciate the volume and difficulty of the order. Over the years, the value market has managed to buy high volumes to secure cheap prices and to move to locations where the labour cost is very low. This has been a successful strategy for brands in the UK, with very large orders being commonplace for successful styles. "Apparel inventories have been crawling up for decades," Zhou, Chen and Xu (2020) noted, known as the bullwhip effect.

Buying in high volumes does not come without risk. The MOQ can be achieved by adding in colourways, which may result in excess inventory, markdown and the ultimate cost of investment. This has been prevalent by High Street department stores (BOF 2020).

The volume of the order has a large part to play in price negotiation where economies of scale apply. The fashion industry has largely relied on mass production of garments through large-scale suppliers to achieve low prices overseas (Doeringer and Crean 2006). The issue this creates for smaller brands is meeting the MOQ of Far East suppliers, as the orders are less important to the factory.

Therefore, volume is the starting point for understanding the cost and price significance and their connection. Identifying the retailers' approach to retail prices and their design development method, which will always contribute to the final cost. It is also worth considering the indirect or hidden costs, such as head office overheads, which can be lost in the final margin calculation.

Cost Prices can be further defined in this way:

Pricing decisions: In many direct-to-retail situations, which are now facilitated by online marketplaces, the retail price will be a direct margin added onto the baseline cost.

Target prices: This can apply to any number of brands at different levels of the market. The retailer will set a target price based on their planned target retail selling price. For the manufacturer to achieve the goal target cost, it will depend on their willingness and ability to manage their costs to meet the target price and make a profit. These sit with the current move to FOB-based negotiation.

Cross costing: This is not a usual method for the fashion industry and sits with tendering, where you might try a new group of suppliers, giving them the same design pack to compare prices. An example of this might be a cotton supplier in India being compared against a cotton supplier in Turkey to make T-shirts. The price and timing would be different, and these can offer a straightforward comparison and depends on the needs of the retail business.

John Thorbeck, chairman of supply chain analytics firm Change Capital said in an interview with *The Business of Fashion,* "Brands must break down and break through the adversarial bargaining that is focused on the price of finished goods out of the factory" (Thorbeck 2020). The quote here links back to the sourcing model discussed before in Chapter 5, where buyers have more appreciation of the whole process and every element within the cost. Thorbeck also discussed the reaction to unplanned events in the supply chain and stated brands should focus more on the suppliers' flexibility rather than the lowest cost.

There are notably "problematic pricing practices" rife in the UK High Street, where punitive terms are enforced before or during a negotiated contract (Gooch 2020), such as discounts for late shipment. These can also involve retrospective discounts. For spurious reasons, a common change to the terms and conditions of doing business is extending the payment due date, typically 30–60 days. It is not uncommon now to see enforced 180-day payment terms and this being changed during production. The change to the contract is not legal and neither is imposing fines and retrospective discounts. These adversarial negotiations are well documented and can result in negative perceptions of brands.

Breaking down the elements of the FOB cost price

The purchaser or procurer needs to avoid these issues and by having better information and understanding of the factors influencing the cost price and how to "guestimate" this.

In garment costing, the method of product development and sourcing is key to how the cost and retail price might be calculated. As a starting point, the in-house requirement of a sample room, which may develop a toile and pattern or even a first sample, is a significant cost overhead. In doing this, a provisional cost analysis can be produced, which also means that a supplier can remove the development cost from their quotation. This method is mainly used by high-end brands or where the design idea requires work in the design studio and the brand can exercise tight control on the design. Most London-based luxury brands will have in-house design studios. As mentioned in Chapter 1, the method of purchase might then be "cut, make and trim," where the factory is paid for the direct labour cost and delivery to the distribution centre. In choosing this method, which is close to the traditional sourcing model, a high level of creative control and specifications are required. The add-on costs for the brand involves ordering fabrics and trimmings and shipment to the factory.

Many brands choose product development at a distance either via direct sourcing or using an agent or a buying house (a "super-sourcer") in the country of manufacture. In this case, initially, it will not be known which factory is making the sample and if they eventually will make the production – this will be decided by the supplier. The business relationship becomes more like working with a wholesaler and the supplier might be producing similar styles and products across a number of your competitors.

Own label and direct sourcing operate differently, and you have much more control of the design process with direct sourcing. It is crucial, at this stage, to date stamp and protect your intellectual property to maintain your unique designs.

Relationships

All these relationships indicate a varied cost scenario and there is a need to beware of the hidden costs that might be involved with each of these. Ultimately, it is a choice on how much control and purchasing power is handed over to the supply base, which will, in turn, affect the final cost.

Using an agent or trading house can give more buying power as a smaller-volume order can be combined with other contracts. It might be fabric supply minimums are difficult to meet, but combining multiple brands' orders can improve the cost price.

Factories will give an idea of their MOQ as a starting point and early in the price negotiation. The emphasis here is that this is a negotiation – a conversation – not a confrontation. Nobody should be forced into a corner on price, i.e., forced to accept a price that would not cover the true cost of production. If there is a better understanding of what factors affect the cost, the aim is to have an open-book negotiation and a better relationship.

To start the process of open-book negotiation, each element making up the FOB price will be examined (Miller 2013). This method was explored in open costing as a term where all elements of materials, wages, processes, overheads and markup were broken down by the supplier (Wu, Su and Hodges 2021). Subsequently, the buyer and supplier work together to review and agree on the direct cost and a fair mark-up to arrive at the final cost price. It was found that these collaborative arrangements resulted in greater cost reductions for the buying stakeholder. Open costing shows a supplier's desire to cement a long-term relationship as they are exposed to the risk of exploitation through exposing their full and detailed bottom line.

Factory specialism

How the factory is set up will affect both price and delivery. Too. These models directly influence the throughput time, the quality and the wages that the worker can earn. Flexibility can be built into some production lines, but specialist machinery matched with types of fabric are key to efficient manufacturing times.

Make through: The entire sewing operations are carried out by one operative, exceptions are cutting and final pressing. This can be linked to individual targeted incentives for higher performance.

Progressive bundle unit: The most widely adopted model in less-engineered factories where operations are broken down and managed to allow all operations to happen at the same time and part garments are sewn and passed onto the next machinist. Balancing the number of machines helps shorter and longer operations match the intended work in progress (WIP) and timing.

Unit Production Systems: Handling systems where technology can speed movement of the part garments around the factory floor, observing any in-balances and ensuring swift movement between operations. This requires lower WIP and the movement between operations is managed by computerised tracking. There is often high investment in specialist machinery to complete separate operations with low manual skill required.

The Toyota Sewing System: Machinists stand up to sew and which is often linked to a Group Incentive scheme. This ties in well with ideas of quick response as WIP can be minimised. In this novel approach, the operatives work as a team and in doing this, absenteeism is low and motivation is high, creating a community workforce within the team. The downside is that it can only manage very low-work-content garments with under 10 minute standard minute values (SMV) (Carr and Pomeroy 1992).

It is in the process of product development that will determine the work content of the garments. With good relationships and suppliers understanding this vision, the products should be enhanced in production rather than become watered-down versions of the designer's original concept. The opportunity to add or reduce cost should be considered carefully as the design needs to be a true replica of the original version.

Raw materials fabric cost

Firstly, raw materials are a large part of the final cost price (between upwards of 60%) and a large financial outlay for the supplier of a retail brand. There may be a better fabric cost by pre-booking raw materials in a greige state; many super-sourcers will do this, and this may extend to fibre booking too. Here again, combining with in-house brands on fabric orders to extend your purchasing power might be an option. A new type of collaboration that might be available to you, if you have a suite of brands, involves combining raw materials orders to result in an improved price per metre, easily meeting the MOQ. The Arcadia group had a great advantage in being able to pre-book material for their brands, however, the downside of this is a homogenised High Street, where base fabrics and styles begin to look very similar.

Printing techniques have improved and reduced costs with air dyeing and digital printing techniques, where small units, also known as runs, can be done with an accurate print quality. This saves cost and waste and applies to both knitted jersey and woven garments.

When it comes to print, checks or stripes, these will involve much slower cutting times, and, if the garment requires areas to be matched and lined up, a longer making time. Checks, stripes and placement prints will be more expensive to cut and make over a plain fabric and the FOB cost price will be higher and the production time will be longer.

Size ratios and the need for diverse and inclusive sizing have increased the opportunity for curve ranges, along with petite and tall designs. These are sometimes and add-on to a main range collection, but work best when they are specifically designed for the target customer. Within purchase planning, it is important to remember the fabric usage will be higher if the sizing ratio is higher on the UK size 18 and over. This can sometimes be offset by having the same amount of smaller sizes, but that cannot always be achieved.

It is the task of the retailer to decide if the higher cost will be passed onto the consumer, directly. The fabric usage will increase and a different cost price will need to be quoted for curve ranges. In research and development, the designers can work on more adaptive clothing, which allows for changes in size, such as adjustable waists, shirred panels and stretch fabrics, which can cut down on size options and achieve better fit.

An area for cost efficiency in fabrics is improved by managing computer-aided design (CAD) and pattern cutting with automated lay plans and cutting of bulk production.

Gerber Systems, and similar hardware and software suppliers, can improve raw material usage in pattern-making by cutting the fabric using digital CAD, manufacturing and lay planning. Raw material efficiency and the fabric usage in a garment is a significant part of the cost price and with the capacity to digitally lay plan, the fabric cost saving can be up to 30% per production order (Jessup 2020).

With the notion that 30% is a high target, even a smaller percentage savings would still be a notable cost-benefit. At 5% or less, this could potentially be passed onto the retailer and consumer and still be a significant saving.

Just to note, the historic saving on fabric use resulted in a darker side of the business with over makes, also known as cabbage, being illegally sold in markets. The ability to do this in the current market involves great risk for the supplier who could lose future orders. It is likely now if new labelled merchandise appears on a market, it has come from lost online deliveries rather than factory over makes. With more overseas manufacture, this happens much less frequently as there is less of an obvious route to customers, but is a risk of far and on-shoring. Risk will be explored in Chapter 5.

Labour cost & cost control

Generally, suppliers have small margins and the pressure to reach FOB target prices is constant. To make a profit and continue in business managing the initial and final cost is very important. This has resulted in the science of factory management systems, which applies to many manufacturing industries. The use of methods and machinery to speed the manufacturing process is continuous and a key part of this is the factory's willingness and ability to invest in new equipment. A larger amount of industrially produced garments against artisan techniques were available in the 1970s (White 2000) and by 1980, the management science was perfected when UK production was trying to compete with new sourcing locations and to reduce the labour cost element as much as possible.

For instance, men's suit factories have become highly automated because the product has a high level of consistency and similarity. Sewing machines that complete several operations in one garment can be expensive, but the long-term saving can be worth the initial outlay.

Some simpler sewing aids to achieve speed and consistency that are less expensive include dye cutting, Fig. 6.2, and jig sewing. They can improve the quality of cutting and sewing and save valuable time and SMVs.

In historic settings in European factories, the element of labour content, also known as work content, was assessed by work-study engineers, a management

Figure 6.2

Dye cutting

science in itself. Every product is broken down into a series of operations. In a factory setting, this is following the movement of the garment between machines and operatives. To balance workflow, and very importantly the volume of WIP, many operatives can perform the same operation. So, a standard time for this operation is measured to keep a track of the throughput time and offer incentives to machinists to achieve or beat the target time. In a deeper work-study context, the allocation of the number of machines can be balanced to allow faster or slower turnaround time and ultimately improve the delivery date.

Direct labour calculation

After the garment is broken down into the sequence of operations, the calculation for each operation of making the garment is measured with a stopwatch, then the mean average time is awarded for that process. This would be known as the SMV. In many instances in the Near- and Southeast Asian factories, this is still the case, and with growing wage costs globally, it will gain importance in the future to save valuable minutes and consequent labour costs in production.

There are some synthetic ways of calculating these costs, too. General Sewing Data (GSD) offered by Coats Digital can aid suppliers in assessing the true costs and work content.

Golam Mustafa, Assistant General Manager of the Epyllion Group said, "Once we implemented GSD it became apparent that the data previously used for Line

Figure 6.3

Factory handling system

Balancing and capacity planning had been inaccurate and was potentially damaging our business in terms of late deliveries and lost revenue" (Mustafa 2020).

Factory planning is key to this and knowing how technology can help factory management, with line supervisors and factory managers assessing where the build-up of WIP is and adding extra machines to help that operation. Handling systems, Fig. 6.3, can move the garment parts quickly from one person to the next, and what is visible is the amount of WIP, which is key to overall turnaround or throughput time and maintaining the delivery date to the customer.

There is a wide choice of sewing machinery and factories are commonly set up for certain types of products.

> **Cut and sew jersey:** Using three- and five-thread overlock and cover stitch machines on knitted jersey in cotton, viscose or polyester. The products would typically be T-shirts leggings and nightwear.
>
> **Wovens:** Lightweight, soft separates in silk viscose, polyester, viscose, Tencel or cotton. Great for dresses and summer-weight garments, soft skirts and blouses. Using lockstitch machines and a variety of button hole, hemming and button sew equipment. Requires a highly skilled and dextrous workforce, able to add embellishment and processes such as pleating and embroidery.
>
> **Tailoring:** Heavier weights, from suits to coats and medium-weight skirts and trousers. Many specialist machines in pressing, construction, pockets, stitch types and interior components. Wool and blends with polyester.
>
> **Specialist:** Knitwear, bras, swimwear, shoes and hosiery.

The future technology for garment construction involves 3-D printing and there has been a limited amount of research into producing garments from this method. This does apply to shoe design – you can see a lot of brands using fly knitting techniques to reduce cost and waste in parts of shoe and trainer construction with 3-D knitting. **Fig. 6.4** shows a Santoni TOP2V, a single jersey electronic circular machine used to produce single seamless garments for underwear, outerwear, beachwear and sportswear. The Santoni machine offers the following benefits:

- 20% additional production
- Cost reduction
- More environmentally sustainable due to 30% lower energy use

In general, these single jersey and knitted products all require specialist equipment often over several locations, depending on dyeing and finishing.

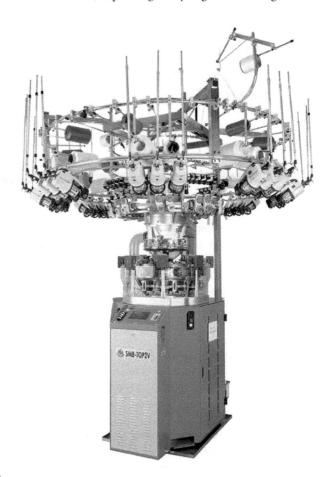

Figure 6.4

3-D knitting machine Santoni (https://www.knittingindustry.com/santoni-introduces-x-machine-for-footwear/)

The cost of a woven garment

As mentioned with open-book costing, to achieve a specific target cost price, a buyer needs to understand how this is broken down for the negotiation on reducing the amount of fabric or changing the fabric used or simplifying the design and work content to save money. This skill is vital to non-adversarial price negotiation and to maintain a profitable relationship for both parties.

The production of garments has not changed much over the past 50 years and lock-stitch sewing machines are mainly used for woven garments. The number of garments we buy from cut-and-sew jersey, which uses overlock, cover-stitch machines and single-thread chain stitch machines, have increased and these machines are very fast.

The cost of knitwear

Plain knitwear in a fine gauge can have many machine processes if fully fashioned. A good example of this luxury process is John Smedley, the yarn is exclusive and construction and dyeing can happen during production.

It is a complicated equation that considers the type and thickness of the yarn, the gauge of the machine, type of stitch as well as then factoring in the number of colours and patterning techniques; one calculation does not fit all. The yarn count of 30 and amount of yarn by weight at price per kilo will give the material cost, then consider the time spent on the machine. The main part of the knitted piece could be one type of yarn, then there are processes in dyeing, finishing, packing and labelling duties that will need to be included.

Again, a throughput time, type of knitted product and the logistics of the factory setting will also affect the price, as dyeing and finishing can occur in various locations. Knitting generally has a variety of stitches, yarn thickness and patterning techniques, which will all add to the cost of the garment; also consider some sweaters can be fully knitted by hand too.

Jersey fabrics

In the UK, jersey fabrics can be dyed to order but the origin of the yarn and knitting is not in the UK. The fabric price per metre would include the Landed Duty Paid (LDP) UK price for manufacture on-shore and the UK dyeing or printing process. It is a good idea to be clear about the timeline and processes that are being covered in your cost price per metre to avoid any surprises.

The technology to produce garments has improved in knitwear with 3-D knitting (see **Fig. 6.4**), which has increased the speed of production and reduced the waste produced for knitted garments. It is fast and requires fewer physical workers or operatives to finish the garment.

The cost of cutting & sewing garments (from knitted or woven fabrics)

The starting point is a T-shirt, a low-work content garment in cut-and-sew jersey.

A basic crew-neck T-shirt can be one of the lowest work content garments, starting with circular knitting so there are no side seams. After the body shape and sleeve are cut out, the sewing operations would be:

1. Attaching the sleeve
2. Attaching the rib at the neck
3. Hemming the cuff
4. Hemming the body
5. Labels

These could be achieved by Sewbots, sewing robots that have been used by Adidas, a pioneers in automation using its "Adi Lab" in Germany to help set up a factory using robotics. The shoes produced with Sewbots were a specific running model, with the production intended to supply short runs, quickly, close to the market and beat increasing costs in China. The idea has been developed to use the robots in existing Chinese suppliers to offer wider types of style manufacturing and reduce costs. The "Adi lab" has now closed this production line in Germany (Thomasson 2019).

High-work content garment

A high style change and short production run will impact price. Measuring the amount of work content in sewing has lost importance as manufacturing moves to ever-cheaper labour cost countries. The time pressure of fast fashion might not give the chance to allow for full measurement and planning production in a work-study setting. However, tracking the flow and labour cost of manufacturing can reap benefits in efficiency and managing your deadlines and relationships.

These sections can be combined in a cross-costing guide (Fig. 6.5)

Garment	UK- make price	EU	China	Cloth usage
Dress	£20	£10	£4	1.80
Coat	£50	£25	£10	1.60
Blouse	£30	£15	£5	1.20
Trouser	£20	£10	£4	1.20
Skirt	£15	£7	£3	.90
Jacket	£40	£20	£8	1.30

Figure 6.5

Fabric use and make price

Typical work content for a cut-and-sew jersey body-conscious dress would be 20 minutes. A standard pair of trousers would be SMV 30 minutes and a tailored jacket would require SMV 90 minutes (Carr 1992).

The chart here shows approximate fabric uses and making prices based on South Asia, near-shore European Union (EU) and UK manufacture, this is linked to the living wage in the country of manufacture, which should be updated annually. The wages will increase and fluctuate over time.

In reviewing the products, they can have high variables such as dresses and blouses, with a large scope for fabric use and labour cost. Always consider this as it is a way of over- or under-spending. As mentioned, an open-book negotiation with a better understanding of how the cost price is achieved will help the buyer to have the confidence and knowledge that everyone is being paid fairly for their contribution.

When the fabric usage is reviewed, these are ball-park averages or a "guestimate" at the likely comparison across various locations. In both woven and knitted pieces, the colours that are chosen also require a MOQ for the dye batch.

Using an analogy here, a costing sheet can be compared to making a cake: you put the ingredients together and calculate what they would cost. Then, consider the time it takes to bake the cake and the energy used for cooking it. This applies to the garment – all of the ingredients are components – and the time it takes to construct it with any extras such as transport, labelling, inspection and additional variables must be considered. The supplier must make a profit, the wholesale margin of 20–30% is usual for a supplier to add on to their basic cost price. This costing sheet, which can be used in a numerical software format such as Excel, will help prepare to cost information and can be shared via a cloud-based IT connection. Any metreage used for a garment is affected by the garment's length and fullness. Jackets and coats can remain quite stable, but dresses and skirts can be flared and use much more fabric. This applies to the labour cost and cloth usage, depending on the wages in the country of manufacture and the amount of work in the garment, which can vary widely. You must consider extra processes, too, such as embroidery or pleating and the type of fabric, as checks and stripes require longer cutting and sewing time. Again, the idea here will affect the making cost or SMV, which will be improved if the factory has invested in modern equipment for cutting and manufacturing. A guide for calculating cost price using Excel is Fig. 6.6.

Work content & wages

The wages and pay of garment workers need to be considered. It is not enough to elevate the wages of workers with excessive overtime and enforced extra hours. Wages can also be improved with incentives, which should be added to the already minimum wage rather than to bring people up to the minimum wage. Issues around minimum wage and living wage have been widely discussed by NGOs. Linking to incentives gives machine operators the chance to improve their weekly wage. Historically, operatives are not fond of incentives at first, as the measurement of GSD or work-study is based on the average comfortable time to do that operation. When the employees understand that they can achieve an improvement in their take-home pay, beating that target quickly becomes something they are much more familiar and generally satisfied with.

STYLE NO / NAME _____   COLLECTION _____   DATE _____

FABRIC

Name	Quality No / Name	Colour No / Name	Supplier	Width	Fibre Content	Price per mt	Costing	Total

TRIMMINGS

Name	Quality No / Name	Colour No / Name	Supplier	Size		Price	Costing	Total
								Sub Total
								Make Price
								Total
								% Mark-up
								Selling Price

Figure 6.6

Excel spreadsheet for costing

This does not take away from the fact that modern slavery and the intention to underpay below the minimum wage has been prevalent in many sourcing locations around the world, including the UK. In 2015, the Modern Slavery Act for the UK was introduced and is seen as a benchmark act that encompasses all of the darker sides of the industry it covers:

- The business model and supply chain relationships
- A businesses's policy relating to modern slavery including due diligence and auditing processes
- Training for supply chain management and the rest of the organisation
- The principal risk to slavery and human trafficking includes how the organisation evaluates and manages those risks
- Relevant key performance indicators will be produced annually, demonstrating progress from one year to the next

The Modern Slavery Act covers organisations carrying any or part of their business in the UK – all sectors of the organisations and both goods and services. Despite this landmark act, which has been seen as a beacon amongst other European countries, there are still many instances of underpayment in garment factories. This can be broken down into a couple of scenarios that may lead to lower wages.

One scenario involves the intention of manufacturers to offer to employ people who are claiming benefits (Universal Credit) in the UK. That person would then be only allowed to work for 16 hours per week but is willing to work more than 16 hours. Typically, these extra hours are paid in cash at well below the minimum wage. This has happened in the UK and is widely regarded as benefit fraud by both the employer and employee.

In another scenario, European destinations, particularly in Turkey have seen issues around modern slavery and employing refugees in factories. There had been a study about migrant workers and child labour in Turkey and the government took action "to allow work permits for foreigners under temporary protection," which means refugees have been forced to leave their country and cannot return or cross borders (Turkish Labour Law 2016).

Then there is the very ugly side of modern slavery, seen in its worst case in the UK with the drowning deaths of cockle pickers in Morecambe Bay (BBC Morecambe Bay 2014). In 2020, Vietnamese workers were found dead on arrival when the lorry in which they were being transported arrived at a port along the Thames close to Purfleet in Essex (BBC 2021). More on the industries and activities around modern slavery are covered by the Salvation Army in the UK, as they are a big part of rehousing and recuperating some of the individuals involved in these cases due to their government award of the modern slavery contract (Salvation Army 2020).

The Environmental Audit Report of 2019 found that out of 27 clothing factories three, (Creagh 2019) were operating under illegal conditions. Additionally, in the summer of 2020, garment factories in Leicester in the UK were found to be working throughout the COVID-19 pandemic, running the factories with disregard for health and safety and breaking minimum wage legislation (Levitt 2020).

Typically, the gangmaster would take the passports from the workers who may have been brought into the country with the hope of gaining a good job that is well paid and satisfying. However, the scenario means once their passports are removed, they live in a house of shared accommodation and their wages are managed by the gangmaster at a very low amount, well below the minimum wage. The best way of auditing this is to ask for proof of right to work, but also to see bank details for each employee and to know that the wages being paid to the employee are going straight into their bank account and not to a third party. The auditing must take place for the brand, the manufacturer and any sub-contractor. In the book *Sustainability and the Social Fabric*, Jenni Holloway of Fashion Enter talks about the relationship they have with ASOS as a supplier. "ASOS undertake and a Fast Forward audit and we have leading status with that audit" (Whittaker and Padovani 2017).

Time

As retailers eased themselves out of sampling costs, new technology has emerged to enable remote sampling and garment fitting. The ability to live-stream a "fit meeting" with a live model enables suppliers and key personnel, such as the garment technologist witness, a first-hand look at the issues of fit, fabric and construction. This can be as simple as using a camera phone, but having an in-house meeting room screen with audio-visual capacity improves the quality of the meeting and process. This can speed up the delivery and return of physical samples, especially if the meetings can be staged in the supplier's location. It is important to approve hand-feel and see the drape and movement of fabrics, so this needs to be factored in. However, this system has the potential to cut down on the number of samples seen and the time it takes to review these, which would of course save significant cost. Many brands adopted this technology due to remote working and now have made this part of their ongoing sampling review process.

Bill of materials & components

Apart from the traditional cost of fabric, there are many key components that form parts of raw materials Fig. 6.6, which can cause long delays in controlling the delivery of parts of a garment to coincide with the fabric delivery.

Examples include materials such as lining, interfacing, shoulder pads, buttons, zips, thread, embroidery or pleating, labels and packaging. Some brands will use specific house colours and certain suppliers, with logos and development of unique components, and this will be a factor in price control and the ultimate cost and delivery. Extensive lists of these components can elevate the cost price without careful control and delay the delivery. Almost all of these would also need to be approved for colour and quality with a laboratory dip for colour approval or sample. Again, the expense and timing is important, and notably, the issues around MOQs apply to components too.

Transport

Thankfully, the prevalence of air freight for garments is in decline due to concerns about cost, carbon footprint and air pollution. As a hanging garment, this transport remains only for the luxury industry. Mostly, garment freight is flat-packed and boxed and for container shipping and is calculated by weight and volume.

In recent years, there have been fantastic improvements in the cost and carbon efficiency of transportation with combinations such as sea–air, sea–land and train–sea. The use of electric vehicles in delivery to the consumer is to be applauded and retailers and supermarkets have improved the efficiency of online fulfilment.

For large consignments of garments, the planned "One Belt One Road" initiative that follows the traditional land route from China to Europe could see improvements in the cost and time issues of delivery from Asia. Carrai discusses the initiative in the book *Belt and Road Initiative and Global Governance*. The implementation of this transport route by both sea and land follows the Silk Route mentioned in Chapter 1 (Carrai, Defraigne and Wouters 2020). The plan to develop the transport connections from China through numerous countries requires investment, planning, collaboration and cooperation from all the countries involved.

Lead times are affected by the method of shipment. In the era of quick response, a trend can have appeared and waned in the five weeks' shipping time from a far-sourced location. It is worth noting that customs paperwork after Brexit requires extra information, including country of origin, in certain products and this needs to be correct to avoid delays.

Many near-Europe suppliers will offer services in addition to transport such as picking and fulfilment selections for store delivery. With the surge in online and e-commerce activity, it is likely these activities and costs might be passed onto a supplier, as discussed in Chapter 1.

Fit technology

A number of software developers proposed new ways to review and fit garments, however there will always be an issue looking at a 3-D product in a 2-D format. This presents an opportunity to try 3-D sampling, which has proven to work on quite simple styles. Although this has been in existence for several years, it has made little progress in high-fashion clothing due to the complex nature of fit and aesthetic; to commit money to a virtual product involves quite a high amount of risk. Optitex technology has found a solution to this with an avatar that can develop samples, show tight areas and is particularly useful for cut and sew jersey (Optitex 2022). The software called Revu can "Save time by reviewing different variations of your 3-D samples simultaneously" and "create seamless collaboration across your supply chain as the 3-D assets can easily be shared with your team, external suppliers, and vendors" (Optitex 2022).

This technology has been supported by many brands and suppliers, most notably Marks & Spencer and Fashion Enter in the UK and Li & Fung in China (Optitex 2022).

In the *Sourcing Journal*, Optitex stated, the "2-D and 3-D design tools that seamlessly turn flat patterns into 3-D models and make adjustments in style, fit, colour, prints, fabric type and features – all in the push of a button, which reduces the need for wasteful physical samples by 50 percent" (Sourcing Journal 2018). Optitex indicates that quality is key in the fast-paced fashion industry, responding to consumer behaviour and fast drop-ship models. The use of this product development technology could save 50% of resources "in time, money and fabric waste" (Sourcing Journal 2018). This is an indication that this method is both fast and sustainable, cutting down on sampling and waste.

Additional costs

In this section, there are several variables to point out, notably Duty on imports to the UK and the EU; for China, it is 12%. The UK government has up-to-date tariffs for all countries from which you might import clothes. As an encouragement to trade with poorer countries, Bangladesh remains duty-free, which enhances its already low labour cost and the benefits of manufacturing there.

Technology to aid transparency

Any enterprise resource planning (ERP) system can hasten the need for investment in transparency and technology in the supply chain. This can be managed through cloud-storage techniques, where information is shared on the critical path. This is a general measure that most brands will adopt. For most retail head-office scenarios, a common spreadsheet in Excel – a line sheet with style numbers and stock keeping units (SKUs) will be sufficient. However, technology has advanced with product lifecycle management (PLM) software being adopted by brands to share real-time information on the product development stage through to final production. This is very much dependent on the software that you choose and the readiness and capability of all parties to be able to engage with the software and keep it maintained. Good examples of this adoption of technology have been seen in the UK by Ted Baker and Burberry.

PLM and SKUs can lead to complete transparency and a design-focused bill of materials, where purchase orders might be raised and tracked in software sites such as Shopify. Technical packs could then go out to suppliers using with software such as Zedonk, as previously mentioned, Excel spreadsheets and sharing simply on Google Docs can have the same results. Companies may have to consider all these factors and analyse where the financial saving is going to be. PLM offers opportunities for shared documentation but there are other ways of doing this, with starting PLM, the set-up of design packs, colours and fabrics can be very labour intensive. There has also been a lot of recent discussion about blockchain technology, widely adopted in the financial sector. An opportunity and market for this in fashion was shown with software called Provenance used by Martine Jarlgaard (Design for Longevity 2020) for her alpaca knitwear brand. This is a locally sourced, transparent product with small runs available and thus has given this the potential to use blockchain software to show the beauty of a transparent supply chain. The more complicated the supply chain, the harder it is to use this software with so many tiers of manufacturers to manage.

Sizing & the cost of returns

It is widely estimated that online shopping causes garment returns of up to 50% of the original purchases (Commercetools.com 2022). Many business-to-consumer models increase their costs vastly by offering free returns and consumers can make good use of this. There have been initiatives to minimise these costs with limited success and the shocking stories of brands burning unwanted returned stock has added to the poor reputation of the industry encouraging excessive consumption and unmanageable waste. A new circular economy law being discussed in Scotland in the UK plans to outlaw this practise (Bbc.co.uk), which would work by ensuring brands give away or recycle unwanted clothes; similar proposals may be taken up by the EU. The reason for the returns often lie with consumers buying multiple sizes and selecting the size that fits, but the starting point lies in how the brands communicate fit and sizing in the first place.

There is room for more digital applications here too. Using 3-D body scanning and a mobile imaging device has the potential to reduce the return rate and ensure the consumer is more confident in the size of garment they have chosen. Early technology developers working in this field are starting to solve issues around medical prosthetics, but this can be transferred to other products and support inclusivity of fit and sizing. Size Stream 3-D body scanning can link the data directly to a factory for made-to-measure items and can support 3-D product development. In the purchase solutions, it enables "scan to size solution using our measurement technology, designed to collect your customers' sizes in minutes. Not only will you be able to provide a contactless way to measure bodies, but you will also be able to manage your inventory and cut down on costs" (Size Stream 2022). This addresses issues around the high cost of returns processing, the creation of waste and an increase in transportation costs and emissions.

Theory of hidden cost

The Iceberg theory was first discussed by Hemingway, Fig. 6.7, in the fashion industry, it shows that the tip of the iceberg you see above the water level is where your visible costs are. The larger portion of the iceberg under the water represents the hidden costs in any business, which might be excessive sampling transport, time lost, sales lost in delays to the critical path, excessive communication by telephone, travel to sourcing locations and the list goes on. One of the biggest head-office costs in research and development is running a sample room and design location; this cost has generally been passed onto suppliers. With this comes risk of paying for a sampling cost in the cost price; this will be hidden unless there is an open-book costing scenario. Some brands require excessive numbers of prototype samples or they require numbers of the same product in fitting samples. This is expensive and after three or four fitting samples, it really is far too expensive to carry on with an order. There are ways of circumventing these product development costs with technology like Optitex (2021), which allows a virtual fitting on an avatar, as previously described. Much of head-office retail costs are now being swallowed up in customer returns and this links to the success of product development and how "right the first time" the product is when it reaches the consumer.

The larger costs below the waterline are what you do not see or account for (Fig. 6.7).

Figure 6.7

Theory of hidden costs – iceberg

Conclusion

In this chapter, we have discussed how to define the cost of a garment and the process of negotiation including fabric usage and labour content. The process of managing these costs and creating a successful supplier and buyer relationship has been reviewed and the issues that might cause problems have been highlighted. Technology that can help aid the smooth running of a purchasing pathway, and the pipeline of suppliers, which may involve many tiers of manufacture, is complex. This technology could be the way to minimise anomalies in these areas. It is worth considering that although clothing production has not changed extensively in the last 50 years, machines are faster and quieter. The cost of the technology is reducing. In a survey of manufacturers, there are also many fewer humans involved than there were many years ago, indicating perhaps a reduction in work content in garments and a preference for buying cut-and-sew jersey products, or that the advancement of some processes fully completed by machines has reduced the manufacturing workforce in the fashion industry. Either way, the outlook is set to look at a cost more forensically in the future as poorer countries will grow their wage prices and negotiation and work content will be on the agenda for future buyers.

Activities & exercises

Costing exercise

CASE STUDY

Pursuit swimwear – using data and product lifecycle management software to review global wage and work content assessment

Figure 6.8
Pursuit the label product

Costing from Pursuit the Label – Radical transparency

As a team, the task is to simulate a product sign-off meeting, and each person can have the role of designer, buyer, supplier and garment technologist.

Review the range of garments – these could be all dresses, trousers or co-ordinates.

It will be possible to work out a target cost price based on the ideal retail price and then break down the FOB cost price using the tables and examples given in Fig. 6.5.

The teams can either create flat drawings or use actual garments to develop documents from a flat drawing, follow the critical path with the supplier and finally the costing sheet.

In doing this, consider the PLM that tracks a flat drawing through its critical path by listing all the components on the costing sheet, the labour cost, the final price and delivery to the consumer.

In this exercise, students should take a flat drawing of three types of garments: one with a low work

content, one with a medium work content, and one with a high level of work content and work through the labour costs.

With each garment, it is important to review how this can be engineered to achieve the best retail price, by recognising the work content and fabric usage. This is where the negotiation begins.

> Are there any details that can be removed, i.e., pockets or stitching?
> Is the garment the right size, or is it too long or too wide?
> Where could fabric be saved?
> If the fabric is patterned, does it need matching?
> Can the base fabric be made from an alternative material?

There is a great deal to consider here and an example of this is in the cost breakdown as shown in

What's in a £155.00 Pursuit swimsuit?

£62.47
To help cover overheads: photography, marketing, website & salaries

£31.00
VAT/Taxes

£10.00
Shipping cost average

£4.00
Recycled packing

£17.53
Sustainable fabric & trims

£30.00
UK garment worker & manufacturing cost

Figure 6.9
Pursuit the label – cost transparency

Fig. 6.9, the Pursuit label example. There might be different manufacturing locations with varied wage costs. Calculate the fabric usage and "guestimate" the wage cost, estimating the cost of components, shipping and any duty that might be paid as if it was being imported into the UK.

You can create all of this in a spreadsheet in Excel with an image of the garment and all of the costs broken down using the example of the costing sheet and using the fabric and wage cost handout listed in Figs. 6.5 and 6.6.

Work as a team to hand out the tasks as if this would be in a retail head office.

Use an image-based diagram, as seen in Fig. 6.10, to explore this and show your commitment to radical transparency in costing.

| Fabric | Trims | Labour | Transport | Duty |

Total Cost

Figure 6.10
True cost illustration

References

BBC. (2021). Essex lorry deaths: Men jailed for killing 39 migrants in trailer. Purfleet Peoplesmuggling. https://www.bbc.co.uk/news/uk-england-essex-55765213. https://www.bbc.co.uk/news/uk-scotland-scotland-politics-60691961. Accessed April 2022.

BBC Morecombe Bay. (2014). Morecambe Bay cockling disaster's lasting impact. bbc.co.uk/news/uk-england-lancashire-25986388

Brown, P. and Rice, J. (2001). *Ready to Wear Apparel Analysis*. Upper Saddle River, NJ: Prentice Hall.

Business of Fashion (BOF). (2020). *The State of Fashion 2021*. McKinsey & Company.

Carr, H. and Pomeroy, J. (1992). *Fashion Design and Product Development*. Oxford: Blackwell.

Carrai, M.A., Defraigne, J., and Wouters, J. (2020). *The Belt and Road Initiative and Global Governance*. Northampton: Edward Elgar Publishing.

Commercetools.com. (2022). https://f.hubspotusercontent30.net/hubfs/4784080/Statamic/Files/commercetools-wp-fashion-commerce-EN.pdf. Accessed April 2022.

Craik, J. (2009). *Fashion: The Key Concepts*. Oxford: Berg.

Creagh, M. (2019). Fixing Fashion Report. https://publications.parliament.uk/pa/cm201719/cmselect/cmenvaud/1952/report-summary.html. Accessed 19th February 2021.

Doeringer, P. and Crean, S. (2006). "Can fast fashion save the US apparel industry?" *Socio-Economic Review*, 4(3), 353–377.

Fairwear Foundation. (July 2019). https://www.filippa-k.com/globalassets/filippa-k-ab-performance-check-2019.pdf?ref=9A6A300540. Accessed 14th January 2021.

Fashion Revolution. (2020). Who made my clothes? https://www.fashionrevolution.org/about/get-involved/. Accessed 13th January 2021.

Gooch, F. (2020). Traidcraft in the proceedings of: www.bbc.co.uk/iplayer/episode/m000r68t/select-committees-fixing-fashion-committee. 17th December 2020.

Jessup, R. (2020). Interview Gerber European Sales. 30th November 2020.

Levitt, A. (September 2020). https://www.boohooplc.com/sites/boohoo-corp/files/final-report-open-version-24.9.2020.pdf

Marriot, H. (2021). The truth about fast fashion: Can you tell how ethical your clothing is by its price? *The Guardian*, London, 4th August 2021.

Miller, D. (2013). Towards sustainable labour costing in UK fashion retail. www.capturingthegains.org. Accessed 11th December 2020.

Mr. Porter. (2021). https://www.mrporter.com/en-gb/mens/product/stone-island/. Accessed 8th February 2021.

Mustafa, G. (2020). https://www.coatsdigital.com/. Accessed 13th December 2020.

Optitex. (2021). https://optitex.com/products/revu/. Accessed April 2022.

Optitex. (2022). https://optitex.com/. Accessed April 2022.

Salvation Army. (2020). https://www.salvationarmy.org.uk/news/salvation-army-awarded-new-government-modern-slavery-contract

Sizestream. (2022). https://www.sizestream.com/commercial. Accessed April 2022.

Sourcing Journal. (2018). https://sourcingjournal.com/topics/sustainability/optiex-apparel-sustainability-technology-114791/. Accessed April 2022.

Thomasson, E. (2016). https://www.reuters.com/article/adidas-manufacturing-idUK-L8N13X3CQ20151209. Accessed 2020.

Thorbeck, J. (2020). The Sourcing Journal. https://sourcingjournal.com/topics/sourcing/fashion-supply-chain-inventory-crisis-coronavirus-john-thorbeck-212944/. Accessed 14th January 2021.

Turkish Labour Law. (2016). Turkey grants work permits for Syrian refugees. https://turkishlaborlaw.com/news/legal-news/turkey-grants-work-permit-for-syrian-refugees/. Accessed 11th December 2020.

White, N. (2000). *Reconstructing Italian Fashion: America and the Development of the Italian Fashion Industry.* Oxford: Berg.

Whittaker, P. and Padovani, C. (2017). *Sustainablity and the Social Fabric.* London: Bloomsbury.

Wu, H., Su, J., and Hodges, N. (2021). "Investigating the role of open costing in the buyer–supplier relationship: Implications for global apparel supply chain management," *Clothing and Textiles Research Journal.* https://doi.org/10.1177/0887302X21993501

Zhou, L., Chen, Q., and Xu, Q. (2021). "Joint pricing and inventory control decisions for fashion apparel with considering fashion level and partial backlogging," *Mathematical Problems in Engineering,* 2021, 7092981. https://doi.org/10.1155/2021/7092981

CHAPTER 7

Innovation and the future of fashion supply chains

Summary

This chapter will focus on recent innovations impacting fashion supply chain management such as the fourth industrial revolution and the introduction of robotics and artificial intelligence in manufacturing. Additionally, the interaction and impact of technology and transparency embedded in fashion supply chain tactics and strategy including: blockchain, customisation and 3-D printing will all be investigated. Such innovations will be discussed in the context of their relevance as enablers of sustainability and transparency within fashion supply chains. Collaboration is a key component of much of the implementation of new technologies in fashion supply chains and newer brands and those "born sustainable" are often those making bold moves. After reading this chapter, readers should be able to see the connections between recent digital technologies and transparency and visibility in the fashion supply chain and how these innovations are directly linked through supply chain collaboration.

Learning outcomes

At the end of this chapter, you will be able to:

- Examine business models with sustainable supply chain frameworks
- Explore the technology that can aid transparency in textile and garment manufacture
- Develop ideas on methods of sourcing and manufacture connected to better practices and the circular economy

SDG GOAL(S) – THIS CHAPTER LINKS TO:

8 Decent Work and Economic Growth

12 Responsible Consumption and Production

17 Partnerships for the Goals

Introduction

The last chapter of this book focuses on the future of fashion supply chains and provides indications of where we are likely to go with some of the most recent innovations and drivers impacting fashion supply chains. There is no doubt that fashion industry supply chain management is at a major crossroads and a paradigm shift has occurred that has been evolving over the last decade to provide a more sustainable and transparent future for fashion supply chains, starting with the product development and sourcing policy of designers and brands. The global COVID-19 pandemic has created a renewed focus and interest on global supply chains in the media and the need for changes required for some time has been exposed throughout the pandemic. These include logistical challenges, already fragile sourcing policies and worker exploitation by some fashion brands as well as resultant global stock outs and cancellations of orders created by global revolving lockdowns and labour shortages. As fashion retailers pivoted to online retailing, their customers' clothing requirements changed. Driven by flexible working and less commuting, the new clothing requirements were manifest by a focus on comfort and consumers spending more time in the home. Additionally, overall consumer attitudes on the fashion industry after COVID-19 in the UK during 2020, according to Statista (2021), have shifted and clothing that is linked to well-being such as sports and leisurewear have seen increases in sales whilst formal attire, tailoring and eveningwear sales decreased. The Statista research noted the COVID-19 crisis has led fashion and clothes shoppers to consider serious issues such as sustainability and the social and environmental impact of the clothing industry. In a recent consumer survey, UK consumers were polled, and 83% of respondents agreed that clothing items should be designed to last longer than they do at present. Around 58% of those advocated government regulation in improving the social and environmental impacts from the clothing sector (Statista 2021).

Blockchain & transparency in fashion supply chains

One of the most discussed issues in the fashion supply chain is a lack of visibility and transparency as it can enable unsafe conditions and poor environmental conditions and obscures the power in the fashion supply chain (Fashion Transparency Index 2021). As fashion supply chains are inherently international and complex, the visibility and transparency of each element and process can border on opaque at best. However, there is an opportunity to change this, and the global fashion supply chain is now in a position to move forward to manage visibility more effectively by implementing many of the recent technological advances emergent from the fourth industrial revolution, including blockchain and robotics in manufacturing, which can both enhance traceability in manufacturing. When all stakeholders, shown in Fig. 7.1, in a fashion supply chain work together, innovation can be enabled and much-needed techniques such as recycling materials and moving to zero waste or a circular closed-loop supply chain (Macarthur 2016) can be achieved. Tracking raw materials and recycling these and their reuse brings challenges in fashion supply chains that blockchain implementation can support and resolve (Wang et al. 2020).

BLOCKCHAIN IN THE FASHION SUPPLY CHAIN
DECENTRALISED, VISIBLE AND CIRCULAR

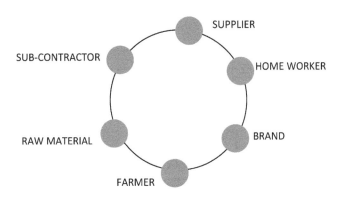

DATA IS SECURE, AUDITABLE, IMMUTABLE AND SHARED

Figure 7.1

Blockchain image

Digital innovation in the fashion supply chain has the ability to generate much-needed transparency and visibility by integrating sustainability into all operations and processes as these are simultaneously highly efficient and can also support zero waste. Many young new brands that are "born sustainable" market entrants with transparency as part of the brand DNA are those that seem to gravitate to blockchain platforms such as Provenance.

An example of a brand applying these new technologies is Martine Jaarlgard. Martine Jaarlgard, a knitwear designer, has created smart labels that can trace the knitwear back to the exact Alpaca farm, and in 2017 created the first blockchain-tracked clothing brand. Every Martine Jaarlgard product has a unique QR code and near field communication (NFC) chip documenting the entire product journey by working with the Provenance platform.

In 2018, the blockchain technology market was estimated to be worth £1 billion and has been forecast to grow to £20 billion by 2023 (Statista 2019; Tapscott and Tapscott 2016).

Another use of blockchain is being applied by Levi's to collect feedback anonymously from their factories in Mexico about their employees well-being, which will further embed transparency into their denim supply chain. In fact, luxury brands are also collaborating with digital blockchain provider IBM to create a tool, "Voyage," that can track a product journey; the Voyage platform creates an immutable trail of data and has been tested by Burberry with an option to add repair and recycling to the tracing system (2021). Other similar technology-based tools are being developed including one collaboration among Stella McCartney, Google and the World Wildlife Fund that focuses on environmental sustainability and embeds pollution and emissions data tracking. The Stella McCartney team is using this new collaborative platform to identify cotton sources in Turkey that are facing water and climate risks (George 2021).

Artificial intelligence

In the late 2010s, much was written and forecast on the drive and potential for the use of artificial intelligence (AI) and the use of this in modern retail procurement. AI offers many faceted perspectives by gauging the customers planned purchases through a variety of retail environments. This can be both in the physical retail space and on mobile technology. The terms that have grown commonplace such as data crawling and use of cookies are widely accepted by consumers. Although the backlash through new General Data Protection Regulations (GDPR) have somewhat curtailed the impact of this. The savvy consumer can operate in the online world with disabled cookies and become an invisible participant. Loyalty for brands is hard fought and the data retrieved and used can be a valuable commodity in planning and delivering fashion products. If brands adopt this technology, which most do, companies can operate in a leaner more sustainable way (Gore and Blood 2018).

> *AI is the science and engineering of intelligent machine manufacturing, particularly intelligent computer programs.*
>
> (McCarthy 1989)

The use of artificial intelligence (AI) in daily life is growing along with machine learning and deep learning and this will play an essential role in our lives and businesses regardless of industry, the flow of information is shown in Fig. 7.2 According to the pioneer of AI, John McCarthy, who stated that:

> *To narrow down the meaning of AI based on literature, it largely has two dimensions which are the process of thinking and reasoning and behaviour. These dimensions bring various definitions sorted in the following four sections.*

> 1. *That is digital software that thinks like humanity*
> 2. *Digital systems that behave as the human being*
> 3. *Technologies that judge rationally*
> 4. *and systems that act logically*

> (McCarthy 1989)

Three-dimensional (3-D) development

In the clothing industry, three-dimensional (3-D) development can strengthen specific aspects of the stakeholders in the supply chain, starting with product development in a virtual form and virtual sampling through 3-D virtual prototypes. There are opportunities for redesign of products, planning for the future life in a circular system, moving into zero waste manufacturing where waste is designed out. This

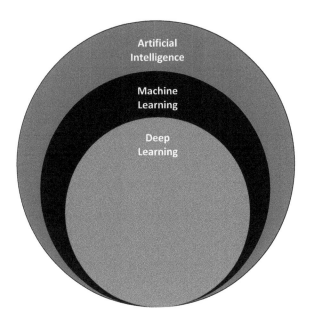

Figure 7.2

Artificial intelligence diagram

can be through the use of recycled materials, 3-D knitting, printing in digital methods into the garment shapes and the use AI to work on successful pattern shapes, predicting customers' needs.

In manufacturing, making actual products that are fully printed via 3-D printing technology can remove a substantial amount of the waste of raw material compared to a traditional method, as 3-D printing has fewer errors than humans (Tarmy, 2016). Three-dimensional printers print a complete product, and although they are quite slow, the potential to customise small parts such as jewellery and homeware is a starting point.

Customisation

New frameworks of supply can include customisation, which can integrate sustainability into the business agenda. Many sportswear brands have offered a level of products that can be customised, such as trainers at Nike (Nike Id [2022])and football shirts within many official sports team kits (Yeung, Choi, and Chiu 2010). They can start with semi-finished goods and through online software, can optimise the customers' choice of colours, fabrics and embellishments and potentially reduce the impact and cost of returns.

To encourage consumers to engage with content through online sampling using this software, the next step could be mass customisation, offering more in terms of sizing the significant gap offered when retailers concentrate on small order quantities and a limited group of sizes (Statista 2020). The fashion retail sector has the largest e-commerce revenue forecast over the next few years and this is further supported by the overall growth in the sector. The Office for National Statistics graph demonstrates the fluctuations during and post-pandemic until late 2021. PlatformE offers solutions to product customisation in larger scale for brands such as Platform E. Ben Demiri, the CEO of PlatformE, stated, "Brands that offer made to order on average reap the benefits not just on full price, but actually super margins" (Demiri 2020). It is an opportunity for consumers to put their own stamp on a product and make it unique. This is a method of managing an overstocked situation along with co-creation and adding value. PlatformE facilitates on-demand manufacturing to minimise high levels of overstock and digital fashion collections (Platform 2021).

Another method of engaging the consumer to minimise stock and customise product around garment fit has grown with innovations such as Size Stream, which has a mobile body scanner and an in-store booth to take critical measurements, allowing a custom fitting without trying on the garment or the need to return it. In the mobile method, 240 measurements are taken and an avatar is used with a connected brand. The early development of the software was in medical applications, but it could give the opportunity for customers to gauge the likely fit and style of a garment without purchasing (Size Stream 2022). This technology does not allow for fabric handle to be assessed, but it might be a solution to the high number of online returns. There is a risk in made-to-measure when a customer does not approve of the subsequent fit. From the chart shown by The Office for National Statistics (Fig. 7.2), the ability to manage the growth of online versus physical retail has varied, but remains higher than two years ago, having peaked during the pandemic. This growth drives the need for seamless omnichannel retail at a fast speed and demand-led production that manages stock levels and minimises returns.

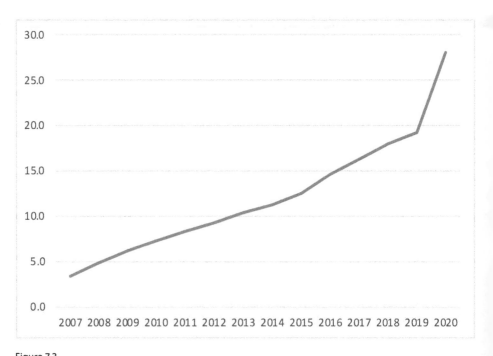

Figure 7.3

Office of National Statistics Online shopping

Physical returns

The logistical challenges of omnichannel and e-commerce brands has shifted more focus onto sustainable packaging, with 43% of shoppers putting better packaging at a high priority (Reboundreturns 2022). Handle Recycling had the aim to recycle 1 million items of beauty packaging in 2021 through a return-envelope that consumers can fill with empty products. Wider adoption of this method is seen with Will's Vegan Store, who allows customers to return their shoes at the end of life to be recycled into new outsoles.

A novel approach to process pre-loved garments through re-processing, such as Reskinned (see Chapter 5), allows collaboration and profit share from the processor and retailer alike. This controls authenticity and ensures the consumer is confident in the provenance of the items.

Many issues with returns being disposed of by online companies has led to outcries and was also mentioned in the Fixing Fashion report (EAC report 2019); these issues can add to reputational risk and diminish consumer confidence. With efforts in ensuring better fit by allowing custom and bespoke items, the evidence is likely to show a decrease in returns and a help to restore full-price sales with less risk and subsequent cost of markdown.

Another area of digital technology is the ability to revolutionise the fashion industry through new modes of design and production that simultaneously streamline supply chains and reduce waste.

Smart brands are implementing digital tools for more sustainable strategies such as unlimited design. Three-dimensional fashion design software CLO allows designers to digitally draw and fit directly onto 3-D avatars. Designs are then used to automatically generate 2-D patterns for production. As well as reducing product lead times, it also eliminates unnecessary physical sampling and shipping costs. Some more progressive brands such as Adidas, The North Face and Timberland are already leveraging 3-D software and digital tools in product design and rapid prototyping processes to speed up the creative process and reduce waste (Stylus Media Group 2021). Figure 7.4 shows the digital consumer, able to view, purchase, track and receive an item anywhere.

Post-Pandemic Consumer

Sustainability matters more than ever 1 in 3 consumers care more.

Prefer re-sellable clothes over disposable ones −43% care more about longevity.

Saving money on clothes is now a top priority–50% of consumers are looking for better value.

They have a newfound disdain for waste– both in garment disposal and wasting money.

Figure 7.4

The post-pandemic consumer

Fibre tracing technology

Chapter 2 discusses the most recent innovations in raw materials and the scientific accreditation for animal and plant-based fibres, which is a potential loophole that can be exploited by "greenwashing" in supply chains and blending fibres. Solutions such as Oritain can aid this problem. There are further digital technologies, such as FibreTrace, that plant a piece of nanotechnology on the garment's fibre.

> FibreTrace® combines traceability with impact measurement. Brands have 20/20 vision of their supply chain in real-time at every step as a product moves from raw fibre to store, and extends to consumer interaction. We add the power of primary impact data from farm and measure quantification of fibre content to ensure authenticity. The technology is indestructible and stays with the fibre from recycle or reuse.
>
> (Fibre trace 2022)

FibreTrace® is applicable to cotton, responsible viscose and recycled polyester, and they expect to complete trials on wool, leather and bast fibres in 2021.

Collaboration

As mentioned earlier, collaboration is required to implement much of the innovation in technology across the fashion supply chain. Co-operating and competing at the same time enables firms to gain common benefits, such as sharing third-party audits and collaborative shipping (Rafi-Ul-Shan 2017). See Chapter 5 for more information on co-opetition in supply chain relationships, sharing audits and supplier information.

> Decision makers should use the pandemic as a catalyst to make structural business changes with less friction from elsewhere within the business, whether that's closing physical stores, focusing on supply chain and fulfilment efficiencies or adapting routes to market in order to stay afloat.
>
> (Retail Gazette 2021)

Similar thoughts echo around the pandemic situation in 2020 being an opportunity to change the way the industry has operated, comparing this era to the bold moves to off-shore clothing production in the 1990s. The move to re-shore or near-shore production of clothing could be the solution to ethical risk, business risk with surplus stock and exercising more control over the complex chains of supply. In doing this, it both increases the simplicity and transparency of the supply chain.

From a business perspective, future planning needs to include sustainability aligned to the United Nations' (UN) Sustainable Development Goals (SDGs) and these should be embedded in every aspect of the business process; having a separate team or department for compliance and codes of conduct is insufficient. The ten principles of the UN Global Compact principles are:

Human rights
Principle 1: Businesses should support and respect the protection of internationally proclaimed human rights

Principle 2: Businesses should make sure that they are not complicit in human rights abuses

Labour
Principle 3: Businesses should uphold the freedom of association and the effective recognition of the right to collective bargaining

Principle 4: Eliminate of all forms of forced and compulsory labour

Principle 5: Work toward the effective abolition of child labour

Principle 6: Eliminate discrimination in respect of employment and occupation.

Environment
Principle 7: Businesses should support a precautionary approach to environmental challenges

Principle 8: Undertake initiatives to promote greater environmental responsibility

Principle 9: Encourage the development and diffusion of environmentally friendly technologies

Anti-corruption
Principle 10: Businesses should work against corruption in all its forms, including extortion and bribery (www.unglobalcompact.org).

New legislation

The International Accord on health and safety in the garment industry is driving further investigations after the Rana Plaza disaster in Bangladesh. Initially called the Bangladesh Accord, the International Accord (since 2021) is now rolling out a feasibility study to take the accord to other countries prevalent in ready-made garment (RMG) clothing manufacture. To encourage brands to sign the accord, it is initially focussing on its predecessor, The Bangladesh Accord:

> *Currently we are primarily calling upon brands that have production in Bangladesh to sign the Accord. As soon as a new country programme is in place, we will call for brands sourcing from that country to sign as well.*
>
> (International Accord 2022)

To date, 173 brands have signed the accord, notably Marks & Spencer, H&M and Next. In terms of what the signatories are accountable for, includes ensuring factories participate in inspections and, more importantly, remediation, giving the supplier a chance to put things right. In a two-pronged/approach, which is legally binding, the factory is forced to address issues uncovered by inspection and the brands can be forced to settle disputes with unions if they do not meet their obligations.

Because of the legally-binding nature of the Accord, tens-of-thousands of potentially deadly hazards have been fixed and more than one million workers have been trained. That is why we will continue to rigorously enforce the Accord and continue to look at innovative, effective ways to resolve disputes with brands.

(Hoffman 2022)

International expansion is needed to address incidents in the garment industry, including countries like Morocco, Egypt and Pakistan where the issues of health and safety are a priority; it seems likely that Pakistan will be the next country to have an in-depth review on worker safety.

Circular production bill in Scotland

Included in the proposals for Scotland's Circular Economy Bill (May 2022) is a plan to ban retailers from destroying any unsold goods; instead, they must offer alternative disposal routes such as donation or recycling. This should avoid unsold durable goods such as clothing ending up in landfill or being burnt. It has similar intentions to the law in France (Love 2022).

European Union

In France, extended producer responsibility has been in law since 1975 and applied to household waste since 1992 (Vernier 2021). Taking this further with legislation, the European Union aims "by 2030 textiles placed on the EU market should be long-lived and recyclable, made to a large extent of recycled fibres' (Rankin 2022). This is along with a disclosure from brands to report unsold clothes sent to landfill. In addition to this, the EU legislation aims to outlaw greenwashing and planned obsolescence.

Ethics, sustainability & greenwashing

When considering the terms used in the conversation about fashion supply chains, ethics and sustainability are quite interchangeable words. Ethics in itself has emphasis on the health, safety and payment of workers in manufacturing, and can encompass animal cruelty too. With sustainable claims, it is better defined as an attitude to reduce waste and over-consumption as a business and might also be a reduction in animal products, making better environmental choices, This is where the crossover with ethics appearing as an environmental impact is a moral and ethical decision. Exploitation of the adjectives surrounding the ethical language has been used in marketing for many years and sets out to engage customers, resulting in consumer confusion. Hence, a number of tools to review brands, such as the Fashion Transparency Index and websites like Good On You, have evolved. Metrics are used amongst all these assessment tools, but they vary, and they are known to credit some fast-fashion brands with better scores than some well-known brands who are more considered as slow fashion brands. Good On You, both a website and application, uses ratings on people, the planet and animals. There is some science to this and it is reviewed more on accreditation, use of materials and managing waste and whether animal products are used. They have scores of "We Avoid," "Not Good Enough," "It's a start," "Good" and "Great," which are discussed in detail later in the chapter. When accessing the information, there is extended detail on the website, but their application enables links with mobile technology. This could be more seamless, however, this allows for a serious amount of progress in transparency. Brands should present supplier lists and accreditation as a standard; they might have this information, but not publishing it results in lower scores based on the lack of available information.

The full guide to the Good On You brand rating system that offers evaluation of fashion brands globally is detailed here.

Further advancements with technology are supported by the use of the Good On You assessment tool, which has been fully developed using and consulting with industry experts.

The data gathered intends to show consumers the impacts of fashion retail products on the environment, workers and animal welfare. This is a laudable and powerful tool if consumers engage with the content and can make a value judgement based on the way the data is presented.

Good On You states its principles as (Good on You 2022):

1. **Transparency comes first:** Brands should publish information about their supply chain and direct operations to increase accountability and drive improved outcomes for the environment, labour and animals. Consumers have a right to know how a brand impacts on the issues they care about.
2. **Consider impact across the product lifecycle:** Companies should be held responsible for their impact on the environment, labour and animals at each stage of the value chain, from how products are produced and distributed to how they are used, and then reused or disposed of.
3. **Be comprehensive:** The rating system should consider a broad range of sustainability issues to give a comprehensive view of a brand's overall impact on the environment, labour and animals. It should be capable of applying to all brands in the market.
4. **Consider issues in proportion to materiality:** The rating system should consider each material issue that impacts on the environment, labour and animals according to an assessment of relative importance.
5. **Ensure an evidence-based approach:** The rating system and its application should be transparent, based on robust research and underpinned by good governance processes.
6. **Be user driven:** The rating system should provide users with data that is accessible, comparable and easy to use. It should inform consumer shopping decisions, provide useful feedback to brands and enable retailers to assess, source and market sustainable brands.
7. **Engage and collaborate widely:** Good On You is part of a global movement for change and should work collaboratively to understand, reflect and drive industry best practice and leadership.

They align their work, as does this book, with the broader UN SDGs, more specifically goal 12: "Ensure sustainable production and consumption patterns." Their hope is by publishing this information, there will be message sent to retailers to encourage positive change. Being pragmatic and thinking about how behaviour change occurred, such as charging for plastic bags, needs to be done more through legislation and self-regulation within the industry. To call out brands for positive and negative practices and efforts, such as greenwashing, the technology and ratings system could become a powerful tool. However, even the highest rated ration brands do not score very highly on their rating system.

Further sub-headings from Good On You measurements cover all published material relating to environment resource management and disposal, energy use and greenhouse gas emissions, chemical use and disposal and water usage and effluent. This information is arguably only likely to be published by Tier 1 suppliers at most, and requires a dedicated sourcing department to analyse and retrieve this data at scale within a retail head office.

Whist using the Ethical Trade Initiative Base Code, brands are assessed on labour workers' rights, living wage, gender equality, worker empowerment, knowing suppliers and supplier relationships, purchasing practices and production risk. Some of these elements are easier to trace, such as unionisation. The living wage is a point of failure for most brands, as evidenced on their website, but this can be achieved via incentives in production, and there are many great examples of this worldwide. Other activities that are more nuanced and somewhat difficult to measure by just publishing a supplier list are the relationship and the risk of production. This can be achieved with better use of technology and more transparency, but there is a long way to go before all brands publish the details of open-book costing.

Good On You's final sector on animal policy, fur, leather, wool, down and feathers, angora, exotic animal hairs, exotic animal skins and traceability absolutely covers many areas of concern, but again, it is not a simple black-and-white issue. For instance, exotic animal hair includes cashmere, which has many recycling opportunities, and leather, which can be certified by the Leather Working Group. There are good examples of farming animals with by- and co-products of the meat industry and reducing the risk of hunting by farming more exotic animals. They are correct to highlight traceability further back than for example, the tannery, but the traceability of all materials should come first in all cases. Again this reinforces the importance of schemes like FibreTrace and blockchain technology to legitimise and control the stakeholders in the supply chain. Along with this, the use of regenerative design linked to regenerative agriculture is far more important as a business model and making the right changes to encourage this way of operating.

In other aspects, Good On You recognises that there are other issues that are important to consumers that do not directly affect the environment, labour or animals:

> In particular, we encourage brands to adopt strong approaches to diversity and inclusion including combatting structural racism and respecting the diversity of consumers in their choice of models and the availability of sizing.

(Good on You 2022)

In this chapter, the offer of inclusive sizing using fit technology and an online platform demonstrates this idea of inclusivity in a commercial sense. There is a suggestion that larger brands have greater influence on their supply chains, which although could be true, the tendency is to operate as business as usual, and small- and medium-sized enterprises (SMEs) are making the most inroads into gaining their accreditation and highest ratings. This is an outline of their rating system (Good on You 2022):

> **Great:** These brands demonstrate leadership in all three areas. They are typically very transparent, and have both strong policies and strong assurance (e.g. from one or more broad-based certification) to address the most material issues across their supply chain.
>
> **Good:** These brands adopt policies and practices to manage multiple material issues across their supply chain and are often demonstrating leadership in one or more area.
>
> **It's a Start:** These brands are transparent about their policies and practices to manage some material issues and are making good progress on one or more of them.
>
> **Not Good Enough:** These brands disclose some information in one or more area and consider some of the material issues, but are not yet adequately managing their impacts across their supply chains.
>
> **We Avoid:** These brands disclose little to no relevant or concrete information about their sustainability practices. In some cases, the brand may make ambiguous claims that are unlikely to have a material impact.

Good On You references the following certifications, accreditations, standards and guidelines when rating brands.

- Better Cotton Initiative
- Blue Angel
- bluesign® system
- Business Social Compliance Initiative Code of Conduct (BSCI)
- Canopy Style Initiative
- Carbon Trust Standard
- Caregora
- Clean Clothes Campaign Code of Labour Practice
- Climate, Community & Biodiversity Standards – CCB standard
- Cradle to Cradle Basic, Bronze, Gold, Platinum and Silver
- Ethical Clothing Australia
- Ethical Trading Initiative Base Code
- EU Ecolabel
- Fair Trade USA
- Fairtrade Textile Standard
- Fair Wear Foundation Code of Labour Practices
- Fairmined Ecological Gold Standard

- Fairtrade International – Small Producers Organizations
- Fedex Members Ethical Trade Audit – SMETA Best Practice Guidance
- Fair Labour Association Workplace Code of Conduct
- Global Organic Textile standard
- Global Recycle standard
- Global Traceable Down standard
- International Labour Organization Labour standards
- International Wool Textile Organisation standards
- ISO 14001:2004
- Leather Working Group protocols
- National Wool Declaration Integrity Programme
- Naturland textile standards
- Naturtextil Best
- Nordic Swan
- OEKO-TEX MADE IN GREEN
- OEKO-TEX STANDARD 100
- Organic Content standard
- Responsible Jewellery Council certification
- Responsible Down standard
- Responsible Wool standard
- Social Accountability International – SA8000
- Soil Association Organic standards
- WFTO Guarantee System
- Workplace Condition Assessment
- Worldwide Responsible Accredited Production (WRAP)
- ZQ Merino Label

Brands' participation in the following initiatives is also considered.

- Action on Living Wages (ACT)
- Agreement on International Humane Trapping standards
- Bangladesh Fire and Safety Accord
- Business for Social Responsibility
- CDP (formerly the Carbon Disclosure Project)
- Child Labour Free
- Detox Catwalk Greenpeace
- Ellen MacArthur Foundation – Make Fashion Circular
- End Human Trafficking Now! Campaign
- Fair Labor Association
- Global Fashion Agenda

- Global Living Wage Coalition
- Global Social Compliance Program
- Institute for Human Rights in Business
- Open Apparel Registry
- PETA Approved Vegan
- Sustainable Apparel Coalition
- Stop the Traffik – Traffik Free Protocol Responsible Sourcing Network
- Textile Exchange
- Transparency Pledge and/or Open Data Standard for Apparel
- Turkmen Cotton Pledge
- UN Fashion Industry Charter on Climate Action
- Uzbek Cotton Pledge
- Zero Discharge of Hazardous Chemicals Programme

From this list, it is easy to see why this level of compliance and traceability is hard to achieve – there are far too many accreditations for both buyers and retailers and this can be a minefield of information. Notably, they do not mention, which offers a more holistic approach and is being taken up by more fashion brands such as Baukjen (Baukjen.com) and Aspiga (B Corporation 2022) in the UK. More could be done to encourage gaining this accreditation, which in the food industry, has been widely adopted and appears to be going from strength to strength, B corporation guidance encourages purpose of the business above profit.

In the near future, extended producer responsibility will be enshrined in law and brands will then need to really consider what they are going to do with garment returns and how to incorporate circular methods in the products they sell.

With news of new fibre recycling in Sweden, the worlds' first Circulose plant, which was completed in order to recycle cellulose garments into a new Viscose fibre (Canopy Planet November 2022) the technology with Renewcell, and at COP 27, Renewcell see Chapter 2 sought more funds for this type of initiative the use of re-cycled materials and minimal waste needs to be at the forefront of any metrics going forward. As this recycled fibre is defined as a Viscose fibre, there is also room to have its clear impacts explained to the buyer and consumer, making the point very clear that this type of regenerated cellulose does not using virgin materials in any form and is curbing deforestation.

But of course this is not always understood by the industry. In the earliest garment trials of this fibre, it was blended with other cellulose fibres, which makes both impact and recycling difficult to measure and is not an ideal answer to better materials. As in most cases, these are small steps to a better cleaner industry, but it is a still an imperfect system with room for improvement.

The Consumer Markets Authority (CMA) has begun a clampdown on unsupported sustainable claims and the intention to confuse the consumer into making an uninformed purchase. The remit for business to progress in the mid part of the 21st century is that brands and suppliers need to align to the fundamental principles as outlined by the principles highlighted next (Rinaldi et al. 2019). The CMA found that 40% of green claims could be misleading, relating to the use of materials or sourcing. Furthermore, the Changing Markets Foundation found in a study of fashion retailers that 59% of claims were not proven and were over-exaggerated.

Labelling & transparency

Reliability: Ensure data and information is supported and genuine

Relevance: Consider the most important areas to improve in and avoid passing on the issue

Clarity: Make this simple to understand and linked to the product

Transparency: Display both the source and the evidence

Accessibility: The information should be easily visible at point of sale

Business model innovation & extended producer responsibility

In Chapter 5, the interview with LMB textiles mentioned the initiative and collaboration with Reskinned. Reskinned's values have set their accountability and actions for the future. Its mission in reducing textile waste involves a service to brands and consumers to "empower people to continue the lifecycle of their clothes." Used clothing that is still wearable and is estimated at £140 million has been ending up in landfill (Wrap). Reskinned will send none of its collected garments to landfill; they ask consumers to return goods in old packaging, with no cost to the consumer, and send on rewards from the brand as part of the Take Back Scheme. If the goods cannot be resold, they can be recycled in fibre-to-fibre recycling plants, and they are keeping on top of the science and innovation behind this. They hope to engage more brands and build a community of like-minded businesses and celebrate the shared values, linking back to the idea of co-opetition to grow new ideas through collaboration. Selling second-hand goods is by no means a new idea, but this platform gives consumers a simple way to return any no-longer-used item and the confidence to purchase an old item that has been cleaned and sanctioned by the fashion brand. They also work with designers who upcycle garments and offer to clean and repair items themselves (Reskinned 2022).

Conclusion

This chapter is the final one in this textbook and it envisions a more transparent fashion supply chain for the future. There is much to be positive about as we are currently in a strong position in the fashion industry (as with many others) as we move out of the pandemic with new mindsets and a renewed focus on values. It is encouraging that, for the first time according to the Fashion Transparency Index, 47% of brands have disclosed primary manufacturers in their supply chain, including: Carrefour, Desigual, Dick's Sporting Goods, Dr. Martens, Ermenegildo Zegna, Fendi, Foschini, Fossil, Gucci, JD Sports, L.L. Bean, Mango, Miu Miu, Nordstrom, Otto, Prada and UGG.

This creates the opportunity to make more use of innovations that have been available for some time to improve workers conditions, the environment and to affect climate change with regard to action and implementation of new technology taken in fashion supply chains. However, these innovations do require collaboration and sharing of data across businesses in the fashion supply chain in a "business as usual" method of working for the future of the supply chain. Brands from fast mainstream fashion and luxury are all taking steps to become more sustainable in managing their supply chain and all aspects of their businesses. The time for full supply chain transparency is now. All fashion brands and suppliers could and should publish data about their supply chain raw materials, workers and interfaces in the chain and could align this data with the Open Data Standard for the Apparel Sector (www.odsas.org). Technology is available to support such transparency and ensure traceability and full visibility in the global fashion supply chain using some of the digital advancements in this chapter.

CASE STUDY

Interview with digital brand Snag Tights – Niki Akrivou (Snag hosiery – interview with Niki Akrivou)

Biography: Snag Tights, as seen in Fig. 7.5, were the first product we ever made and we're so proud to say that we've sold over 4 million pairs so far! Since then, we've created our own range of basics, from leggings to tees to underwear. We're committed to making tights and clothing as sustainably and as affordable as we possibly can, in at least a size 4 to 38.

As a company, we welcome change and innovation, which means we take risks sometimes. In fact, we love ideas that challenge what's been done before. We believe that if you want to achieve extraordinary results, you have to be prepared to do extra-ordinary things – a Snag mantra!

We also believe we should show the work how it really is without bias in our marketing. All our marketing images are of our customers, people who love Snags and wear them all the time. We want to reflect all genders, abilities, ethnicities ages and styles. It's

our job to make the advertising world more inclusive and welcoming. It's just the right thing to do.

We value inclusivity and fairness, along with affordability for all customers and employees. We are also committed to implementing sustainable practices where possible. Our production dyeing systems use recycled water, we never use plastic and are committed to using recycled materials whenever it's possible.

1. You are part of a new online only brand specialising in women's hosiery, can you explain how this business-to-consumer (B2C) model started?

Niki started in 2020 during the pandemic and trusted previous suppliers to work with. The founders wanted to grow the brand, and acquired 1 million customers before then; she was needed to move the brand to the next step.

2. Have you considered the impact of new technology on this business in manufacturing?

Niki set up a studio in London, doing fittings and worked with this large size range. Niki researched data to develop the product, using historical data to improve sizing. She also worked with Size Stream to develop body scanning and going through the application's development. Snag now has 4 million customers globally.

3. What is your most used software to track orders through the critical path?

Once price and lead times are agreed against sales data, the purchase order is raised. Production management comes through Niki's role, using an Excel spreadsheet and continuous communication –

Figure 7.5
Snag tights

WhatsApp, weekly phone calls and "Facetime" – this has evolved hugely during the pandemic and facilitated fast communication and better relationships.

4. What are the benefits or drawbacks of this system?

The benefits are detailed as above, but the drawbacks are not being able to visit suppliers before every shipment, which has been forced by the pandemic. Although acceptable quality level (AQL) reports are carried out before shipments.

5. How do you ensure ethical compliance and transparency in your supply chain?

Niki would be happier to provide more information on the website, but they are reducing plastics and all products are delivered to the customer in paper. SMETA audits are carried out and checked and everyone is paid a living wage. Also techniques used are digital printing on fabrics, recycling the water used in dyeing; tights manufacturers use solar panels and renewable energy. Snag is the first hosiery brand to introduce a recycling scheme – old products are made into bobbins and the yarn is spun onto the bobbins rather than recycled hosiery products, which is still an idea in development. There is a lot of science around higher carbon impact in 100% circular synthetics.

6. How do you develop new products within the range?

Through the studio and developing specific fit for all sizes, mainly relaxed jersey. A new item woven will be bamboo, launched soon to gauge the customer interest in this type of garment.

7. What consumer aftercare do you offer?

Snag tries to minimise returns, ensure good quality, deal with any complaints directly through social media with community champions and respond to all comments. Returns for recycling is a new concept and allows a great method to dispose of worn-out products.

8. How do you book space with manufacturers?

We book greige yarn and look at 6–12 months in hosiery. Otherwise, capacity booking, we have trialled the product and it is planned from there. A lot of product is cross-seasonal and the business analysts are looking at data crawling rather than sales history. We can repeat in-season and our fans, "Snagglers," support the new launches, e.g. Halloween tights that sold 7000 pairs in 24 hours and a further 10,000 in a weekend.

9. What have been the challenges in your current business?

The average lead time has increased if you have greige – it was four weeks, now eight weeks. And knitting has increased to 15 weeks. There are yarn shortages and for elastane. Many brands are moving out of South Asia and this has impacted European factories.

10. What are your most sustainable practices?

Clothing is mostly often made from Ecovero, recycled polyester. Swimwear is recycled as well as lingerie from organic cotton. Also, the factory audits, as mentioned before.

The distribution centres (DC) are in Holland and Livingstone, Scotland – with 100% quality check on hosiery and sent out. Clothing is delivered pre-packed. All shipments are by road to the DC; the largest market is the UK and Europe. Online orders use a variety of delivery methods; the customer chooses the shipment methods.

11. Do you see currently the input of robotics of 3-D printing in this product or a future where this will exist?

Any new machines are not being used yet by our manufacturers, but there is more technology in South Asian factories. Size Stream gives the possibility to use avatars to work on 3-D prototyping and bespoke customisation through body scanning.

12. And finally, what have you learnt during the first few years of the brand's development?

Talking to the customer, engaging, doing focus groups, fitting on real people. Working with three new suppliers, Italy, Turkey and one Chinese supplier and reacting positively and growing the brand during the global pandemic.

Activities & exercises

1. Investigate new developments in technology, both digital and material, for clothing production.
2. Design and plan products using a least one new technology.
3. Plan and define an appropriate supply chain model to meet the needs of this product.
4. Map the lifecycle of this product to comply to circular economy theory.
5. Lifecycle Case Study "Hursuit"

CASE STUDY

Case study activity – Hursuit

Can Slow Fashion and Fast Fashion sit side by side in a product range?

This is about product development issues within design for longevity and circular fashion concepts.

Keywords: Extended producer responsibility, outerwear, coat ranges, woollen fabrics, recycled polyester, circular economy

Table of contents

1. Learning objectives
2. Introduction
3. Business issue
4. Suggested questions
5. Teaching notes
6. References and further reading

Abstract

Issues that have been highlighted in the fashion industry after the Environmental Audit Committee's (EAC) Fixing Fashion report (2019) include the high impact of fashion waste and the need for "take back" schemes from retailers. The case study encourages discussion and decision-making around how design departments can develop product ranges that meet the needs of the consumer and retailer and minimises negative impacts on fashion waste. Designing clothes that last and extending the life of clothes i.e., the 30 wears campaign (Eco Age 2020), is at the forefront of the slow fashion movement, but alternatives exist if brands and customers think more broadly around potential recycling issues and the circular supply chain. There are a number of retailers who are taking aspects of sustainable development into the ranges – Nike is using recycled polyester and Arket is planning and using more traceable wool fabrics – along with collections in global retailers like H&M and Zara that use more sustainable materials. Assessing the best

route to take and the most impactful fabrics is complicated and can lead to green marketing (Niinimäki, K. 2015) where a brand boasts about aspects of the supply chain that are not necessarily true.

There were a number of recommendations from the EAC report, including "take back" schemes, which are the law in France (Tojo et al. 2012). The points are developed in the case study looking at material selection, designing the coat and sourcing the supplier, whilst managing the cost and the timing for a fashion brand.

Learning objectives

Upon completion of this case, students should be able to:

■ Explore research and design within product development to achieve improved environmental impact within an outerwear range, including cost, supply and marketing material

■ Analyse the product lifecycle management of various fashion products and materials and to compare these for different garment attributes

■ Evaluate the supply chain and the complexity of garments and their intended use phase and disposability

■ Review the product offer and suggest improvements to the product range, identifying the sustainable impact of the garments

■ Propose the most effective solutions to the issues raised on lifecycle of the garments, looking at second life and further into the circular supply chain

Introduction

In the current era, at the "tipping point" of sustainable fashion, can a business adopt a mixed method to approach the product development within the range? A brand or retailer might have a focus on re-cyclable materials linked to a "take back" scheme and also look at better-rated fabrics with less environmental impact, however, other strategies could apply to look at the second life of products to keep them in use longer. These options can make a compelling offer to the consumer and can contribute to meeting the long-term aim of minimal product impact. The decision as to whether a brand would choose to run these methods alongside each other within the same retail business forms an as yet unanswered question: product development and sustainability – should the model be circular design or design for longevity?

The fictional brand "Hursuit London" makes a range of outerwear in classic styles and sells through its own label and also will sell to brands using their own label, also known as private label orders, using their specifications. Traditionally in product development, branded clothing carries out a large amount of their range development in house by making toiles and patterns. Some brands will specify fabrics and even supply on a cut, make and trim, where Hursuit only gets paid for the labour cost and trimmings.

In doing this, they have a great amount of control over the product quality and components. They may also produce under a fully factored basis, specifying main fabrics, but allowing the supplier to source and pay for these items themselves. Brands can hand over the sampling stages to trusted companies depending on their relationship and confidence in getting the style right the first time. Hursuit London follows all of the above methods, has a design and pattern set up and can source European and Far East fabrics in small and large quantities.

The slow fashion movement is represented by purchases and items that have been well researched for their classic style and long-lasting quality. The characteristics of slow fashion have been explained by Fletcher (2010) as small-scale production, the utilisation of local materials and production, traditional production and techniques or design concepts that are season-less, slower production times to focus on quality, durable products, prices that reflect true ecological and social costs, and a focus on sustainability in both production and consumption.

Essentially, fast fashion "is a global trend that is characterized by the ability of fashion companies to respond quickly to fast-changing fashion trends and consumer tastes while maintaining low prices" (Hall, 2017). For Hursuit, they have not made any of this type of product, however, they have the ability to respond to new trends and produce quickly with limited supply. An item in recycled polyester can aid the use of renewable materials and contribute to the importance of circular production. An item designed for longevity will stay in use longer and may be passed down through families and generations or be resold and have many useful lives. Here is the crux of the issue: can both these ideas and methods sit alongside each other and how will this be communicated in a retail narrative?

Business issue

With the current range, the items are long-lasting coats in classic styles and fabrics for both men and women. The coats are often made in heavy wool-blend fabrics and last a long time – more than 30 wears – and are not considered fast fashion or disposable garments. The designs are functional and the colourways follow key core colours for the season.

You have been asked by the marketing director to do some competitor analysis to see what is missing from the ranges.

Sales of these heavy coats have been steady, but as the winters are getting warmer, the frequency of new customers has slowed. As you have a passion for research and development, you readily offer some ideas for new products – you can see there is a market for a lightweight duster coat. Many lower priced High Street and online stores have these unlined colourful coats in their range. They are layered with other items and add an injection of on-trend shades.

In looking at these styles, although they are coat weights, the compositions are 100% polyester, however, they have hand-feel of wool. You have an idea to use recycled yarn in this type of fabric weight and finish. The base fabric is more expensive than non-recycled, but you think the customers and brands will buy into the idea as a unique selling point. Many brands such as Zara, M&S and H&M are offering recycled polyester in garments, including swimsuits, schoolwear and soft blouses.

The product development stage

You will need to consider the design and the raw materials of the coat range by looking at the information on fabric inspiration from Premiere Vision (or similar) and the environmental impacts using the benchmark from the former NGO Made-By.

The cost price

You want to ensure the message to the customer is about the transparency of the supply chain. The marketing manager will explain the material choice and the ethics of the manufacturing location.

Here, you consider the supply chain and in which location the garment will be made. There is a small UK factory and they have access to EU suppliers. There are different minimum wages in each country and there may be Duty or tariffs, shipping costs and, most of all, the labour content of the design. The tiers of manufacture can involve component suppliers, for example linings and buttons, and every item will have a source and timeline for delivery. The cost of the product will add all these items together and include the main fabric usage.

Once the average margin is known, this will give an estimated retail price and shipping must be included in this. VAT applies to the retail price and is not included in the cost price. This needs to link to the planned critical path and should sit with the expected delivery timeframe.

There is also an opportunity to market this product with a clear explanation to the consumer of the relative benefits. When considering this area, how should the brand or retailer explain these products – both existing and new – to the consumer?

They need to avoid any hint of greenwashing, which can often be seen through as a marketing ploy (Gowereck 2013).

Future-proofing the products to avoid their ending up in landfill will be necessary; only 1% of garments in the UK are currently recycled into new fibres (Ellen MacArthur Report 2017). Could you offer in-store collection? What would need to be in place to encourage the correct disposal and eventual repurposing of the coat after it has been discarded? May it be passed on for resale or rental?

Can the brand Hursuit London offer both these products – the original classic coats from wool and the polyester recycled version – alongside each other within the range?

You can think about the wider connections with the supplier, merchandiser, quality control and marketing departments. In this you can explore what barriers exist and how can you overcome these.

The brand currently sources fabrics from Italy, mainly wool fibre content at a cost price of £75, Retail Selling Price of £325. They can source fully recycled polyester coat-weight fabric within the UK from Italian recycled yarn. The target retail price for this coat is £125.

Do they need to consider new manufacturing options? What might the design content look like in terms of workmanship and work content?

How could they manage the "take back" option for the products as they have very few retail outlets.

What would need to be in place for this to happen in terms of supply chain, raw materials, logistics, quality, critical path and marketing to the consumer?

Suggested questions

Can a retail brand offer more than one sustainable business model and target new consumers without damaging the brand quality & integrity?

Can you define the carbon impact of wool fibres versus recycled polyester fibres?

Does the garment construction of a wool coat vary from a polyester outerwear-weight fabric?

What needs to be in place in the supply chain for a fully recyclable product?

Can you estimate the cost price and target retail price?

Can you evaluate the timeline of the critical path for each product type, based on the raw material and garment manufacturing location?

Can you propose inspirational images and flat drawings for the intended garments?

Can you develop marketing material for the ranges and indicate their relative environmental impact?

In this study, students will consider the critical aspects of product development at the research and design process and explore the options that will shape the supply chain and ultimately the life of the garment and its ultimate disposal. The goal is to extend the life of the garment alongside minimal use of new materials. You can use images, flat drawings, mood boards and costing sheets. Consider a critical path timeline, marketing material suitable for a website and point-of-sale material

Teaching notes

Students can write short reports. This case allows wider research on coat ranges, silhouettes and pricing using business information on design, trends in fabric and colour, too (**45 minutes**).

■ Use WGSN, Vogue.com and online catwalk and Instagram to research value and slow fashion.

■ What are the likely prices of the fabric and components and how much fabric would be needed per garment? (**30 minutes**)

■ Minimum order quantities: Discuss what these could be by colour and style.

■ Present key items from your range, explaining the design, sourcing and cost scenario including the labour cost from your intended supply base.

■ Discuss the impact of the garments on the planet comparatively.

■ This case has been expanded for an assessed presentation to evaluate the supply chain of a product, its lifecycle and environmental impact.

■ A written paper on evaluating a brand or retailer, using wider research, and suggesting recommendations for improvement to the design supply and marketing of fashion.

References and further reading

Fixing Fashion Report. (2019). UK Parliament [online]. Available at https://publications.parliament.uk/pa/cm201719/cmselect/cmenvaud/1952/1952.pdf. Accessed 27 May 2020.

Eco Age. (2020). 30 Wears Campaign. Available at https://eco-age.com/news/30wears-mikaela-loach. Accessed 27 May 2020.

Ellen MacArthur Foundation. A New Textiles Economy. Available at https://ellenmacarthurfoundation.org/a-new-textiles-economy. Accessed 27 May 2020.

Goworek, H., Hiller, A., Fisher, T., Cooper, T., and Woodward, S. (2013). "Consumers' attitudes towards sustainable fashion," in Gardetti, M. and Torres, A. (eds.), *Sustainability in Fashion and Textiles*, pp. 377–392. Sheffield, UK: Greenleaf Publishing.

Hall, J. (2017). "Digital kimono: Fast fashion, slow fashion?" *Fashion Theory*, 22(3), 283–307.

Niinimäki, K. (2015). "Ethical foundations in sustainable fashion," *Textiles and Clothing Sustainability*, 1, 3. https://doi.org/10.1186/s40689-015-0002-1

Tojo, N., Kogg, B., Kiørboe, N., Kjær, B., and Aalto, K. (2012). *Prevention of Textile Waste: Material Flows of Textile in Three Nordic Countries and Suggestions on Policy Instruments*. Copenhagen: Nordic Council of Ministers.

Bibliography

Baukjen.com. https://www.baukjen.com/pages/b-corp. Accessed October 2022.

Bcorporation. (2022). https://www.bcorporation.net/en-us/find-a-b-corp/company/aspiga. Accessed October 2022.

Burberry. (2021). www.burberry.com

Caldarelli, G., Zardini, A., and Rossignoli, C. (2021). "Blockchain adoption in the fashion sustainable supply chain: Pragmatically addressing barriers," *Journal of Organizational Change Management*, 34(2), 507–524.

https://canopyplanet.org/first-of-its-kind-commercial-scale-recycled-textile-mill-opens-in-sweden/. Accessed November 2022.

www.changingmarkets.org. Accessed January 2022.

Chavez-Dreyfuss, G. (2019). https://www.reuters.com/article/us-usa-blockchain-harvard-idUSKCN1PI2FA

Choi, T. and Guo, S. (2018). "Responsive supply in fashion mass customisation systems with consumer returns," *International Journal of Production Research*, 56(10), 3409–3422.

https://cleanclothes.org/campaigns/protect-progress/qa-extensive. Accessed April 2022.

Creagh, M. (2019). Fixing Fashion. https://publications.parliament.uk/pa/cm201719/cmselect/cmenvaud/1952/report-summary.html

Deacetis, J. (2021). https://www.forbes.com/sites/josephdeacetis/2021/07/02/expensive-designer-nfts-and-how-blockchain-is-wooing-the-luxury-lifestyle-industry/?sh=4b402182d702

Demiri, B. (2019). https://www.stylus.com/future-thinking-podcast-episode-68. Accessed January 2022.

Earley, R. and Goldsworthy, K. (2019). "Circular textile design: Old myths and new models," in *Designing for the Circular Economy*, pp. 175–185. Routledge.

https://www.fashionroundtable.co.uk/news/2022/18/01/cma-greenwashing-fashion. Accessed January 2022.

Fibre Trace. (2022). https://www.fibretrace.io/technology. Accessed 2 January 2022.

Gallarate, S. (2019). https://screenshot-media.com/the-future/fashion/alyx-blockchain-technology/

George, S. (2021). https://www.edie.net/news/6/Most-fashion-brands–failing-to-disclose-supply-chain-emissions-despite-net-zero-pledge/

Good on You. (2022). https://goodonyou.eco/. Accessed April 2022.

Gore, A. and Blood, D. (2018). The Sustainability Revolution has taken off. WIRED.

Hoffman, C. (2022). General Secretary of the UNI Global Union. https://www.industriall-union.org/bangladesh-accord-arbitration-cases-resulting-in-millions-of-dollars-in-settlements-officially. Accessed April 2022.

International Accord. (2022). https://internationalaccord.org/signatories. Accessed April 2022.

Longo, F., Padovano, A., Cimmino, B., and Pinto, P. (2021). "Towards a mass customization in the fashion industry: An evolutionary decision aid model for apparel product platform design and optimization," *Computers & Industrial Engineering*, 162, 107742.

Love, E. (2022). https://resource.co/article/scotland-proposes-ban-destruction-unsold-goods. Accessed April 2022.

MacDowell, M. (2019). https://www.voguebusiness.com/technology/6-ways-blockchain-changing-luxury

Martine Jarlgaard. https://martinejarlgaard.com/

McCarthy, J. (1989). "Artificial Intelligence, logic and formalizing common sense," in Thomason, R.H. (ed.), *Philosophical Logic and Artificial Intelligence*, Dordrecht: Springer. https://doi.org/10.1007/978-94-009-2448-2_6

Nike ID. (2022). https://www.nike.com/gb/nike. Accessed January 2022.

ODSAS. www.odsas.org

Office for National Statistics. (2022). https://www.ons.gov.uk/businessindustryan-dtrade/retailindustry/timeseries/j4mc/drsi. Accessed January 2022.

Platform, E. (2021). https://www.platforme.com/resources. Accessed 16 December 2020.

Provenance. https://www.provenance.org/

Rankin, J. (2022). https://www.ecotextile.com/2022033029161/labels-legislation-news/eu-sustainable-textiles-strategy-unveiled.html. Accessed 30 March 2022.

Rebound Returns. (2022). https://www.reboundreturns.com/blog-articles/how-to-turn-your-fashion-returns-into-a-profitable-and-sustainable-rental-service. Accessed January 2022.

Reskinned.(2022).https://www.reskinned.clothing/the-re-edit-blog/bts-with-reskinned-our-values. Accessed April 2022.

Retail Gazette. (2021). https://www.retailgazette.co.uk/blog/2020/04/the-challenge-of-surplus-stock-in-the-time-of-coronavirus/. Accessed 16 December 2020.

Size Stream. (2022). https://www.sizestream.com/ssah. Accessed January 2022.

Statista. (2022). Fashion eCommerce report 2020. Retrieved at https://www.statista.com/study/38340/ecommerce-report-fashion/. Accessed December 2020.

Stella Mac Cartney. (2022). www.stellamccartney.com

Stylus Media Group. (2021). https://www.stylus.com/fashions-digital-future

Tapscott, A. and Tapscott, D. (2016). "How blockchain will change organizations," *MIT Sloan Management Review*, 58(2), 10–13.

Tarmy, M. (2016). The Future of Fashion Is 3D Printing Clothes at Home. [online] Bloomberg.com. Available at https://www.bloomberg.com/news/articles/2016-04-15/3d-printing-is-poised-to-bring-haute-couture-into-the-home. Accessed 16 December 2020.

Thredup. https://www.thredup.com/resale/#whos-thrifting-and-why

UN Global Compact Mission Statement. (2022). https://www.unglobalcompact.org/what-is-gc/mission/principles

Vernier, J. (2021). "Extended producer responsibility (EPR) in France," *Field Actions Science Reports*, 2021(23), 22–25.

Wang, B., Luo, W., Zhang, A., Tian, Z., and Li, Z. (2020). "Blockchain-enabled circular supply chain management: A system architecture for fast fashion," *Computers in Industry*, 123, 103324. https://doi.org/10.1016/j.compind.2020.103324

Yeung, H.T., Choi, T.M., and Chiu, C.H. (2010). "Innovative mass customization in fashion," in Cheng, T.C.E. and Choi, T.-M. (eds.), *Innovative Quick Response Programs in Logistics and Supply Chain Management*, pp. 423–454. Berlin, Heidelberg: Springer.

Index

Note: Pages in *italics* refer to figures.

For Product Safety Concerns and Information please contact our EU
representative GPSR@taylorandfrancis.com
Taylor & Francis Verlag GmbH, Kaufingerstraße 24, 80331 München, Germany